Lord of the Dance

TO BE
DISPOSED
BY
AUTHORITY

WILLIAM KAY

Lord of the Dance

THE STORY OF GERRY ROBINSON

ORION
BUSINESS
BOOKS

First published in Great Britain in 1999 by
Orion Business
An imprint of The Orion Publishing Group Ltd
Orion House, 5 Upper St Martin's Lane, London WC2H 9EA

A CIP catalogue record for this book is available from the British Library.

ISBN 0-75281-048-0

Typeset by Geoff Green Book Design
Printed and bound in Great Britain by
Creative Print & Design Ltd, Ebbw Vale, S. Wales.

To Betty Robinson, without whom this book
would not have been possible

Contents

Acknowledgements

I would like to thank the many people who have given their time unstintingly to help me research, write and produce this book.

My principal sources have been Gerry Robinson himself, his family, those who have worked with him and those with whom he has crossed swords in the business jungle.

When Gerry Robinson agreed to my writing his biography, unauthorised but with his full co-operation, I felt it only fair to warn him that it would take up a considerable amount of his own time. He immediately agreed, and we have spent many hours talking together, mainly in his office at Granada's headquarters at Stornaway House. This is the legendary press baron Lord Beaverbrook's former home behind St James's Palace in central London. Sometimes we wandered off whatever aspect of the book I wanted to discuss, and fell to putting the world to rights, or simply tearing it to pieces. On many such occasions, I admit, I walked back to St James's with my sides aching from laughter.

Robinson's family has been a joy and a revelation to meet, from his mother Betty and his brothers and sisters, to his wife, Heather, and his children, Samantha, Richard, April and Timothy. As an only child myself, I found it a revelation to get to know such a large family. I learned to think quickly on my feet: the Robinsons are merciless leg-pullers and those who cannot keep up soon find themselves left behind in the onrush of digs, jibes and banter.

I have had tremendous help from Robinson's colleagues, led by Alex Bernstein and Charles Allen but including executives throughout the Group as well as his driver, Jim Walsh. My access to all these vital people has been made infinitely easier by Gerry's unfailingly efficient personal assistant, Suzy Warburton.

Outside Granada, I have had just as much co-operation from Robinson's and the company's advisers, allies and business rivals. They have included Sir Christopher Bland, Sam Chisholm, Jonathan Clare, Michael Green, Sir Peter Hall, Peter Hewitt, John Nelson, Lord Sheppard, Sir Anthony Tennant, Ward Thomas and Eric Walters. I thank them all, and others who have also offered invaluable insights, for helping to make this a better-balanced and more rounded work than it would otherwise have been.

While all opinions and factual errors are my own, I would have stumbled into some terrible blunders without the vigilant gaze of my literary agent, John Pawsey, my editor at Orion Business Books, Clare Christian, and, not least, my partner Lynne Bateson.

I

Dunfanaghy

If it had not been for the need to find bedding for horses on the battlefields of World War One, it is more than possible that Gerry Robinson would not have become the ultimate pay-master of *Coronation Street*, *Blind Date* and Britain's leading painters, sculptors, actors and opera singers.

He grew up in Dunfanaghy, a picturesque village on the Atlantic coast of Donegal in northwest Ireland, which until the 1920s was the area's commercial centre. There are relics of its busy past in the stout buildings in the Market Square and overlooking the now-bare pier. It is hard to imagine today that this quiet haven had once been a bustling crossroads for farm traffic ringing with the noise of horse-drawn carts and the cries of their drivers setting off along the narrow coastal road with coal, maize and fertiliser from Liverpool, Glasgow and other British ports. The sailing ships were then loaded with local meat and dairy produce for the return journey.

All that activity came to end after World War One. During that war the bent grass on sandhills near the village had been sent to France for horse bedding. But that grass had held the sand together. Without this natural binding, the next big gale that whipped through Sheephaven Bay drove the sand into Dunfanaghy's little harbour, silting it up and denying it for ever to deep-water shipping. Because the port business was gone, the gale also swept away much of the work that a busy commercial centre needed to keep it going in those days: making and repairing carts, equipment and even the ships if they had had a rough crossing from England. Although Robinson's father was not yet born, this was to have a crucial impact on the scope for his natural skill as a carpenter. He helped to build the row of tiny houses in which he brought up his family, but there was not enough work for him in Dunfanaghy and increasingly he had to go first to Scotland – 'tatty-hawking' in Glasgow, lifting potatoes and selling them – and then England to find enough work. That led to what eventually became the total exodus of the Robinson family to the London area.

Northern Donegal is reckoned to be the rawest part of Ireland, with its bare limestone plains and steep cliffs, studded with thatched stone cottages and peat fires. Dunfanaghy stands on a long, winding inlet from Sheephaven Bay, said to be the only place in Ireland where the corncrake can still be heard in its natural habitat. Adding to the untamed feel of the place is a natural oddity: McSwine's Gun, a rock blow-hole which used to give a loud report like a gun when the wind and tide played over it in a certain way. Nowadays the noise is largely gone, but it can still throw up a dramatic plume of water.

Dunfanaghy is protected from the Atlantic by Horn Head, a high windswept headland which nowadays attracts carloads of bird spotters, as it includes Ireland's largest mainland seabird-breeding colony. Guillemots, gannets, puffins, stormy petrels and others nest there when they are not circling overhead, searching for food. Stand on top of Horn Head, more than 200 metres above sea level, and you can see for miles, for there are few trees. Even further down where habitation begins, there are only a few farmhouses to obstruct the view. But footing can be treacherous, as there are often peat bogs on the heights. Over the centuries rain has drained from the hills to form streams, which have eroded the land, making pools and waterfalls, surrounded by the occasional clump of trees.

However, Dunfanaghy has had its share of Ireland's turbulent past, from those early settlers to the potato famine of the mid-nineteenth century and echoes of the Irish struggle for independence from the United Kingdom. Even before the famine, Robinson's forebears had a tough time scraping a living from the miserly conditions. Thomas Campbell Foster was appointed by *The Times* newspaper in London to inquire into 'the condition of the people of Ireland' in 1845, just before the potato crop failure that produced the famine. He wrote from Dunfanaghy on 10 September that year:

> It is the nature of the men on the west coast to cling with strong affection and prejudice to old habits, to their land, to their kindred. Enterprise is forced upon them; they do not

seek it as one of the pleasures of existence. The middle classes live by subletting, and subletting, and again subletting the land at increased rentals. This is the extent of their enterprise.

As the poor increase, they divide and subdivide the patch of land they possess; they submit to live on poorer and poorer food; still they cling to the land, and subdivide it with their children till rent no longer exists, the land will not keep them, and all starve together. Their highest ambition is to obtain 'a blanket and a shelter for Sally,' and potatoes for themselves and their children.

The people, being left to themselves, were found a year or two ago by the Poor Law Commissioners lying in their huts, without food or clothes, all starving together in the most frightful state of destitution.

The famine is commemorated by a permanent exhibition in Dunfanaghy's former workhouse on the edge of the village, near the schoolhouse that the Robinsons attended.

These days Dunfanaghy is a golfing and trout-fishing resort, with grocers, craft shops, two thriving hotels and several pubs. It also has the now-obligatory trail of American tourists coming to trace their ancestry. Donegal is gaelic for *Dun na nGall* – fort of the foreigner, harking back to the original Viking settlement there – so the county is well used to coping with visitors of one sort or another.

The birth of Gerrard Jude Robinson on 23 October 1948 was of no great concern to the mixed Protestant and Catholic community of Dunfanaghy. There was no shortage of children among the twelve families who lived alongside the Catholic Robinsons in Cottage Row, which is set back from the rest of the village, and in 1999 still had houses on only one side of the narrow street. On the other side was a row of trees shielding a farmer's field. Another birth – at home, the tradition in that part of the world, rather than the antiseptic surroundings of a hospital – was almost an everyday event. Gerrard was the ninth of what was to be a brood of ten in the Robinson household, although by the time he appeared most of the elder half had fled the nest to seek their fortunes in England. When Gerry was born, as was the custom he was handed from one to another of the local women who had been awaiting the new arrival in the Robinsons' tiny front room. The nurse came into the room with the infant and, pointing out that his head had two crowns, said, 'This baby will go places.' His was the first birth in the family for five years – to the fury of his sister Fiona, the previous youngest. She hated Gerry because he was the new centre of attention. But she took her jealousy too far, so her father sent her to the local grocery shop for a bar of Lux soap to bath Gerry. But as a punishment he sent her five times before she was actually allowed to buy the soap. This, though, was mild by the standards of the retribution their father was capable of dispensing.

Robinson's parents, Tony and Betty, were a contrasting mixture. Tony, who was born in 1902 and died in 1988, was raised in Dunfanaghy. Betty, seven years younger, had sailed across the Irish Sea from Glasgow, where she had been brought up in a well-off Scots family. She went to Ireland on holiday in 1931 when she was eighteen, met Tony and they fell in love.

Said Betty, 'I was a Stuart, brought up in Crown Street on the south side of Glasgow. It was a fair-sized house, because my people were fairly comfortable. I was coming down in the world all right when I went to live in Ireland, but I loved it! My father was a warehouse superintendent. We got all our clothes from the warehouse as children. I had two sisters, and a brother who died in infancy. I was the second last.'

But Betty's upbringing was to change dramatically. Her mother died when Betty was only five years old. Her aunt, who was a nun, stepped in and obtained special dispensation from Rome to leave the nunnery so that she could look after the children. Then, within a year, Betty's father remarried and she did not get on so well with her stepmother, particularly after she had children of her own. Gerry said, 'My mother had a sense of being let down and felt her stepmother's children got the best of it. She had a lot of hurt about her father remarrying and that feeling that she didn't get her share of things.'

At eighteen Betty trained to be a nurse, specialising in fever nursing – measles, whooping cough, mumps, typhoid and so on. 'There are so many injections now for these things,' Betty pointed out, 'that you don't hear of fever nursing any more. But my first five children had measles and whooping cough.' Nevertheless, nursing was to be only a stopgap. Marriage and the move to Ireland gave her the opportunity to make a fresh start.

'I was on holiday in Donegal when I met Tony,' Betty remembered. 'He was in a car and we asked for a lift because we were quite a bit away from where we were staying and there was very little transport – it happened just like that. I liked him as soon as I saw him. We got married six months later. I was twenty-two, he was twenty-nine. I always liked the scenery and the hills in Donegal. It's a lovely part of the world, entirely different from Glasgow. It was more or less primitive in those days, everything was very plain. But I didn't mind – I was happy. It was exhausting, having all those children. But the older ones helped with the younger ones and we regulated them: you had to give them jobs, tell them what to do. They were very good and they are now, and keep together.'

Betty's nursing training naturally came in handy for dealing with a large family, as did her normally calm temperament in the midst of the sudden squalls that arose all too frequently. One day Gerry and his elder brother Pat were chasing another boy, who was throwing bits of mud back at them as he ran. As the mud did not stop them, he picked up a jar and threw that back. It caught Pat in the face, just near his eye, and blood flowed. When he got home Betty just put a towel on it as a makeshift bandage to staunch the flow, and went back to whatever she was doing.

While Tony and Betty's marriage seemed an unlikely match, it was apparently based on genuine mutual affection. Their skills and temperaments complemented one another. 'Tony and I were very different from one another,' Betty confirmed, 'but they always say that different people get on best.' Naturally, Betty – cool, calm, almost calculating – was the one who usually got her way. 'She thinks things through,' said Gerry, 'and my father would be entirely passionate and rage about things – and always lose.'

Tony and his father worked with their hands, Tony as a highly skilled carpenter, his father as a baker. Like Tony, he had had a large family – eight children: six boys and two girls. He was by all accounts a soft man, who spent a lot of time helping plant potatoes and taking care of Tony and Betty's family. Some of Gerry's elder brothers and sisters believe that he resembles his grandfather. Tony's father baked in Dunfanaghy for years, and then he got a skin irritation known locally as baker's itch, like eczema, and couldn't work any more.

Said Betty, 'He was a lovely man, and he and his wife got on very smoothly. I got on well with my mother-in-law. She was a dressmaker, the only one in the town. She was expert at it, having learnt at a time when dresses were very difficult to make, long and elaborate with plenty of frills. I helped her with a bit of sewing because I was handy with a needle, and did things like putting pockets in suits. She appreciated that.'

Tony did seven years' apprenticeship as a carpenter. Gerry's brother Pat, recalled, 'He could make a spoked wheel by sight, completely without plans or measurements. He used to make them all finished and painted. And you know what he got for that? Ten shillings. And sometimes it took the farmer who bought it six months to come up with the money. It was hard making money in those circumstances.' On the other hand, food was cheap and for many years the rent at Cottage Row was 4s 6d (22p) a week to buy the house on a rental-purchase scheme – so ten shillings (50p) for a cartwheel was a valuable piece of business. And if there was anything in the house that needed be made Tony could make it, including furniture of all kinds. This was of course a huge help in such a big household, where every penny mattered. Betty just had to tell him they needed a cupboard here or some shelves there and Tony got to work – though not without the odd grumble.

Although the Robinsons were slightly better off than

others in the neighbourhood, by modern standards their lives were a mixture of hardship and modest comfort. With only one source of income in the family for much of the time, there was very little spare money to go round. Even though the whole family never lived at home at the same time – there is twenty years' difference between the oldest and youngest children, Tony and Paul – it is hard to imagine even half a dozen of them living together in the tiny house, even though it later became more spacious when its boxlike front rooms were knocked into one. Behind the house was a workshop for their father's carpentry, and beyond that a long narrow garden where the washing was hung out to dry. That led to a communal field which sloped up to the main road out of Dunfanaghy, where the workhouse and schoolhouse were.

Like thousands of families in Ireland at that time, the Robinsons had to make do and mend where they could. If they had trouble with their teeth they had to go to the dentist at the former Victorian workhouse, and he would pull them out with a pair of pliers. They lit paraffin-fuelled Tilley lamps at night and drew water from the green-painted pump outside their cottage. They were thought fortunate by their neighbours because their home had the pump right outside, so they did not have to carry the water far back to their house. Nonetheless, the lack of running water meant the family sharing a dry toilet, which had to be emptied regularly. Gerry and the other children in the family had to take turns to empty the waste on to the dunghill at the back of the garden.

Gerry and one or two of the others would cry their eyes out when it was their turn. But that cut no ice with their father, who was liable to beat them for disobedience. John, the fifth eldest, who now lives in the New Forest, said, 'Dad had to be a disciplinarian, but maybe too much so. I thought he took it too far and it was one of the reasons I left. The elder children, Tony, Maureen and Jean, each used to sit on a stool at mealtimes, and the rest of us had to stand around the kitchen table. There simply wasn't room to do anything else.'

Yet Gerry's sister, Evelyn, insisted, 'We weren't born with a silver spoon in our mouths, but we weren't dragged up either. The children had to work around the house. We had a wooden table which had to be scrubbed, and a black-leaded range with steel fixings which had to be cleaned and polished. Mum did the cooking and ironing. We had porridge in the morning, cheese sandwiches for lunch, braised steak, chicken or rabbit at night. The butcher called twice a week with sausages and mince. We were better off than some kids, who were living on dry bread and black tea.'

The Robinsons even joined modestly in the advancing consumer society, buying a radio in 1952 and a car five years later, becoming one of the first families in Dunfanaghy to have their own motorised transport. They used to sit round the radio listening to Radio Luxembourg, and everyone had to be quiet when the news was on. And they could afford a daily paper – the *Irish Independent.*

Tony's carpentry was not enough on its own to pay for even this modest lifestyle. Betty brought in some money from her sewing, but ultimately Tony had first to go to Glasgow, pulling and selling potatoes, and then to London, doing building work to earn enough to feed the family. In the meantime they had help from an outside source. Meg, Betty's sister, used to come on holiday to Ireland and bring two suitcases – a little one for herself and a great big one full of clothes and shoes for the growing Robinson family. The children went through shoes very quickly, on the rough roads in and around Dunfanaghy. Meg worked in a clothes factory as a cutter, cutting patterns from measurements, and she sent new clothes and castoffs for the kids, Stuart tartan kilts and velvet jackets. 'Ours were the best-dressed children in the village,' Betty insisted. 'I would cut down the second-hand clothes for the children, trousers, jackets, coats, that sort of thing. One teacher at the school was the son of a tailor and would put new seats in his own trousers – we used to do that in those days, to save money – and he used to admire the seats I put in the kids' pants.'

Betty chose to throw in her lot with a complex man. Tony was unlike his father in several ways. Although his father was easygoing, he was supposed to be the wild one of his family. And, while he was very strict with his own children, by and large they were pretty sunny-tempered. Gerry's sister Fiona said, 'Dad was strict because of Mum. He wanted to please her, and was strict partly because she wanted him to keep the children in order – starting with Tony, the eldest, who was a real rascal when he was a boy. Mum didn't like Dad bringing his friends back home, farmers and the like, even though they were always well behaved, not drunk. She just didn't get on with strangers.'

While many Irishmen have a reputation for being fond of a drink, Tony senior rarely touched a drop, yet could be very bad-tempered. 'He was unusual in Ireland in that he didn't drink much,' confirmed Gerry. 'I don't ever remember him being drunk. He would sip a whiskey but get little pleasure out of it. Perhaps if he had he would have been more mellow.'

Jean, the third child, remembers, 'Dad was Mum's orbit. She worshipped him. So she didn't want to share him with anyone else. And Dad was terrible: at one time I was going out with a schoolteacher who came to collect me from home one evening and Dad said, "Mind you bring her home on time – and no pokin' her!" I could have died with embarrassment. He was quite outrageous as a boy, very unlike his father, who was very quiet. Dad's sisters were gentle, too. Dad was the black sheep.'

Nevertheless, he may have had to wield the big stick to keep the brood in line. Tony, the eldest child, set a yardstick for unruliness that his father would not have wanted to see repeated. A farmer called Moore owned some petrol pumps next to the Arnold Hotel on the main street because he needed petrol for his tractors, so he sold the petrol as well. Then he used to bring his cows down there for milking, and sold the milk. Clearly something of a self-made businessman, he was a strong British Tory and proudly hung a photograph of Winston Churchill outside his shop. Even as a lad Tony leaned more towards republicanism, so he used to take some small, hard potatoes and throw them at the picture – breaking the glass time after time. Tony told me, 'Dad was doing a lot of work in Glasgow when I was young, and I think it frustrated him, having to go there to earn a living, but being away from Mum and the family. Then he would get back and Mum would tell him what we had got up to, and we'd get a real hiding. One time we were playing football on the front green and the ball went through a window. I got real hell for that, because we couldn't afford to pay for it to be repaired. Another time there was a man sitting on a horse in the square and I whacked it with a stick. The horse reared, and it put its two front hooves through a window. I got a hiding for that, too.'

Betty added, 'My husband didn't drink but ruled with an iron rod, and wouldn't let the children do certain things they weren't supposed to do. He was a good father, though they didn't appreciate it. He didn't let them go out with the dogs in the farms in case they worried the sheep, especially when they were lambing. He made them follow the rules as far as gates and ditches were concerned. The children would take a dog to catch rabbits. The farmers didn't mind, because rabbits were vermin as far as they were concerned. They would bring them home and we used to cook them for dinner – and very nice they tasted, too!'

Gerry and his brothers used to go blinding rabbits with lights to flush them out of their hiding places. They would go into one of the fields at the back of Dunfanaghy and make a noise. A rabbit would look up, startled, and the boys would catch it in the beam of a torch. Then they set the dog on it. On one occasion, according to Neil McGinley, a childhood friend, 'Eddie and Pat Robinson just fell on a rabbit as it ran towards the torch. We had to toss a coin for who got the rabbit.'

The Robinsons had a succession of dogs, mainly terriers, but an Alsatian and an Old English Shepherd gave them headaches. The Old English Shepherd came to town with the local circus, attached itself to the Robinson family and the circus left it behind. But they couldn't afford to keep it, so they gave it to a local farmer. The Alsatian was a more serious problem. Like many of the breed it was subject to epileptic fits, and there were no vets in the area to help because the local farmers just used to help one another. On one occasion Tony tried to control the dog and his face was ashen white with the effort. He was a danger to the children, so they had to put him down.

The young Gerrard took his time joining in the rough and tumble of life in such a family. For the first year and a half of his life he just lay back and watched the world go by, showing no inclination even to crawl. His mother, Betty, said, 'He was lazy. I would sit him up and straightaway he would lie down again. But he could talk before he could walk, rattling off little rhymes. He could talk nineteen to the dozen. He was a real chatterbox. We used to wonder how he could talk so plainly at such a young age.' However, the infant's apparent inability to walk became such a source of concern that Betty took him to the doctor. 'Don't worry, Mrs Robinson,' said the medic, 'the boy is just bone idle.'

In the end it took something remarkable to attract his attention and get him on his feet. It is a tradition for Irish communities all round the world to hold a big parade on St Patrick's Day (17 March), Ireland's national day, complete with marching bands, floats, acrobats and clowns. But Dunfanaghy in 1950 was too small and too poor for such extravagance. The boys in the village just used to walk through the streets banging tin lids. 'As they came up the road,

Gerrard was sitting on the mat indoors,' Betty recalled. 'Everyone else in the family was standing at the gate watching the boys go by, and we suddenly realised he was coming out of the house to see what was happening. He fell at the doorstep, but he began to walk from then on.'

Once he was able to make his own way out of the little cottage the Robinsons owned, Gerrard had no shortage of friends to play with, nor things to do: fishing from the pier, going out to the wide, scenic Killyhoey beach, exploring, playing childhood games. In the much harder winters of the 1950s there would be six or seven inches of snow falling on Dunfanaghy, and it would pack frozen hard. Gerry's father used to make a sleigh, complete with steel shoes so it would last longer, and two wooden guiders so it could steer round corners. That was vital, for the slope down into Dunfanaghy high street contains a sharp right-hand bend. Gerry and his brothers used to sleigh down the hill into the village, past the shops and – with a good push-off and up to four aboard – beyond the market square.

A fortnight before Christmas Gerry joined in the activity known as mummers, when a bunch of the kids would knock on doors wearing false faces, to recite rhymes. After the little show one of them would say, 'Here comes Johnny Funny, I'm the one that collects the money, all silver no brass and bad money won't pass.' They would often walk as far as ten or twelve miles in a night doing mummers round the village and surrounding hamlets.

Danny McFadden, who is the same age as Gerry, remembered, 'He was in the forefront of any devilment. His mother used to make a pudding every day for a woman down the road who wasn't able. She gave it to Gerry and Paul to take round to her and they used to eat a bit of it and tell the woman, "Not as much today for you: it's worked out a smaller portion." We used to knock on doors and hide, and sometimes there was an Irish showband in a tent on the golf course. A friend used to let us sneak in and we used to steal Cokes and other soft drinks. So when he said he was going to be a priest, we just didn't believe it. It didn't seem like him at all. But Gerry had a great gift of talking to people. And he had that angel face, that got him out of scrapes time after time.'

Life in the Robinson family was run on strict Catholic lines, guided by a vigorous concept of right and wrong. The children were brought up in the Catholic faith, with no meat eaten on Fridays, Mass every Sunday, and a firm belief that wrongdoers perished in the fires of Hell. If it is delivered with enough force and repeated regularly, this is liable to make even the most headstrong lad think twice – especially if all his friends have been subjected to the same uncompromising indoctrination. That, however, did not stop them getting in trouble. In church they used to take turns to hold the candles representing the stations of the Cross. One time Gerry and Pat were rowing about whose turn it was. They started wrestling and Pat reached for the candlestick and ran out, with all the other boys streaming after them in their white surpluses. When they caught up with them, Gerry was hitting the bigger and older Pat with the candle.

While Gerry lived in Dunfanaghy that indoctrination was confined to church and home. He went to the village school across the road at the head of the Plot, the stretch of land that sloped up from behind the houses in Cottage Row.

Two teachers shared fifty pupils across the age range, in a small but imposing building that had been a fever hospital and later became a gallery selling paintings and *objets d'art*. In the same class they were dealing with children of different ages so they were divided up according to their age and ability and worked side by side on different projects.

Gerry was taught by Mrs Boyle, on the first floor of the school. On the ground floor were the boys' and girls' cloakrooms, where they had their lunch if they were staying at school. If the weather was fine, the Robinsons would take the short walk back down the Plot to have lunch at home. Gerry's elder sister, Maureen, recalled, 'It was a very good local school. We had one big room with a huge fireplace and all the kids brought pieces of turf to burn. Turf doesn't throw out as much heat as coal – it's much slower – but it was all we had.'

Turf was money in those days, and John and his brother Tony took some of the family's turf and sold it so they could run away to England. 'Tony knew better than to go back,' recalled John ruefully, 'but I was younger and had to return to face the music.'

Smoking was a great source of crime and punishment in those days. Neil McGinley, a schoolfriend of the elder Robinson boys, said, 'We used to smoke at school. But at first we didn't know how to smoke. When we heard the teacher coming one lad was tossing the lit butt from hand to hand because he didn't know how to put it out. So he got caught, and so did James Brogan, the lad who gave it to him. You had to hold both your hands out to the side and you would get ten on either hand.' It was no less serious for the Robinsons at home. One evening when Betty was out visiting and Pat,

Gerry and Fiona were in bed, the ever-mischievous Pat pulled out a packet of cigarettes and gave one each to Gerry and Fiona. 'I think it was Gerry's first,' said Pat. 'He was coughing, so he said "nick my fag", meaning pinch the top of it and put it out. I flicked the top and the ash burnt the sheet. We didn't want Mum to find out because it would have meant a hiding, so we buried the sheet in the midden at the back of the house. And as far as we know she never found it.'

Parts of Donegal are said to be among the last regions in Ireland where Gaelic is still spoken as a first language, but that made little impact on Gerry. 'As a child I learnt Gaelic,' he recalled 'but I can't remember any of it as no one talked it at home, though it is still taught in that part of Ireland. It was a very parochial education, very narrow. I knew the geography of Ireland pretty well, but I would have struggled to tell you where London was. Ireland was the centre of the universe and nothing else mattered – especially if it was English. I remember being quite shocked when I went to school in London, learning English history and the immensity of the British Empire and what had gone on and the smallness of Ireland in the scheme of things.' In such unpromising circumstances much can depend on how well the rudimentary formal education is supplemented at home. Robinson did not shine at the village school, but the family reckon that he got his mathematical and analytical skills from his father, and his determination from his mother.

His brothers gave him a well-practised survival instinct. He and Paul dreamed up a boyhood fantasy to steal all the school's pencils. They hid a large collection in a rabbit hole at the back of the Plot. Later their father was giving Paul a talking to and, to get out of it, he blurted, 'Well, what about Gerry. He's stolen a whole load of pencils.' This had the desired effect, in that their father demanded to be shown the cache. Gerry was ordered to stay in the house while his father went up the Plot with Paul and Pat. Gerry recollected, 'I was shaking in my shoes, waiting for them to come back and for me to get the inevitable hiding.' But, amazingly, they came back empty-handed! Someone had heard about the pencils and secretly removed them. Consequently, Paul got the thrashing for lying and trying to get his brother into trouble.

Gerry has credited much of his drive to his need to compete for his parents' attention – and there was often only one parent to appeal to. To make ends meet, Tony would spend months at a time working in Glasgow or London because there was not enough demand for carpentry in Dunfanaghy. His return could be a mixed blessing, for the family missed him but feared the return of his accompanying tirades. 'It was jubilation when he came back,' said Gerry, 'for he was good fun to be with, but then he couldn't find a tool or something and the world would fall in. He would lose his temper very quickly.'

Evelyn recalled, 'The younger children had it easier than the first five – and I was in the middle! Dad was more affectionate than Mum – he would be the one putting his arm round you. Mum was more distant. But, if you upset Dad, you upset him. On the other hand, none of us brought home unpleasant children or got in trouble with the police. It was a very free and easy life, a bit sheltered because going to London was quite a shock.'

As Tony was increasingly away in England, the children

became used to their mother running the place. And, if she had to go away as well, the elder sisters, particularly Evelyn and Fiona, had to become surrogate parents.

Fiona admitted, 'I felt very hard done by. Mum was ill having Paul – she was forty-three by then. So I had to help bring up him and Gerry and consequently I only had six years at school. I resented that. It was expected in those days if you were the girl. The three of us would feast for two days and then starve, because I would blow what money Betty sent over from England. Paul and Gerry played me up something awful. Gerry didn't want to go to school, so I had to beat him up the Plot with a Sally rod. It swung beautifully.'

When Betty went to England to have an operation in 1955 it fell to Evelyn to help her father to look after Paul, Gerry, Fiona, Pat and Eddie. But when Betty returned she learned that Eddie was dead.

2

Eddie's death and the boating accident

On one of the rare occasions when Tony was in sole charge of the family there was a tragedy that has to this day cast a shadow over Gerry, his mother and his brothers and sisters — and was very nearly repeated in 1998.

When Gerry was seven one of his brothers, fourteen-year-old Eddie, drowned in the sea. Eddie was apprenticed to an architect at Newtoncunningham, a town near the head of Lough Swilly, thirty miles away along the coast of Donegal. Eddie wanted to be a draughtsman, and an architect's firm in Newtoncunningham gave him a summer job to see what he was like. If he looked promising, they were going to help pay his fees to go to college in Letterkenny, the nearest large town. On the evening of 11 July 1955, Eddie just didn't come home on the bus. That was the first they knew that something was wrong.

Then their Uncle Hugh, Tony's brother, came puffing up

Cottage Row. He was the local postmaster and had received the fateful telegram. Pat was playing with a ball in the front garden, and Fiona was sitting on the wall by the road. She turned round and saw Uncle Hugh coming up the street. 'Where is your father?' he demanded. Tony was working in the shed at the back of the house. Pat and Fiona carried on playing until their father came down the broad, sloping pathway at the side of the house. His face was ashen. He took his spectacles off and said, 'Come on in, children,' in a low tone that he never normally used. Pat said to Fiona, 'Something's wrong.' They went indoors and Tony told them that their brother was lost. That evening Tony went to meet the bus from Letterkenny, in case it had all been a mistake and Eddie was going to be on the bus after all. Fiona remembered, 'He came back from the bus looking immensely forlorn. After that, he suddenly became old. He was never the same again.'

Eddie had been out swimming in the sea with a friend working in the same firm and he drowned. Said Betty, 'He was in difficulties and waving his hand, and the other person thought he was just waving to say hello as he was just coming into the water. But he had taken cramp. The problem had started the previous day. At Horn Head, on the coast near Dunfanaghy, there was a hole that used to collect water. Eddie took cramp there and Pat had to pull him out, but they kept quiet about it because they didn't want their father and me to stop them going there. If they had mentioned it, Tony might have warned Eddie not to go swimming at Newtoncunningham.'

In fact, Eddie had been prone to cramp while swimming, but had kept it from his parents for that very reason. Tony went out on the boat that searched for and found the body, led by one of the locals who knew the tides in the area where he had gone missing. By the time the body was pulled out of the water it was already bloated, a sight to break any father's heart.

Betty was in London at the time, visiting her daughter Maureen. When the children had seen her off on the bus she put her hand on the window to wave them goodbye, leaving an imprint on the glass. She insisted that she was ironing at the precise moment when Eddie drowned and she had this overpowering feeling that something was happening. 'I had just had an operation,' Betty recalled, 'and they sent me a wire to say Eddie was ill because they didn't want to tell me he was gone. Fortunately I had convalesced, so I immediately set off back to Ireland.' Tony was taken in a taxi to Letterkenny to meet her, so he could break the news to her in private. There was a letter on the table at Cottage Row, addressed to Eddie from Betty in London. She opened it, and it said, 'Is something wrong? You haven't been writing to me lately.'

There was a huge funeral. In such a small community, everyone knew Eddie Robinson and the whole of Dunfanaghy turned out for it. The tiny churchyard was packed, and the walled lane leading to the churchyard entrance was lined with mourners. The nearby school, which Eddie, along with the rest of the Robinson family, had attended, was shut for the day. Tony made the gravestone, putting the inscription into a mould he made. It said, 'In loving memory of a beloved son, Edward.' Pat was the brother closest to Eddie. During the funeral one of his uncles asked

Pat to hold his trilby. Pat held the hat tight against his chest with his head bowed while the tears poured down his face.

The tragic episode hung around the family for a long time. It brought Tony and Betty closer together in their grief. 'It ruined my dad,' said Gerry. 'He absolutely fell apart. He felt terribly guilty, as he was in charge of the family just then. He was never the same. He became more subdued, less joyous.' Betty reflected, 'Eddie was so quiet. His father just had to tell him to go and weed the spuds and he would do it. He wouldn't say so, but you wouldn't know by his face that he didn't want to do it. It took me years to get over his going like that.'

While some of the family had grown up and moved away by the time Eddie died, there were several children still living in the cottage, including Gerry, who struggled to cope with the disaster. Pat was a year younger than Eddie. Fiona was twelve and Paul four.

'It was a horrible, black thing,' Gerry recalled. 'I know when people die everyone says nice things about them, but I think he was particularly nice and gentle. It was hard for me to understand that Eddie had just gone and wasn't coming back. It gives you some sense of what can and does happen. You realise that there are some things you cannot guard against. You can't make sense of it. There's something shocking about seeing your dad cry. I remember my uncle coming to see my dad, and having this terrible sense of something being wrong. I don't think my parents could get to grips with it at all. It was a subject you dropped because he couldn't handle it.

'Pat was given to shocking people, especially younger

brothers, and he was himself terribly shocked by it. Pat and Eddie used to fight a lot but were very close. My younger brother Paul was too young, and so I really had no one to talk to in the family about it. There was none of the counselling you would get nowadays. Nobody thought about explaining it to me, and I was too young to take part in any family discussions. It was a horrific, horrible experience. It's the thing that sticks in my mind more than anything else.

'I have since explored Eddie's death with my mum and how she felt. I still go to the grave occasionally when I'm in Donegal. It's daft on one level, because you know there's nothing there, but it touches something. And paradoxically as I have got older I have remembered him more. I suppose you just shut it off and get on with other things.'

But, while nothing else on that tragic scale has happened to the Robinson family since Eddie's death, the episode has echoed down the years, striking a chilling chord on at least two occasions.

By 1957 money was becoming slightly easier, thanks to contributions from some of the older children who had moved to London. Tony and Betty could afford to buy a small car, a Baby Austin, and got into a habit of going for a drive on Sundays with the three remaining youngsters, Fiona, Gerry and Paul. 'He had a terrible combination of high speed and no driving sense,' said Gerry. 'We must have visited every church in Donegal. This was Mum's idea of a fun day out, but the three of us sat in the back and usually had the sandwiches eaten by eleven o'clock in the morning. When I drive around Donegal nowadays I still see a church I vaguely recognise and think, 'That's one we visited with Mum and Dad in the car.'

It seems that most weeks the Sunday jaunt turned into some sort of disaster, with Betty saying to Tony, 'I'm not driving any further with you at the wheel.' Betty learned to drive too, and was apparently a much better driver, but of course in those days it would have been out of the question for Tony to let her drive him.

On one of these Sundays they stopped for their picnic by a river. Gerry and Paul were dressed in their Sunday-best suits, but forgot about that as they were trying to get something out of the water by crawling along the branch of a tree that hung out from the river bank. Gerry was further out than Paul, who was egging him on, telling him to go on and go on, further out along the branch. Eventually Paul gave him a shove and they both lost their balance and fell in. They were soaked through and – with the still vivid memory of Eddie's accident in mind – Tony went berserk.

'When Paul pushed me in the river,' said Gerry, 'the water was not deep and I didn't feel at risk. But I was flung in the back of the car like a bedraggled dog! Dad was furious beyond the norm, even allowing for the fact that we were wearing our Sunday best. It was only much later, when Paul mentioned it, that I realised he had had in mind Eddie drowning.'

Tony drove everyone home in a fury, with Betty at his side desperately telling him to slow down. If that was no more than an understandable overreaction to a basically trivial incident, in April 1998 Gerry had a real scare that he will never forget for the rest of his life – and a scare that was made all the worse by its terrible reminder of Eddie's death …

•

On Friday, 17 April, Gerry and his wife, Heather, drove from their holiday home on Mulroy Bay to view a new speedboat they were buying. To show its paces, the boatbuilder took them out in it through a treacherous channel, full of reeds, hidden sandbanks and fast-flowing currents, to the open sea beyond the bay. The following morning Gerry decided to go out in their existing vessel, a modern, white, fibreglass speed-boat with an outboard motor and two white-cushioned bench seats, one in front of the other. He waved goodbye at the kitchen door as he left, saying, 'I've got my mobile phone.' Gerry's sister Fiona and her husband Ray were coming for lunch and Heather thought they would picnic on one of the small islands in the bay. Fiona and Ray arrived, and the children were playing in the garden. Lunch was ready: no Gerry.

Heather, tears in her eyes and her voice breaking as she relived the incident, said, 'I phoned him and he said, "I'm fine, but I'm taking my time because I don't know my way through the reeds and sandbanks." I phoned him twice more. I was more irritated than concerned because he was going to be late for lunch. Then he phoned, embarrassed, and said "I've run out of petrol. But I can see the house – I'm not far. Can you ask someone to take the spare can of petrol out to me." It was in the workshop, where he had left it because he had forgotten to take it with him.

'They went out, but no one could find him. It went on across the afternoon, hour after hour. The blokes were radio-ing in, saying they couldn't find him and Gerry didn't have a clue where he was because he was beyond the narrows out at sea. Then I phoned him and got the recorded message saying it was switched off and please try later. I could not believe he had switched it off. But then I started panicking. After all, professional fishermen were saying they couldn't see him. People were standing on our pier with binoculars saying they thought they could see him, but of course they couldn't have.'

Gerry had not taken any precautions with him – no spare petrol, no oar, no two-way radio – because originally he had not intended to go far. But it was a pleasant day, nice and sunny, so – like a fool, as he later admitted – he thought, 'I'll just go a bit further' and sailed through one funnel of water, and then another. And suddenly he was out at sea and the tide was much faster than he had expected. Then he ran out of petrol. Oarless, he was completely adrift and at the mercy of swirling currents. To his horror he realised he was being taken out to sea and could not do a thing about it.

'I'm still shaking to think of it,' Gerry told me two days after the incident. 'I nearly drowned. It's very tricky there: there are two narrow channels where the water rushes through and there are a lot of rocks. I called Heather and she sent two guys down to rescue me. I could see them coming over the hill, but they were too far away to shout to, and too far away to do anything for a good few minutes. So I thought, I have to secure the boat, and I tossed the anchor over the side. But because of the current all that did was to drag the back of the boat into the water, and I was sinking. I couldn't bail out the water anything like quickly enough, so there was nothing for it but to swim for the shore. I had a lifejacket on and I took off my shoes - everything else was lost. It was the most terrifying swim of my life. It was exhausting fighting against the current and for a time I didn't think I was going to make it. I have never felt so relieved as I did when I reached the shore.'

He walked back home, barefoot and soaked through, to an emotional reunion with his family. Ironically, had he only realised it, he could have stayed in the stricken boat without any risk of drowning, and waited until his rescuers reached him. For, like most modern speedboats nowadays, this one had an air tank built into the hull to prevent it sinking. That is why a local fisherman was able to recover it later, sitting a few inches beneath the surface, but easily visible and virtually undamaged. They even found the abandoned mobile phone. But it is all too easy to forget such factors when panic sets in.

Heather recalled, 'The last thirty or forty minutes before Gerry returned was a horrible time. I got really frightened. After Eddie dying at sea, I couldn't think beyond thinking, How am I going to tell his Mum? We had a late lunch and everyone else left quickly. Then Gerry just sat down and cried.'

3

Darling Row and the seminary

Four of Tony and Betty's children – Tony, Maureen, Jean and John – had left Dunfanaghy by the time of Eddie's funeral, and Evelyn and Pat would not be long behind them. They had been steadily departing from as young as fourteen. Their father was quite happy not to have the children hanging around the house, so he did not try to persuade any of them to stay. The first to leave was Maureen, who went to train as a nurse at St Andrew's Hospital, Devons Road, in what is now Tower Hamlets. She was followed two years later by Jean. Irish girls were attracted to cross the Irish Sea because they were paid to study nursing in England while *they* had to pay in Ireland. But Maureen met Stan, a porter at a nearby hospital, and quit her job to get married.

Maureen gradually became the family's unofficial immigration officer, welcoming the others to London one by one. Stan was a painter and he heard of a one-bedroom flat going in Shenley Road, Shoreditch, a rundown district of east London where, according to Maureen, there was a thriving trade in stolen goods. 'Of course, they would never burgle the local houses,' she recalled, 'and once you became part of the family they would get you anything.' After Stan heard of the flat going, Maureen took their two-month-old baby and hurried to the agent in nearby Kingsland Road. He showed her the flat, just a day or two after the previous occupant had died. Nothing had been moved. 'I think the agent saw my face fall,' said Maureen. 'It must have told a story, because he said, "Blank it from your mind and I'll have it cleared out by tomorrow." We went back the next day and it was completely empty, but it took my husband and a friend six days just to make it habitable.'

So Shoreditch was where they first established themselves, and that was why the rest of the family started off living in east London. Maureen and Stan would put them up until they had a chance to find a place of their own, and help them find a job. Jean remembered, 'After she married Stan, Maureen became a mother to the rest of us. And Stan was very generous. Once he met me in the street and said, "Have you got any money?" I was horrified because I thought he wanted to borrow off me and I didn't have a penny on me. I told him so – and he gave me seven and sixpence!'

In line with the custom for Irish immigrants to Britain in the 1950s, the girls tended to train as nurses while the boys found work on construction sites in the postwar building boom. Evelyn's shock at arriving in London from the Donegal countryside was typical of the family as they got off the train from Liverpool. She said, 'I stood at Euston station and thought, What have I done? Maureen and Stan took me from the station and bought me egg and chips, because it was a Friday and we didn't eat meat that day. It was the first time I had had chips!'

Pat went into the Irish Army, leaving only Paul, Gerry and Fiona in Dunfanaghy. This made it harder for the family to keep in touch and their father's prolonged absences were becoming a strain, especially as he was in his mid-fifties by this stage – though there is a suggestion that he secretly enjoyed the excuse to get away every so often. So instead of his winding down to a gradual retirement on the Irish coast they decided to join the exodus to London. 'My mother was instrumental in that decision,' said Gerry. 'Being Scottish, she was comfortable about the move to the mainland. My father called her "the old imperialist", something between a term of endearment and I'm not sure what.'

On the morning of 4 November 1959, Mrs Robinson took Gerry, Fiona and an outsize leather suitcase to the main road of Dunfanaghy to catch the bus to Londonderry. Paul had gone on ahead because he had had to go to hospital in London for a minor operation. Gerry's sister, Fiona, remembers locking the front door shut with a loud click and realising that a stage in their lives had come to an end.

'I walked down the road with Gerry's hand in mine,' said Fiona. 'while Mum walked on ahead, carrying the bags. And that's my memory of her. Dad was very strict, but a gentleman. He never raised his voice, either to the children or to Betty.'

Their father had gone on ahead to sort out a job with an

Essex building firm. 'We had been trying for a long time to get to London,' Betty remembered, 'to be with the rest of the family, but Tony didn't want to leave Dunfanaghy. He would come to England to work and said he would look for a place, but he never did. Eventually Maureen found a place for us and helped to furnish it.'

The Robinson family, what was left of it, moved into a tiny flat in Stepney. It could not have been more different from the life they had left behind. In Ireland they had been used to fresh air, wide open spaces, going to the beach and playing with their pals. At 32 Darling Row, just behind the roar of east London's Whitechapel Road, they had a bedroom and a sitting room on the first floor of an old house. They had to share a toilet with a Mr and Mrs Edwards, who lived on the same landing. 'Mrs Edwards used to talk to us while she was on the toilet,' Paul recalled. Paul had been staying with Maureen and Evelyn, and by the time Gerry arrived he greeted his elder brother with a thoroughgoing Cockney accent. He had acquired the nasal twang to stave off cries of Paddy – a lesson that the nine-year-old Gerry had to learn fast.

For three years Tony and Betty shared their bedroom with Gerry and Paul in bunk beds. Fiona went to live with her eldest brother, Tony, and his wife Kath in north London. She said, 'It was like opening a door on the world after living with Mum and Dad. It represented freedom.'

With two boys running around in Darling Row's cramped rooms, there was bound to be some noise from time to time. An aged couple were living on the ground floor, and they found plenty to complain to their new neighbours about. Gerry had a notion to write short stories to sell to magazines and the like, but he discovered that magazines would not even look at them unless they were properly typed. So his parents bought him an ancient typewriter, but that did not last long because the clacking used to annoy the old couple. Said Betty, 'They complained because they were convinced it sounded like a table-tennis ball bouncing against the wall and we couldn't make them believe that it wasn't. It was a bit noisy in our flat with two boys, but we tried to be as quiet as we could and I often told the boys off if they were getting too noisy.'

Gerry added, 'Darling Row was far from darling to me. It was exciting at first, what with the move and making all the new friends and getting used to a new school, but it became terribly enclosing. My father was never happy there. He died aged eighty-six in 1988, still living near London, and the great sadness was he had always intended to go back home.'

But there was some relief from the cramped conditions. Tony and Betty Robinson kept on their little house in Dunfanaghy, and would take the two boys back there for the summer holidays. Said Paul, 'As we went back to Ireland each summer we gradually turned into local superstars – look, here come the Robinsons from London, they'd say. In your memories of childhood holidays the sun is always shining, isn't it? As far as I was concerned it was just great. We played with hoops, running them along the road just like in Victorian times. If we got sent on an errand we were much quicker if we took a hoop to bowl along. In later years we'd turn up wearing cheap versions of all the latest gear from Carnaby Street – button-down collars, flares, kipper ties – which the locals had never seen before. Then we'd relax into the holiday and by the time we got back it took a week to get my wardrobe right again.'

Back in London Gerry at first went to St Anne's School, attached to St Anne's Catholic Church in nearby Underwood Road. Gerry was officially not old enough to sit the eleven-plus exam, then the mandatory route to a prized grammar school place. He hadn't studied for it and the school liked to prepare the pupils themselves for the exam. He sat it, but did not pass. So he moved to a Catholic secondary school, St Bernard's in east London. But he was to stay there for just a year. One day the Holy Ghost Fathers, from St Mary's College at Grange-over-Sands in Lancashire, visited the school look-ing for promising raw material to mould into priests.

'I decided I wanted to become a priest,' Gerry recalled. 'It had been in my mind that maybe it would interest me. I did it and thought about it afterwards. Like so many things I have done, I didn't think it through. My mother was absolutely delighted at the idea of having a priest in the family, after my brother John having tried and given it up, but it was entirely my doing.' So keen was Betty to see Gerry realise his – and her – dream that she took a job as a tea lady at the local Midland Bank to help pay the fees. Betty insisted, 'We had enough – we always had enough.'

Gerry was at Grange-over-Sands from the ages of thirteen to seventeen, and he emerged with eight O levels, four A lev-els and a love of painting that has stayed with him throughout his life. There were around eighty to a hundred boys in six classes there, all heading for the priesthood. It was a very disci-plined, very heavily structured and very narrow education, but with tremendous concentration on study. They would get up at about 6.15 a.m., wash and dress very quickly. Within half an hour of waking the boys were in church for Mass. Then they had three-quarters of an hour of study from about 7.30, breakfast at 8.15 a.m. and classes began at 9 a.m. The school day went through pretty much as normal, then there was an hour or so of free time after school. That was followed by an early supper and three hours of study before bed. This was the basic routine for five and a half days a week, breaking only for a half-day's games on Saturday afternoon. They spent most of Sunday in prayer.

'With all that enforced studying,' Robinson explained, 'you had to be a complete dunce not to pass your exams and it was not exceptional to get a lot of O and A levels. I was always first or second in class. I did well in that sort of structure, but the difference between the top and bottom was pretty narrow. My big regret is that I didn't do sciences, because that wasn't covered there. I did Latin, Greek, English and mathematics to A level, but I did not study pure science at all. I felt the effect of that. I have become more interested in astronomy in particular and I am an avid reader of New Scientist. Science may never have fitted with Catholic teaching, but it may not have been as cynical as that. It was about a philosophical difference, rather than some long-standing fight with Galileo!'

Many of the boys made the most of their opportunity to run off excess energy by throwing themselves enthusiastically into sports, particularly soccer and cricket, and the teams did well against opposition from nearby schools. Robinson preferred cricket, cross-country running and gymnastics. He said, 'I was a batsman, but pretty far down the order, and my bowling was just horrific. I never did master it. But I was a good long-distance runner.' They also did a lot of serious walking to local places like Kendal and Scafell – both more than fifteen miles away from Grange-over-Sands.

Said Robinson, 'People knew exactly what you were doing every minute of the day. It was very close control. And there was a kind of zeal about the education, that it was very important, and passionately imparted. Teaching has never been very well paid, but the teachers at the seminary were certainly not attracted by the pay – it was the zealous sense of preparing people for the priesthood that drove them. We had a Father Holmes who taught English. He just had a fantastic passion for literature that really, really made you enthusiastic. He really brought Kenneth Grahame's *Wind in the Willows* alive. There was one passage in particular that always stuck in my mind, about

> a plate piled up with very hot buttered toast, cut thick, very brown on both sides, with the butter running through the holes in it in great golden drops, like honey from the honeycomb. The smell of that buttered toast simply talked to Toad, and with no uncertain voice; talked of warm kitchens, of breakfasts on bright frosty mornings, of cosy parlour firesides on winter evenings, when one's ramble was over and slippered feet were propped on the fender; of the purring of contented cats, and the twitter of sleepy canaries.

'That conjured up wonderful pictures for us, and made our mouths water, because the food at Castlehead was pretty spartan, ordinary and repetitive. Pot Luck, we called it, because you were lucky if you got anything from the pot! It became a bit of an obsession. There was a pat of butter

47

between six at mealtimes, and it had to be split exactly six ways – the trouble we went to, to make sure that no one was diddled! They had calculated the food pretty well, because it was just about all right. But we looked forward immensely to the goodies parcels that we got sent from home – they were enormously important and fought over.'

One of those parcels got Robinson into serious trouble. When he was fifteen or sixteen, like many other boys he was intrigued by the idea of smoking. But there was no chance of any of the Castlehead pupils acquiring any cigarettes by their own efforts, because they were not allowed out of the school grounds unsupervised: they could not just pop down to the nearest tobacconist. One day a friend of Robinson in London, Pat Doran, gave his sister Fiona a box of chocolates to post to him.

Eagerly opening the wrappings, Robinson was delighted to discover what was inside. However, he painstakingly husbanded the contents, taking two or three days to munch his way through the top layer of chocolates. He then lifted out the paper divider to get at the bottom layer – and found two packets of cigarettes nestling in the bottom of the box! Robinson could not resist trying one, and shared half a dozen with his mates. They did not have matches, naturally, although with all the candles around the place lighting the contraband was no problem. But the boys were discovered immediately. They went into assembly and the head teacher, Father Pass, walked by and began sniffing. Among all those nonsmokers, the acrid smell of cigarette smoke must have stood out a mile. They froze. Father Pass had a reputation for being a fair man, but he was also a figure of fear who was not shy of administering the cane.

'We didn't get caned on that occasion,' said Robinson, 'but I was warned that if I were caught smoking again I would be expelled. The other thing was that Father Pass told my parents. They wrote to parents every week with a card marking us all for the standard of our behaviour, dress, achievement in class and so on, and if you had a bad report you would get a letter from your parents telling you to buck up. It was just a list of marks out of ten for the different categories, but it was a very good discipline. You lost a point for talking when you weren't supposed to, or if a prefect saw your tie was loose. And we had to mix, to stop cliques developing – it may also have been a precaution against homosexuality, though I don't remember homosexuality being an issue. If you were caught grouping, as it was called, you lost points for that. So naturally it went back home that we had been caught smoking. It felt like the end of the world.'

Betty confirmed, 'I remember the smoking episode. I was disappointed, but you get over it.'

However, Robinson did not entirely escape the dreaded cane at Castlehead. It happened when, of all the jobs to have around the school, he was the school barber. He recalled, 'It wasn't a bad job, but there was no training – your predecessor simply handed you the set of clippers. There was a guy called Quigley who had been quite a pain – I think his nickname was Smelly, so he wasn't too popular. So I gave him a haircut where I went right up the middle of his head, with tufts sticking out on either side. We were both called before Father Pass and Quigley was given the opportunity to cut my hair but he said no, it was all right. I felt about an inch high after he passed it off so lightly – and because I would otherwise have gone unpunished I was caned.'

But they were, after all, teenage boys who – although they were studying for the priesthood – were as much on the lookout for fun as any other bunch of adolescents. An unpopular caretaker was whacked over the head with a heavy bag of blood when he was caught unawares in the seminary's abattoir. And when they held a Whitsun fête it attracted people from Barrow-in-Furness and all around, including girls good-looking enough to have the boys' tongues hanging out.

'When I was in my second year,' said Robinson, 'we took a school play to Barrow, a farce where I hugely enjoyed playing a woman, and again there were girls in the audience. And one time we were taken on a trip to the circus in Blackpool Tower, which had girls on a trapeze – in leotards! We were just open-mouthed. Father Pass was with us, but he would have made a wonderful poker player. You just couldn't tell from his expression what he was thinking.'

Nevertheless, Robinson really did not like the seminary. 'Once the gloss was off it, six weeks in, I was terribly homesick,' he admitted. 'I didn't enjoy it, and I never looked forward to going back there after the holidays. My worst memories were of the second week of the holidays, because it was beginning to face me that it was all going to start again. And I literally used to count off the days to the end of term, just like being in prison. That can't be a good sign, can it?'

In his last couple of years at Grange-over-Sands Gerry came to a realisation that, as with his brother John, the priesthood was not for him. It didn't feel right. Instead he found that, through going back to Ireland occasionally and sneaking into dances at the age of fifteen or sixteen, girls seemed a much more attractive option. 'I think I saw the light in an entirely different way to St Paul,' Gerry explained. 'It all just struck me as wrong – I don't think it hangs together. I think religion is all a load of nonsense now. Comparatively few from the seminary make it to be a priest.'

Once Betty had got over her disappointment at realising she would never be the mother of a priest, she decided to get Gerry fixed up with a job. After the financial strain of putting him though the seminary, even with his four A levels university was never going to be an option.

'University literally never occurred to me,' said Gerry. 'With my A levels I could have chosen to go almost anywhere, but I didn't have that sort of conversation with my parents, and as I had left the seminary I had no advice from there, in the way that a lot of people got from their schools if their parents had had no university experience. My parents had no guidance for me, beyond being a priest, because they had not had that sort of background and none of my brothers and sisters had gone to university. So in a way I fell between school and home advice and just never thought about going. Looking back, I miss it. I'd have appreciated having those three years to study and think about things free from outside pressure. And going to university in the late 1960s would certainly have been a huge change from the seminary!'

His brother John had become a senior site agent with

Tersons the builders. He tried to interest Gerry in becoming an architect, but it didn't grab him. After his disillusionment with the priesthood, he was probably wary of committing himself to another lengthy period of training. But his academic successes were powerful cards to use to attract employers. So, with a sheaf of St Mary's College reports in her bag, she marched Gerry up the road to the Youth Employment Bureau at Hackney Town Hall.

'Gerrard got very good reports every week,' Betty recalled. 'I had collected them all while he was at the seminary, because they were very impressive and I thought they might come in handy. He was a great fellow for the books, wanting to learn all the time. So I took the reports with me when I went with Gerrard to the Youth Employment Agency and they were so impressed that straight away they got him a job at Lesney.'

This was the East End company that made miniature cars and vans under the brand name Matchbox Toys. Gerry's sister Fiona, then twenty-two, was already working in one of Lesney's factories putting rubber wheels on the cars. When she was only seventeen Fiona had been running a branch of Maple Dairies in Harlesden, northwest London, but she moved back to live with her parents when they moved to more spacious accommodation in Bethnal Green. So Fiona reached Lesney, a big local employer, before Gerry, but when he started there he used to give his big sister a lift to the factory on his motor scooter. 'I went to work on the shop floor while he went upstairs to the office,' she recalled.

There were three thousand other women working on the production lines, most of them considerably more worldly-wise than Gerry. 'It was heaven for a young lad like me,' he said.

4

Lesney and Lex

Lesney was a near-ideal place for Gerry Robinson to start his career. The company's share price was beginning to take off, the management had the confidence to feel they were doing the right things, demand for Matchbox Toys was soaring, so the business was expanding rapidly, creating plenty of opportunities for an ambitious young man like Robinson.

With the help of their postwar gratuity, Leslie Smith and Jack Odell had started Lesney in 1947 in a bombed-out pub in Tottenham, north London, when they were both in their late twenties. At the company's peak, in the late 1960s, Odell and Smith each owned shares in Lesney worth around £30 million – at a time when a pint of bitter cost about 10p, a bottle of champagne £1 and a decent car just a few hundred pounds – and they could see no end to it. 'Our sales just go on and on increasing,' Smith, the ebullient salesman of the two, told me in 1968. 'There is a worldwide vacuum in the supply of toy cars. We've got more orders than we can fulfil for some time to come and we're continually increasing our capacity.'

By modern standards Lesney was run on a wing and a prayer. Using the shy, introverted Odell's engineering skills, they had started by making die-cast components for washing machines, freezers and record players. But they hit a quiet patch and orders dried up, so they made a few toys to keep the machines running. It was a line of business that in any case appealed more to the flamboyant Smith than selling anonymous components to other manufacturers. Then Smith had the brilliant idea of producing a miniature coach and horses to commemorate the coronation of Queen Elizabeth in 1953, and its high standard of workmanship put them on the map.

When Robinson joined Lesney in 1965, the place was throbbing. And, even though he was a newcomer, because the company was run on fairly informal lines, he could see at first hand how a business operated. Robinson recalled, 'I learned a lot at Lesney. Because it was a raw company, it didn't have layer on layer of management. You could feel it was something raw and you got decisions out of these people pretty crisply. There was no subtlety attached to these guys and it was therefore a very good way of getting exposed to the harder end of business.

'There was an East End feel of the older guys looking after you. It might have been attractive for them to have someone there like me, who was not worldly-wise but who was very enthusiastic about what was going on, and eager to learn. It was exciting to get up in the morning and go to work.'

Robinson took to working life with the same thorough-
ness with which he had tackled school. He was delighted to
start at Lesney on what for him was a fortune of £7 10s
(£7.50) a week, paid in cash, soon raised to £10 a week as his
bosses realised they had a promising recruit on their hands.
He started modestly, cutting out pictures of toys from the
company catalogue and sticking them on to cost sheets.

Meanwhile, Robinson was as entranced as the rest of his
generation by the rising tide of 1960s pop music – and, like
thousands of others, he got together with some mates and
formed a group. He became singer and rhythm guitarist in a
foursome that called itself Musical Catastrophe. Robinson
recalled, 'It was a right disaster, but we spent a lot of time
rehearsing in the local school hall and, though I was no good,
I can still pick out a chord on a guitar. Other than a few
appearances at the church hall and one or two pubs, we never
played anywhere in public. But it was terrific fun, because
Britpop was where it was at. We were more Rolling Stones
than Beatles, but we did both and a lot of Chuck Berry. We
had all the inevitable difficulty of getting kit anywhere,
because none of us had cars. But we had great comradeship,
big rows and falling out over girls.'

The venture did nothing for Robinson's relations with
his father, who saw the band as little better than a bunch of
hooligans. 'It was difficult for Dad,' Robinson conceded. 'One
time I brought home this parka, then *the* thing for a young guy
to wear, all the rage, and Dad said, "Unless you stole it, you
were robbed." I remember him watching me watching the
Stones on TV and he couldn't understand it. He wasn't
horrified: he was just thinking, What *is* all this? It was a time

of a sea change in attitudes, quite unlike today when the kids still listen to the Beatles and the Stones and so on. In the 1960s we would have never dreamed of listening to the bands or singers of thirty years before we were kids.'

Pat, Gerry's elder brother, was living in London at this time, and with Paul they would go to Highbury to see Arsenal play football. They had a few scrapes, especially when Pat taught Gerry to drive. While he was learning Gerry scraped an Austin Westminster and he was just about to stop and apologise – when Pat reached over and put his own foot on the accelerator!

While Robinson was working for Lesney he met Maria, who was to become his first wife. It happened by chance when he borrowed his brother's minivan. He had passed his test, but could not yet afford a car of his own. A fellow member of Musical Catastrophe, Terry McAndrew – known as Mac – had a girlfriend who lived in south London, so Robinson gave him a lift down there from the East End. But one of the tyres on the van was punctured and while they were repairing it Maria Borg turned up, as she was a friend of Mac's girlfriend. Her father was a Maltese who had a small jewellery business in Bishopsgate, in the City of London, and so was well off compared with the Robinson family. She lived near the two boys in Whitechapel and had been in the year below Robinson at St Bernard's. 'She says she remembers me chasing her and kissing her at school,' said Robinson. 'I honestly don't remember that!'

As he was working in Lesney's cost office, becoming an accountant seemed the natural thing to do, even though he had not had any thoughts in that direction before he had arrived there. However, he soon realised that the numbers game took him to the heart of a business and Lesney had the foresight and generosity to give him a day off a week so that he could obtain a qualification from the Association of Cost and Management Accountants. He said, 'I wanted to get the exams out of the way. I knew I couldn't face up to studying throughout the year, so two months before the exam I blocked everything off and went for it. I left Paul to go out on his own, locked myself in my room and played Beatles records to keep me company.' Maria would sit in and knit or read while he was studying, and be there for him. 'It never felt like Maria was pushing me,' Robinson explained, 'but she was keen for me to do well.'

Like most successful careerists, Robinson had a succession of mentors who helped him at important stages of his climb up the ladder. The first was Bob Tanner, who worked in the cost office at Lesney. Said Robinson, 'He was very paternal towards me. I was in his section and he was very encouraging about getting my ACMA qualification, otherwise I probably wouldn't have done that. Bob had some sense of my lostness, my being very uncomfortable in that environment. Rather like moving from Ireland to being in this flat in Stepney, it was quite a change to come out of that seminary environment, very regimented, into making your own choices in a company like Lesney.' But, once Robinson got used to the setup at Lesney, he took one liberty too many with his mentor.

'We used to do overtime on Saturday mornings, when Bob almost never came in. We started having a game of cards just for ten minutes at lunchtime, but it got longer and longer until it ran for about an hour out of the four hours we were there on a Saturday. I was just the junior, but I still felt guilty about it. We got caught – I think it came back to him via someone else who noticed us playing cards for so much of the time – and I always felt awful about letting this great guy down. He told us off more in sorrow than in anger – that was what got me. In that sense it said more about him than about the incident itself. I had a huge feeling of letting him down. It was not the event, so much as "how could we have done this to Bob?"'

When Robinson was still in the seminary at Grange-over-Sands his parents had moved from Darling Row to a council flat in a tower block in Bethnal Green. But he left home within months of getting the job at Lesney. Perhaps it was significant that the trigger was a row with his father over a TV programme, *Sanctuary,* that had a strong Catholic flavour. It was a realistic drama series about life in a small convent – where, controversially, the nuns were allowed to smoke and break other traditional rules. Its creator, Philip Levene, said at the launch in 1967, '*Sanctuary* will be strictly true to life. The cast have visited convents to see how nuns live and work.' The first episode was about how nuns consider whether a novice has a true calling or is being influenced by a psychological whim concerning a love affair. One episode was about a young girl, played by Sinead Cusack, who wants to become a nun but her family disapprove. Other episodes covered birth control, faith healing, a visit to Lourdes and the consequences of a nun being raped. It was designed to provoke controversy – and surely most of all in thousands of Catholic households throughout the country.

'It was a close thing between me walking out and being thrown out,' Robinson admitted. 'It was just the tip of the iceberg, because there was a growing feeling between my father and me. And just about every one of the boys had a row with Dad, about getting home late or something, and left home in those terms. Dad was strict about time: he was master of the house and he decided what you watched on TV and when you should be home. There was a definite pattern to it, so maybe he wanted more time to himself – I don't blame him, with all of us running around getting in his way!'

He went to live with his sister Evelyn and her husband Julian Tims in Rainham, on the London–Essex border, and lived there for nearly two years until he married in 1969. Evelyn worked as an office accounts clerk for the Council of British Shipping in the City, and Gerry had introduced her to Julian, a Catholic of Anglo-Indian descent.

In their first few years in London the Robinsons had become immersed in the Legion of Mary, which tried to help people. Julian was living in a hostel attached to St Anne's Church, and one evening Paul and Gerry brought him home. Julian was an accountant who also worked in the shipping industry, first for Fred Olsen and then for Transatlantic Freight Company. He was a very calm man and in some ways Robinson represented, or so he felt, the teenage son Julian and Evelyn never had. 'He could always put things in perspective,' said Robinson. 'It was not that he always let me do what I wanted – you couldn't tramp in at all hours – but it was done with great care and patience.'

The three of them moved from Rainham to Stanford-le-Hope, further out of London on the Essex coast, to what was their first house after living in flats in London. It was very small, just a three-bedroom semi, part of a modern development, but Julian put a lot of work into it and built a garage on to it. Said Robinson, 'Julian taught me how to play chess well and helped me with my accountancy lessons. He would drop me off at clubs and pick me up at three o'clock in the morning. He put a hell of a lot of effort into that, though perhaps I didn't realise it at the time. It was a great time for me, living with them. It was a time that I really enjoyed. There was not that slightly brooding feeling of not knowing where Dad was coming from.' Julian died of a heart attack in 1989. Nine years later Evelyn moved back to Donegal.

After Robinson left his father he bought himself a scooter, partly for the freedom it gave him to get around, and partly because it was a great way of getting girls. 'It was a pretty explicit time,' he recalled, 'and I think back to those times with a lot of affection, especially when I had much more freedom living with Evelyn and Julian.'

Robinson and seven or eight of his pals used to stack camping kit on the bikes and pitch tents for the weekend in a field on the Norfolk Broads or near Hastings, in East Sussex. 'I was never in any mods-versus-rockers sort of scene,' he said, 'but I had a hell of a good time around the edges of the whole mods thing, without ever getting involved in the seaside brawls there were at the time. We used to take the girls back to the tents. We were eighteen or eighteen and a half, and after the seminary I felt I had a lot of time to make up. There was also rebellion about my dad not liking scooters.'

But the scooter also gave Robinson an early taste of the capital's low life, because he was arrested twice in a month for speeding down the Mile End Road in east London. That meant a visit to the magistrates' court among all the drunks, prostitutes and other ne'er-do-wells, to collect a £10 fine plus an endorsement on his driving licence.

When Gerry and Maria married they set up home in Roundwood Park near Harlesden, in northwest London – a safe distance from Gerry's father. They rented a two-bedroom maisonette, up stairs that were on the outside of the house. If his parents still harboured any illusions about their son's dwindling devotion to Catholicism they were shattered soon after Gerry and Maria moved to Harlesden.

'I was still pretending to go to church,' Gerry recalls, 'and I kept that up for quite a long time. I would not have spoken to my Mum and Dad about not going to church, and needn't have said anything about it now I was living on the other side of London. But when they came to see us in Harlesden, I was driving them home and stupidly pointed out this church along the road and lied, "That's where we go." Dad saw instantly that it was a Protestant Church of England church, and he gave me this look that just said so much. My brother Paul married a Protestant girl, and that caused a bit of a stir in the family. But in those days you had to get married. It would have been very uncomfortable to have lived with someone without marrying, as people often do nowadays.'

As with Robinson's next two jobs, at Lex and Grand Metropolitan, he spent nine years at Lesney. He progressed from cost clerk to senior cost clerk at the Hackney-based toy maker, eventually becoming a works accountant in one of the factories. The promotion ladder took him all the way from Hackney to the group's Edmonton factory, via Eastway. He moved up to section leader first, and then management accountant with two or three people reporting to him. Then he became accountant for the Eastway factory, which was very much the foundry section that actually moulded the toy cars' little metal bodies under the die-cast process. Then he went to Edmonton, final assembly point for the larger toys, boxes of twelve toys, and fancy goods like ashtrays with the Matchbox logo on them. 'I was separate from the head office,' Robinson pointed out, 'and so I was the big finance cheese there! But I missed being part of the larger central role.'

Lesney was basically a one-product company. The US giant, Mattel, came along with Hot Wheels, toy cars that had pin-thin spindles so that there was much less friction than with Lesney's and consequently they could go faster and even loop the loop. Suddenly, from selling all they could make, Lesney saw its stocks starting to pile up in the warehouse. Although Smith and Odell came up with their own version of Hot Wheels, known as Supafast, they never made up the lost ground and eventually went into receivership.

Long before that happened, though, Robinson was on his way to a more promising employer – which, crucially, gave the staff use of a company car.

'Before we got married we scraped together the money for a battered old red Mini,' said Robinson. 'It was a right old banger: I was banned from driving for a month because it had a bald tyre. That was a real nuisance, because of having to get to work by public transport, all the way from Harlesden to Edmonton. The need to have a better car was behind my looking for another job, because repairs were a real financial blow on the money I was earning then, and I was too junior to get a new one from Lesney.'

He saw an advert by Lex, the motor dealer and Volvo concessionaire, for a job with a car attached – a sand-coloured Mini, as it turned out, but all the costs were taken care of. 'That was far more important than any career consideration,' Robinson admitted. 'I didn't even want to know that much about the job, which was to be a management accountant with Lex Service, the motor dealer. I just followed the car! Money was quite important, and knowing that if the car broke down, or you needed new tyres, it was taken care of, that was a big thing. Bob Tanner at Lesney made me feel quite bad about it, tried to say there was no future in car dealing compared with a proper manufacturing company, but Maria and I wanted the car that came with the job.'

Lex had been started in 1928 to run five garages in London. The company took its name from its chief outlet in Lexington Street, Soho, where even as late as the 1950s customers could park their car, have a bath, change clothes – and leave their dogs in a kennel. In 1944 two brothers, Norris and Rosser Chinn, joined the board to revive the business after the losses it had run up during World War Two. In the often rough-and-tumble postwar years they had to make their presence felt and when Robinson joined in 1974 there were still awe-struck stories circulating of Rosser Chinn turning up at a garage at three o'clock in the morning to fire some hapless minion.

But the brothers developed Lex into a substantial company until they were able to pass management control to Rosser's Harvard-educated son, Trevor, who in 1959 became a director of Lex at the age of twenty-four, and was made managing director eight years later. He was knighted in 1990. By the time Robinson arrived, Trevor Chinn had embarked on a rapid expansion which for a while took Lex into US electronics distribution and hotels, at one time owning the prestigious Carlton Tower Hotel in London's Belgravia.

After Lesney the twenty-seven-year-old Robinson found the work at Lex a doddle – perhaps too much so. He was with Lex Brooklands, which held the main Volvo concession, and was responsible for four garages, selling cars, petrol, accessories and parts as well as wholesaling cars to other dealerships. Said Robinson, 'Compared with accounting in a manufacturing business like Lesney, it was very simple accounting for an organisation that just imported cars and sold them. I found it easy work. Lex paid its people at the upper end of the scale, so you got some very good people attracted there. You also met some interesting people in the trade – it's a right ruffian's game. There were some comic types, especially those buying second-hand cars. They didn't want to be accounted for. VAT came in just as I arrived and it was calculated on the profit margin, so if these lads knew the VAT they knew how much you were making on the deal. It caused a lot of worry among the Lex management. They came to depend on us quite a lot to organise them and keep the books straight.'

The garages Robinson took care of were at St John's Wood in north London, Mayfair's Albemarle Street, Elgin Avenue in London's Maida Vale district, and Reading. Robinson was based at Lex's Wembley office, which was a convenient four miles or so from his home in Harlesden, but the accounting centre was in Ipswich. That gave him regular treks round the North Circular Road and up the A12 to tie up records and make sure everything was in order as far as his clutch of garages was concerned.

At Lex Robinson met not one but three mentors. 'The managing director of Lex Brooklands was Ken Burr, who was a real enthusiast,' said Robinson. 'He made you feel really good about it when you did well. He was a very strong manager. You didn't mess about with him because you were in trouble pretty fast if you did. He was a man of huge integrity, very straight, very demanding. And I was taught a lot by Alan Costin, the financial controller of Lex Brooklands. A lot of my systemised approach has come from him – his filing system, the way he followed things up. If you said you were going to do things, you had better have done them. Ken Burr called him the man with a bucket of cold water because he was always saying that so-and-so might not work.

'It really stuck with me that the numbers have to work, that the first thing you have to do is to have really good financial records, so they lead you to decisions rather than just tell you what has happened. You need very good information, well presented and honed down. Alan hugely influenced me over a period of time. He was very dogged. Lex's real success was Volvo, that was the big money-earner. The safety aspects of the car were very well marketed.

'There was a time when people couldn't get the cars, so we were sitting on the cash for months before we had to hand it over to Volvo AB, the Swedish manufacturer of the cars. It was, like Lesney, basically a single-product company. The motor trade is notoriously very cyclical because people usually need finance to buy a car, so sales go up and down with interest rates, but demand for Volvos was so high that people would pay over the odds.'

Commercial vehicles were handled through Lex Tillotson, Lex Commercial and Lex Mead, the British Leyland dealer.

Robinson became a senior management accountant, then Divisional Accountant of Harvey Plant Hire, a successful business which leased out forklift trucks and earth-moving equipment, and also owned Lex Vehicle Leasing.

There Robinson met mentor No. 3. He recalled, 'I worked for a very good guy there called Eric Walters, who was running the specialised transport division consisting of Bees Transport, a very successful parcel business called Albany Freight and Albany Travel in London and Tel Aviv. Eric was incredibly straight. He had a very scientific mind. I learned a hell of a lot from him and if you were delivering he wasn't in your hair. Eric had that capacity to make things happen and be very clear about what was wanted. He was a big influence on me. I remember spending six weeks in Israel, after the accountant there was dragged off to the army. It was left to me to put things right and it took six weeks to sort it out and it added up to bugger all in terms of the group's finances. But I had a wonderful time going round Israel, the Dead Sea and the Mount of Olives. The people were wonderful and I stayed with some of them.

'But there were problems. I came back after two weeks and told Lex that it was all sorted out – then found out that nothing I had said would happen actually happened. The people out there argued over every bloody thing, and after I had come home they just went back to their own way of doing it. I had been so cocky about the whole thing. You had to be incredibly precise about what was agreed, in writing, or you would get fifteen different interpretations. In the end it didn't matter because it didn't add up to a row of beans, but I had to go back there to sort it out and it was a tiring job.'

Robinson became Financial Controller of the Commercial Division, covering Harvey and Lex Commercial Distribution, and eventually became Financial Director and Financial Controller. That meant he was senior enough to have to make presentations personally to Trevor Chinn two or three times a year.

'If the corporate centre wanted something, it had to be done pretty smartly,' Robinson recalled. 'Oddly enough, although I got quite a way up the organisation, I never worked at the centre. I enjoyed Lex, though. They were a nice lot and it was pretty undemanding work. There was never much in the way of late hours. Sometimes it was frustrating because you could get everything done that you needed to, with time to spare. I never have been a long-hours person. I have always been like that. I have always felt promotion comes from doing what you are doing, well.'

Gerry and Maria were married for over five years before they had their first child, a daughter called Samantha, but the marriage was already hitting difficulties. 'I was quite a difficult partner because I was vaguely discontented at the time,' said Robinson, 'and very unfaithful; I still thought of myself as free and single. I didn't settle, other than for the odd six months. I think I tried to blame that on Maria – I was ill at ease, and didn't want to be tied down. There's an immaturity about still chasing women after you are married, the ego thing that was still there. It probably goes back to childhood. You have a child and the child gets complete attention and that means a back seat for fathers. About six or seven months after Sam was born, we almost got divorced and even got to the stage of seeing solicitors. As that became more and more real and it became clear that I was going to lose that closeness with Samantha, I made an attempt to give up my philandering. That lasted six months and then I was off again. It was my fault, no doubt about it, but I felt Maria should have questioned me because she never knew where I was in the evening. That might have made me make some choices, realise that it couldn't work like this. Instead, it sort of petered along.'

A developer bought the building in Harlesden where they were living and was naturally keen to get people to move out. Robinson cannily refused to move unless they offered compensation. Eventually they handed the Robinsons £500, which paid for their move to Mary's Mead in Hazlemere, near High Wycombe in Buckinghamshire. Not long afterwards they moved home again – from Hazlemere a few miles up the road to Hughenden Valley, just south of Great Missenden – they had a son, Richard.

They were beginning to move up in the world. Their new home was a modern detached house, built about 1970, two-storey with dormer windows, that cost about £25,000, and they added an extension to it. 'There was a time for a couple of years when it was a bit more settled,' said Robinson, 'but not much. One of the huge things at Lex was that you got a second car once you reached a certain level, and I got an MGB for Maria, and she loved it. But it was still not a relationship that I put a lot into. I never came to terms with being married. I was never contented when I was just at home. I was ill at ease. That goes back to Ireland, I think: if the weather was OK, you were sent out of the house – and that is what I kept doing.'

Despite Robinson's restlessness, Samantha has happy memories of her father at around this time. 'We would listen to Lord of the Rings on the radio,' she said, 'and he would read to us endlessly. But he also used to tell my brother Richard and me stories that he would make up as he went along. He would sit on the bed and say "This bed is a boat and we are all sailing off to sea – but the sea is infested with crocodiles" – and we'd say, "No it isn't!" Then he'd say "All right, no crocodiles, trust me, you'll be quite safe, you can go out into the sea," and I'd gingerly tiptoe over to the corner of the room, and he'd say, "Watch out! I was wrong: there really are crocodiles!" And I'd scream and rush back to bed.

'When I was about eight I'd be like a little wife to him. I used to put toothpaste on his toothbrush before he was awake in the morning, and lay out his towel, then climb into bed with him. Then when he had a shower I would be waiting for him with a towel to wrap round him and he'd go "Oooh, that's lovely!" But he was away a lot and Richard and I never had enough time with him. I suppose I was trying to get his attention.'

After Hughenden Valley, the unhappy couple and their two children moved to Penn, just down the road from Hazlemere. They bought an old farmhouse for £75,000, enough of a jump in value to stretch them financially. Said Robinson, 'It was in a terrible, terrible state and we had it refurbished. It was fun to do it up, and it certainly needed it – rewiring, decorating, and carpentry. I did a lot of it myself.'

Penn, near Beaconsfield in Buckinghamshire, was classic executive commuter belt. The Robinsons' farmhouse was not far from where Ernest Saunders and his family lived when he was running Guinness, and Robinson even turned up at some of Saunders' Sunday afternoon open-house parties there.

Meanwhile, though he hardly realised it at the time, Robinson's career was about to take a sharp upward turn.

5

From Coke to Compass

The catalyst for Robinson's career lift-off was Eric Walters, Robinson's old boss at Lex's specialised-transport division. He had left Lex to run the soft-drinks business of Grand Metropolitan, embracing Club mixers and the South of England franchise for Coca-Cola. Grand Met was having trouble putting these two businesses together, and one of the first headaches he faced was the finance department, where stocks and invoices were all over the place. There were 200 people in the department, chasing everyone from huge pub chains to tiny corner shops. So in 1983 Walters pulled Robinson across in his wake, to clean up the mess.

'It was not about getting the numbers right, so much as getting a sense of teamwork going, so that we could all tackle the problems,' said Robinson. 'It was better for someone like me to come in and say "It has been a mess, now let's get on with it." We spent six months getting it right, and another six months catching up with the backlog. You could easily identify with the brands and there were no negatives attached to them, like with alcohol or tobacco. I just remember enjoying it a lot. It was good from Eric's point of view, because he could make plans and he was there when you needed him and not when you didn't. He knew me and knew it would probably be all right, and after just over a year it was humming and going very well.'

So well, in fact, that Walters took the big chance that lifted Robinson out of the counting house and on the track that led eventually to the chairman's suite. He asked Robinson to run the sales and marketing division, where instead of keeping an eye on the pennies he was responsible for spending them. It was a big job that needed more flair than the average finance director was capable of, and it was a daring piece of lateral thinking on Walters's part to go for Robinson – as well as provoking suspicion within the higher management echelons of Grand Metropolitan.

'He was clearly going to be in general management at some point,' said Walters, 'but it was a question of convincing Allen Sheppard, who was in charge of the division at the time. They were suspicious about why I was trying to put Gerry into line management. So I said "What about sales" and he said OK. Gerry was very good at the big picture, but he was also good at going into detail. He has no side to him, and will talk to anyone. But if someone is bullshitting him he will say, "Let's go through it point by point," and they don't do it again in a hurry!'

'Taking over the sales side unnerved me at the time,' Robinson admitted. 'There was a lot to learn, from drawing up a marketing plan to controlling the advertising and sales teams, even the timing of the ads. What I remember most was this incredible sense of getting something to work with a team of people. There's something about a brand like Coke that makes people feel good about working for it – like your country, it gives you something around you. People knew it and liked it, and it left you feeling good. It has a bonding effect. It was a fun thing to do. Unless you can get that type of approach it is extraordinarily difficult to get going. But that's why I loved working with Eric Walters. He was brilliant at leaving you alone, but if it went wrong he was crisp. He was extraordinarily fair and nonjudgemental. Making a financial guy like me a sales and marketing director was a brilliant leap.'

As in the finance department, Robinson felt he inherited a sales team who were not at all clear what they were supposed to be doing. As he put it, 'There are always people who try desperately hard and it's still not working – that's the most difficult type of situation to deal with. There were a lot of people in those roles at Coca-Cola.'

So he did what in retrospect looked like the obvious thing and split the team into different sections: first, selling to the on-trade – pubs, restaurants, hotels and so on - secondly, large retail such as supermarkets, and then the corner-shop accounts.

'Some of the retail concessions, like around the Tower of London in the summer, were big-volume sellers,' said Robinson, 'and if you tried to muscle in on one of those patches you would probably get your legs shot off!' Most of the time it was a question of getting what Robinson called 'a bit of ra-ra' into the operation, running Top Seller of the Week contests and getting the telesales staff motivated.

Robinson explained, 'We sent out cards to the customers with pictures of the half-dozen prettiest girls, and said, "Mary (or whoever) will phone you next week." And we had a system where we made a note if Joe's wife was ill, so that next time the girl could ask Joe how his wife was. A telesales operator made a hundred and fifty calls a day, so they couldn't possibly remember everyone and they needed some kind of hook. Salespeople are often insecure, because they get rejected all the time, so getting them to feel part of a team was important.

We had people come over from the US for training on selling Coke, because Club soft drinks had been sold almost entirely in the on-trade and their idea of a sales drive had just been to have a drink with a pub landlord. And there had been no link between advertising and sales before, so we started telling them things like that there was an ad campaign breaking soon, so they had better get the customers to stock up. Not surprisingly, we increased sales by nearly fifty per cent a year.'

Walters then gave Robinson yet another leg-up – into his own job as chief executive of the soft-drinks operation. Walters was promoted to run a bigger part of Grand Metropolitan, including some of the pub and lager businesses as well as soft drinks. Robinson took over as managing director of the soft drinks, which gave him his first taste of being the one running something.

'It was a good move, but I'm not sure I enjoyed it because it was rather lonely,' Robinson recalled. 'Suddenly I was dealing with a group of former colleagues that I was in charge of, and however much you want to be one of the lads you are not any more. It's something you just have to get used to in senior management.'

However, Robinson had only about a year as managing director before the business was sold over his head to Coca-Cola. 'We had sorted it out and Grand Met sold it for about £36 million,' he said. 'It was absolutely the right decision, but I was bitterly disappointed.'

In 1984 he was moved to Contract Services, the catering operation – a fateful move which resulted in Robinson later and notoriously being labelled an 'upstart caterer' by the comic actor, John Cleese. It was another activity that had gone out of control. The business had been making money hand over fist, mainly in the Middle East, on the back of the 1973 oil-price hike. Money meant little when the oil-price quintupled in a few years, as many of the local inhabitants became rich virtually overnight, so it was easy to charge high prices in the region. But when profits race away like that, managements have an uncanny knack of finding ways to spend. Robinson's predecessors managed to lose money all around the world, including catering for hotel chains around the US. The Middle East and Alaska were going well, but the rest were losing money.

Said Robinson, 'For me, it was like going around the world closing small loony bins. I went to Hong Kong and the chap there gave me a lecture on the whole area, including the Chinese mainland. I asked him how many hotels we had contracts with, and it turned out to be just one or two. It was the same in the Middle East, America and South America.

And you had people having a wonderful lifestyle in Bahrain, when it could have been run by one manager. It was plainly a business that was going to die in due course. It had already sunk into losses. Anthony Tennant was given control and he asked me to run the catering side, Compass et cetera. And we owned a substantial Mechanical and Electrical Engineering business because they thought they could replicate the catering success all over again in that area. But it was an astonishingly difficult business to get right. The UK catering was all right, M&EE was losing money hand over fist, and the private-hospital business was beginning to look interesting. We did the stupid thing of sorting out Compass, putting up its value, and then buying it from Grand Met – although without some sort of track record the financecompanies would probably have been very nervous about lending us the money. I remember going to Anthony Tennant and saying the best thing would be to sell it to the management because it was surely taking up too much management time, but he said, "It's not a lot of management time at all, it's just half an hour of my time three or four times a year having a chat with you, and I rather enjoy that." Drat! I thought. That ploy won't work! But Anthony didn't waste a minute of my time. He could get right to the heart of things.'

Sir Anthony said, 'Gerry and I had a very happy relation-ship, and he has often agreed with me that the best thing that happened to him was me leaving Grand Metropolitan, because he would say he would like to buy the catering services business and I would say, "Bad luck, it's not for sale because it's a good business and you go on and run it!" As soon as I left, Allen Sheppard [chairman of Grand Met] agreed to sell it. Grand Met did have a very wide conglomerate-type range of activities and it did need to streamline, but catering was a business I would have kept. During the time we were together we were discussing acquiring other businesses. It gave us the thought that if we were in one type of contract service we could just as well go into other types of contract services.

'We discussed funeral services and it seemed to us that this was a fruitful area for consolidation, involving similar skills and so on. In the end we didn't think funerals were quite in the Grand Met style. Gerry has a very fertile mind, both lateral and very straightforward, so we talked these things through quite a bit. He was very ambitious – he conceals that a bit now. That easy-going manner is very deceptive – blarney, really.'

In 1987 Allen (now Lord) Sheppard beat Tennant to be chairman of Grand Met and did not mind selling the catering business. 'Allen Sheppard is a good example of someone who can take a subject down all sorts of routes and bring it back and make it work,' said Robinson. 'Allen recruited Eric Walters from Coca-Cola. He had a memory for numbers that was astonishing, and could really catch you by surprise. He was very good at getting you to do something even if you didn't want to do it. When they sold Coca-Cola, Allen was instrumental in getting us all to come to Grand Met, and persuading us that everything would be fine. Contract services was the last thing I wanted to do. And he almost persuaded me into going to Intercontinental Hotels instead of doing the buyout. He was a great believer in just pushing people and getting them to try things.'

But by that time Robinson had done his sums, saw there was a fortune to be made from a Compass buyout, and was serious about wanting to give the buyout a go. He had finally been persuaded by Compass's finance director, Francis Mackay, who had been with Global Travel and had unsuccessfully tried a management buyout.

'He was instrumental in getting me from thinking about it, like many managers, to actually doing it,' Robinson admitted. 'He didn't see any barriers and I'm very grateful to him for that. Once I know what I want to do I'm very singular about it and just worked at it to make it happen. We did the buyout between us with Rodney Hall and Rupert Wiles at 3i, the venture capital house, and it was a great success. The easiest part was raising the £160 million to buy it. The difficult part was persuading Grand Met to sell it to us. It's tricky, because the company selling it knows the guys buying it are going to make a lot of money out of it.

'In the lead-up to the buyout you are intensely tied up with it. The whole legalese thing, and getting advice from merchant banks and stockbrokers and accountants, was difficult to get used to because it had previously been done by other people in the company. It was a very intense time. It's very messy and you are up all hours. You are trying to negotiate what you get out of the deal and at the same time persuade both your employers and the potential investors and lenders that this is a good idea. We were very lucky in our timing, because a lot of the big finance houses were very keen to do big MBOs.

'Our £160 million deal was a record at the time, but it was soon overtaken. Soon there were MBOs worth

£1 billion. They lent me £87,000 to buy my shares, and just allowed the interest to roll up. Compass was a very predictable business, overseas catering, Rosser and Russell and the other overseas remnants, hospitals and the UK catering. Every single part of it performed.'

But to cash in on that fine performance they had to float Compass on the stock market. Rupert Wiles recommended they get in touch with John Nelson, then with the corporate finance department of Lazard Brothers, the City merchant bank. 'We were particularly targeting MBOs to advise on future flotations,' Nelson remembered. 'There was a long line of MBOs coming to market at about the same time as Compass. I went to see Gerry and Francis Mackay at their office near Hammersmith Bridge. Compass was then a catering business with private hospital management. It was very fragmented.'

They floated Compass just one year after the buyout, in 1988, for £158 million. On the day dealings began the shares went above the offer price and they took off from there.

Robinson admits that he was unused to the responsibility of taking a company forward as an independent entity, rather than part of a bigger group with others calling the shots. Nevertheless, everything worked well at Compass until 1990, when they made a £100 million takeover bid for Sketchley, the dry cleaning group, which had already seen off a £126 million bid from the Godfrey Davis car-dealer group. Sketchley's big shareholders were up in arms at the lower bid, and instead installed a management team of their choosing. On top of that, however, there was strong opposition to the bid from Compass shareholders.

'We saw a company that was very badly managed,' said Robinson. 'One of our guys had gone to Sketchley and we thought all we had to do was take it over to make money out of it. Sketchley had a big retail side, together with some big commercial cleaning contracts for uniforms – including a large contract with British Coal. But sadly our shareholders weren't happy with it, and our shares fell from about 400 pence to 290 pence. I remember doing a presentation to Standard Life, with all sorts of stuff about the advantages of the bid to Compass this way and that, and the senior manager just turned round when I'd finished and said, "What the hell do you think you are doing making this bid at all" I might as well have saved my breath! So we walked away.'

Not long after that, Robinson walked away from Compass. After allowing for some sell-offs to tidy the business, Robinson simply ran out of ideas for what to do with it. 'After the Sketchley bid failed the shares just took off again,' he recalled, 'and I thought, What do I do?, because I wasn't going to make another bid if that was going to be the reaction.' Meanwhile, the Compass businesses rolled on with very little effort on Robinson's part. So he in effect took eighteen months off, working at most a couple of days a week at Compass. This provided an excellent opportunity for him to get closer to his daughter, Samantha, who was living with him but struggling with her GCSEs, so she was glad of help from a father who had all too often been too busy to see much of her. Robinson's second wife, Heather, was pregnant with their daughter. That brought her closer to Sam, who came up with a name for the baby: April.

Said John Nelson, 'When Gerry took things easy at Compass he was going through a difficult time in his personal life. I think he just wanted some time to think. And he and Francis Mackay, whilst they got on well, felt there wasn't room in the company for both of them. Francis is a pretty strong character. They came to see me about this, and they were fairly frank. They thought about selling Compass, about one of them leaving, and about carrying on as they were. So one reason for Gerry spending more time at home with his family was partly to give Francis more space at Compass.'

Inevitably, Robinson began looking around at what he might do next. As word spread around his close circle of business acquaintants, he was approached by headhunters to see if he could be tempted into another top job. He went to talk to BET, the former British Electric Traction, which had turned into an all-round mops-and-buckets firm – a jack of all trades that was master of very few. The share price had slumped in February 1991 on fears that the company would need a £100 million cash injection to keep going. The chief executive was Nicholas Wills, son of the group's effective founder, and he was under pressure to leave or go upstairs as chairman. So Robinson was interviewed by the then chairman of BET, Sir Timothy Bevan, former head of Barclays Bank. In the end the job went to L. John Clark, a tough ex-US Marine who set about the most savage cost-cutting programme in BET's history. Despite that, BET was taken over by Rentokil Initial in 1996.

'Although I didn't get offered the BET job,' said Robinson, 'I thought, Why did I go for that? I realised it was because I wasn't totally happy at Compass. Then Miles

Broadbent, the headhunter, approached me to see if I would be interested in being chief executive of Granada. Alex Bernstein was the chairman, we met a number of times and hit it off – he is one of life's gentlemen – and the whole Granada thing started from there. He was very cautious: apart from taking up references, I met him several times before he made his mind up. It was unusual to have started Compass as an independent company only four years earlier and not go on with it, but I didn't really think much about going to Granada. The only thing that occurred to me was that it had had a pretty bad run and I could do quite a lot with it quite quickly. After a detailed review of the numbers I felt I could do different things with it, that I could sort it out.'

Or, as John Nelson put it: 'I had a word with Gerry and said, "I think this is more interesting than it looks, because under the surface there are some reasonable businesses here."'

The approach caught Robinson at the right moment, because just then he was beginning to be fed up with feeling that he could not do much more with Compass. He recalled, 'I think Francis Mackay was quite keen to get the opportunity to run Compass and, as it turned out, he had more aggressive ideas for the business than I did and has done a brilliant job. All round, it seemed quite a sensible thing to do.'

So Robinson quickly relinquished the reins of Compass and made a clean exit to leave Mackay to get on with it. The great Granada adventure was about to begin.

6

Death, Divorce, Remarriage

Robinson left Compass in 1991, at the end of a huge series of upheavals in his private life: he became a multimillionaire, his father died, he divorced from Maria and met and married Heather.

Five years earlier his father had a prostate operation at the Whitechapel Hospital, east London, from which it seems he never fully recovered. Robinson remembered, 'I went there with my children, Samantha and Richard, and he was a bit gaga, mouth open, toothless, singing Irish rebel songs which the mainly Irish nursing staff found faintly amusing. I felt ashamed, hurt, angry and overwhelmingly sad all at the same time. I was torn between being embarrassed and thinking "You poor old bastard" … I cried buckets, which was very alarming for the children. I hugged him for the first time in my life. It was a bitter pill to discover that I loved him at the moment of losing him.'

Robinson's father lived for two years after he left hospital. The rest of the family increasingly noticed that he became prone to more and more frequent bouts of dementia, eventually diagnosed as Alz-heimer's disease. 'I had nearly three years of Tony not being well,' said Betty. 'He used to get out of the house and I'd have to go looking for him, so eventually I had to lock the door.' It was becoming steadily more difficult for Betty to cope. So in 1988 Robinson bought them a little two-bedroom house at Haverhill in Suffolk, on the borders of Cambridgeshire and Essex, to be near their daughter, Fiona.

That made life more bearable for Betty, who was by then eighty-one years old. Fiona had wanted to see more of her parents, and as she was helping her husband, Ray, to run his electrical business she could organise her time to visit them and help Betty. Tony's prostate problem meant he was going to the lavatory every other minute. And as his memory went he began to turn on Betty and other family members with the chilling question, 'Who are you?' He developed a paranoia about losing his wallet, and insisted on having a lot of cash on him. 'One day he was lost completely,' Betty recalled. 'A neighbour took me in a car round the village to look for him. Some man met Tony wandering along the road and took him into an old people's home. He had four hundred pounds in his pocket. He had to have money in his pocket – he was a devil that way towards the end. After a while I just used to give him fifteen pounds to keep him happy.'

Within months of their moving to Haverhill, taking care of Tony became altogether too much for Betty, so the family clubbed together to move him into a home nearby called Anne of Cleves House, an old house from Henry VIII's time.

He died after about two weeks there, in November 1988. Robinson realised that his father meant far more to him than he had believed.

He said, 'He felt terribly betrayed, going into a home. When things were getting really bad there was the unspeakable thought that it would be better if he went. But when it happened I was enormously shaken. There was something terrible about seeing him being given a bed bath at the nursing home. He fought mightily against being helped to use the toilet, a child again but with a man's sensibilities. The loss of his dignity was, I know, humiliating to him even in his demented ramblings. He had the shakes, it was pathetic. He was completely helpless, and it was such a stark contrast to the man who had been so dominant and feared for most of my life.

'There were moments of wry humour in his conviction that the young nurses were "after him" and they humoured him in his youthful advances. Despite so much of what had happened in the past, I loved him. I was not all that close to him, but I did care for him. I would happily have taken the brunt of his anger again to see him his old self, but it was never to be. During my last day with him, the day before he died, I helped him to the toilet, chatted to him in an incoherent way. He was talking about his brothers and sisters like he was a boy and they were still alive, and on that basis we had a strange conversation.

'Then, disconcertingly, he would turn round and say, "What are you talking about Alice for? She's been dead forty years!" It was a very odd day. His death had an enormous effect on me, much bigger than I had anticipated because I had never felt that close to him. He was a very tricky man to deal with. You never quite knew where you were with him. But when he died, amid all the usual jocularity at family funerals, I was amazed at how much I missed him, and how sad I was at the fact I had not been close to him during his life. My sense of the loss of him was far more powerful than I could ever have imagined.'

As the purchase of the Haverhill house showed, this was a time when Robinson was in the first flush of considerable wealth from the buyout and subsequent stock market flotation of Compass. He would never have to work again, but he was just beginning to get to grips with the problems riches were presenting.

'It's like winning the National Lottery because you are suddenly worth a lot of money,' he said. 'It moved my own personal position from relative poverty to what seemed like immense wealth. It's hard to deal with, like the stories I've read about Lottery winners trying to cope. It takes a long time for it to really dawn on you. It was very unclear at the time of the buyout what it was worth. In these buyout situations it's very hard to know what it might be worth. However, when you realise that there is considerable personal wealth there, you start to have a sense of independence that comes along with it.

'The value didn't actually crystallise until the flotation of Compass a year after the buyout. Even then it was still something of a paper exercise. You've got the shares, but it's still a slow process of getting acclimatised to their real financial value. There are significant adjustments required to make sense of all that. It's just hard to believe that you have got all this money. You don't have to restrict yourself to a semi-detached house: instead you can have a very nice house, and three of those, and six of that – and the upshot is that, at least for a while, you don't know where you are. By the time I came to realise it in a real way, I found it didn't matter to me all that much. I could gear myself up to finance some project or other, because I now have assets the banks could lend against, but the money per se doesn't really seem to interest me. I didn't want to make a billion pounds, or anything like that. The fact is that I don't spend the money I have, and there is nothing I am yearning to do. People with six houses and huge yachts, I have always suspected, are rather unhappy.

'I could of course do things for the family, sort out issues, help them buy a better home: I bought Mum and Dad the house in Suffolk. I'm not sure, however, it doesn't simply create more problems. People come asking for money, and I have helped, but I believe everyone has to fend for themselves. To have someone giving you substantial amounts of money, solving your problems by bringing out a cheque book, can take away your pride. Sibling rivalry is not about making money – at least I don't think so: it's more about where you are in the family. It's often more awkward than helpful, to be able to do things to help financially. You've got to have your own pride in achieving things. It's easier to give to children and parents, but there are even risks associated with passing the money on to your children. Although I'll obviously pass it on to them, I think it's important that my children don't start out in life thinking everything's laid out on a plate for them.

'What does work for the family is to do the odd thing for them that they wouldn't do themselves. For Mum and my sister Evelyn's birthday one year we took the whole family for a weekend in Paris, stayed at the Hotel George V, boat on the Seine, up the Eiffel Tower, and a trip down to Versailles. It was a real treat for everyone, who wouldn't have done things in that style normally. And more recently we went to Rome for Mum's ninetieth birthday. I don't sense that my having money is a problem for any of the rest of the family: I do my share but I don't try to take over. I don't think people in the family spend their days thinking about me and my money – apart from the odd joke about me tripping over my wallet! I don't think it matters all that much. I can see that members of my family, brothers and sisters and cousins and so on, who are not wealthy are just as happy as I am. If money becomes your method of deciding how important you are, then you're probably in a lot of trouble with yourself.'

As it turned out, some of the greatest demands on Robinson's new fortune arose in the first year or two of acquiring it. While his father was falling deeper and deeper into his illness, Robinson's first marriage was breaking up.

Robinson said, 'I met Maria when she was twenty and I was twenty-one, and we married a year later. She was pretty, very giving, very exciting to be with. She put herself out a lot so that we could be together. But almost from the day I got married I had the feeling it was not going to work. We had five years before we had children and if I had had the courage I should have tackled it then, and allowed Maria to go off and have children with someone else. We nearly divorced before our first child, Samantha, was born. But it was me who stopped it and said "No, let's try and make it work." I tried to be faithful but it was no good. It was of course a kind of sexual immaturity, and certainly not helped by starting late with girls after being in the seminary. Maria firmly believed that you had one person you shared your life with and that was how it worked. I think she was very faithful and very much wanted it to work. Although Maria must have known about my unfaithfulness, she never tackled me on it. It was never therefore an open marriage.'

In 1987 this rocky relationship was confronted by a double challenge: the enormously time-consuming Compass buyout and the emergence of a woman for whom Robinson was willing to go through the pain of ending his marriage with Maria and leaving Samantha and Richard. The buyout process meant he was spending very, very little time at home – even less than he had been in the years before. The strains became intolerable.

'The corporate buyout process just sucks you in,' he said, 'taking up an enormous amount of time with lawyers, accountants, bankers and so on. That was the end of the end as far as Maria and I were concerned. We had had a pretty fragile relationship for some time. We were not really sharing much, we didn't do anything together. I never made enough effort to make my first marriage work like that. There is then nothing to stop you seeking other sexual outlets and other interests, and becoming wrapped up in other relationships. I was cowardly about it. I was picking and mixing about when I was and wasn't there. For a very long time I had lost connection with Maria and had I been her I'd have been unhappy about that. She wanted things to work, and somehow it just wasn't possible. I had a number of affairs, one or two quite serious.'

•

Robinson met his future second wife in the summer of 1986, when he was running what was then the Contract Services division of Grand Met and he placed an advertisement in *The Times* for a secretary. Heather Robinson recalled, 'I was sitting outside a conference one day and picked up *The Times*, which I never normally read. There was an ad in the "Crème de la Crème" section for a secretary to a chief executive, so I phoned the agency. I didn't care what the company did.'

Heather had trained as a PA and had a business studies diploma. She had been a sales administrator with a water-cleaning company, then a technical administrator with a computer software firm. At this time she was living at home with her family in Pinner, northwest of London. She later shared a flat with a girlfriend in Acton, west London, to be nearer the office, which was by Hammersmith Bridge.

'The relationship with a secretary is a very close one,' said Robinson, 'especially in a buyout when she knows the detail of it and can talk about it. Nowadays Heather and I share virtually everything and therefore the relationship is alive: we are very much together on things. I'd never had a relationship with anyone in the way I now have with Heather.'

There was clearly an immediate working friendship between Gerry and Heather, who remembered, 'I was very taken with Gerry right from the start. He was quite unlike any other businessman I had met, very relaxed and willing to let people get on with things. He didn't need someone with shorthand, because he doesn't dictate letters. He either writes them out in rough or says, "Reply to this person and tell them this is what we'll do," or whatever, leaving the wording to me. That suited me, because I hadn't used my shorthand for about three years. I have also never met anyone who can keep things so simple and prioritised as Gerry can. He only had fifteen files at Compass, and I don't think he has many more now. For a secretary, it means you know where everything has to go. He was just very organised. The buyout was very hectic, especially as nothing like it had been done on that scale, so we were very involved with lawyers and accountants and so on.'

Chats between Gerry and Heather about the latest meeting with the lawyers or the venture capitalists were gradually replaced by more intimate dinners. Gerry spent an unhappy Christmas with Maria, Samantha and Richard at the end of 1986, and a few months later bought a flat in Chiswick, west London, from money raised from exercising some Grand Met share options. That was when he left Maria.

He remembered, 'After I told the children that their mum and I were splitting up, I went back to the flat in Chiswick and cried for several hours. It was amazing how painful it was. It was horrible, and I had a headache for days. The worst thing was that I had a mini-version of that every time I went to see them because of the antagonism and the questions about "What have you been doing?" But I am glad I did it and that I didn't simply wash my hands of them, because it would have been very difficult to get back in touch with them if I had done that. It was important to let them see just how important they were to me. There was never really any danger of my just sliding off – I couldn't have done that. There were very few Sunday nights, when I dropped them off at their front door, that I didn't feel great pain. If I missed a week it felt terrible. But I was there two or three times a week through that first year.'

The tension transmitted itself to the children. Samantha recalled, 'After Mum and Dad broke up we'd have these terrible Sunday lunches together at a local restaurant, and it would be all false bonhomie and it didn't mean anything, because at the end of it Dad would have to go off and leave us and we were all sad. Mum didn't want him to go.'

Robinson's younger brother, Paul, and his wife, Jean, felt some of the effects, as they had been in the habit of going on holiday with Gerry and Maria as a foursome. After the break-up Maria tried to persuade Paul and Jean not to see Gerry and Heather, apparently because she thought that that might encourage Gerry to come back to her. But it was no good. 'She was heartbroken when he left her,' said Paul.

Robinson was wary of hopping straight from one marriage into another, after eighteen years of playing hide-and-seek. He also had relationships with other women to sort out, so he spent several months on his own in Chiswick thinking about his future. 'I took time to think about this one. I didn't want to jump into it again,' he said. 'I lived for a while on my own so that I could think about it differently. Once you have handled the difficult bit in telling the children what has happened, you really are free to make a choice. Of course, with an old and a new relationship, the old one is going to struggle because the new is always more exciting.'

Heather for her part had things to resolve in her own mind before committing herself to the idea of becoming the next Mrs Robinson. As his secretary, she had become used to taking phone calls and opening letters from his other

girlfriends. 'When we got serious, that was certainly something I wanted to discuss,' Heather said. 'We had some black
moments, because I overlapped with some of his other
relationships and I said they had to stop. Now, if he went off
with someone else I would be sad, because it would mean that
our relationship had failed.'

It was, then, a crossroads for Robinson. Not only would
he be ending a marriage that had lasted most of his adult life,
and jeopardising his relationship with his children, he would
also have to rethink his happy-go-lucky lifestyle if he was
going to keep Heather. After several months of returning to
his lonely Chiswick flat, he made up his mind.

'Being with Heather has worked out enormously well,'
Robinson said. 'For the first time in my life I have been faithful
and haven't had the inclination to be otherwise. There is a
relationship here that matters to me and I don't want to put it
at risk. From that moment I was very clear that I was not
going to go back to Maria.'

He bought the Chiswick flat in spring 1987 and Heather
moved in that autumn. Meanwhile, he was making progress
towards the management buyout of the Compass group of
companies from their parent, Grand Met, for £160 million.
Although he would have to borrow to buy a block of shares in
the newly independent Compass, he knew the likely profit on
that stake would eventually yield him a fortune of several million pounds. That would eventually enable him to buy himself
out of the marriage to Maria, which had shackled him for so
long. But Richard and Samantha were on the verge of their
vulnerable teenage years. Much as Robinson wanted to end
what he saw as his sterile relationship with Maria, he did not

want to fall into the traditional male lot of losing contact with his children. 'The most important thing is your position with them, maintaining that dialogue and that connection,' he said.

He was initially clear that Sam and Richard should stay with their mother, so they could continue at their schools and keep in touch with their friends. The Compass buyout made it easier, because he did not have to take the children out of their home or school, as millions of other divorced couples are forced to do. So Maria and the children could stay in the same house in Buckinghamshire and Sam and Richard could stay on at the same private schools.

'But', said Robinson, 'I think in many ways, through her anger, Maria may have handled it badly. I think it's very easy for parents in these situations to assume that the whole thing is almost the only thing that matters to the kids, and of course on one level it is; but they have their own friends and their own lives to lead, and in the end they make up their own minds about what they want to do and even about the rights and wrongs of it. It's too tempting for parents just to take over and try and tell their children what to think. They come to their own conclusions soon enough, for good or bad. It's hugely important to allow them that space.'

Like many other divorced husbands, Robinson felt the strain at Christmases. He spent a miserable Christmas with Maria and the children in 1987, without Heather and aware of Maria's bitterness at his decision to leave. For the next two years, until they were married, Gerry and Heather spent Christmas ferrying disabled people to and from their families. But they also took the opportunity to get away from the pressures and spend time together.

'Heather and I spent a lot of time in Italy before our children arrived,' said Robinson. 'We went to Rome, Florence and Venice. It was a way of seeing a lot of Italian culture and art in a very relaxed way. We must have spent a fortnight together at the Uffizi gallery alone. You can go back and back again and again. Like me, Heather is very interested in art. As for Rome, it was just great for clothes – shirts, ties, dresses, shoes, you name it. The Italians spend so much on their appearance, as opposed to their homes, and we in Britain are virtually the opposite. You are often ripped off in Italy, but it's done in such style!'

Compass was floated on the London stock market in December 1988, at a price that confirmed Robinson's multi-millionaire status. Gerry and Heather married in November 1990. They moved from Chiswick to a substantial house in London's fashionable Holland Park district, near Kensington. It was big enough for Sam and Richard to live in too, if they wished. As, gradually, they did.

'Although I put little pressure on them,' said Robinson, 'I was very keen for them to come and live with me. They decided for their own separate reasons to do so. I loved it. It was fantastic to deal with them in a natural way, day to day. Samantha still maintains a good relationship with her mother. Richard, I think, finds it more difficult. Richard and Samantha gradually developed a relationship with Heather. Sam pretended at first that everything was fine but bottled it up. Richard was very honest and decided it was terrible to start with, but then got on well with Heather. I think Maria blamed Heather for everything, which was not a balanced judgement because of what I had been up to myself. Maria couldn't contain her own hurt and left Richard and Samantha feeling that they couldn't clear off to handle things for themselves. In the end it probably cost Maria dear, because kids have their own way of working these things out. They want to be off doing their own thing and they get angry if they feel they have to see you.

'Sam came to live with us so that I could help her with her GCSEs. It was nice to come back home to them, and I had a lot of time at home at that time. I was genuinely able to help her because she had had a lot of trouble with her studies. It had its difficulties, having a sixteen-year-old living there, and it coincided with the birth of April. That whole issue of another family arriving is very tricky. When I told Sam that Heather was pregnant, she burst into tears. I realised later that she had felt she was being put aside, and that I was simply abandoning her to start another family. But she was great to have around, and when April was born it was Sam who thought of her name.

'It was a halcyon time: I was spending less time at Compass and instead did a lot of painting. Of course, we also had plenty of rows because Sam is pretty instant: she reacts fast. She needed a tight regime to get her through her exams, but I think my persistence with her work made it plain to her that she really did matter to me. It showed I cared. I prepared exam papers for her, and set up mock exams. She had *Far From the Madding Crowd* as a set book, and we really enjoyed working on it together.

'April and Heather were around and relationships were good. It will remain in my mind as a key time of peace, when things were pretty well together. I was relaxed about not working hard, something I had never really done in this way before. Sometimes I would feel ill at ease if I had time on my hands, but this was the exact opposite. I was helping Sam, and April was a very young baby. It continued because Richard also then wanted some help with his studies and also came to live with us. He was heading for very good results, and went on to get As and Bs in his GCSEs and then had to make up his mind what to do. It was the route by which he came to us.

'In the nature of these things, having lived for a while in London, neither Richard nor Sam went back to Maria after their exams. They had made their own decisions. By the time Richard came to stay, Jack, Maria's second husband, was already on the scene and he had had children by a previous marriage. I have never been in any doubt that Maria's concern for our children was complete. That was probably the driving force. They always went back to see Maria at weekends. It was not a case of them walking out on Maria, but it must have been difficult for her. I never had that sense that she was hugely put out, because I always kept her completely informed about them. Our interest in the children was unquestioned – we both wanted it to work.'

Of course, there were tensions and problems as Samantha and Richard separately adjusted to life with Heather. Samantha came to stay in the house in Holland Park a week or two before April was born, in May 1991. This was an additional factor for Heather to cope with, in the run-up to the birth of her own first child. 'It was difficult living with Sam,' Heather recalled. 'At first we were dancing round one another, trying to be nice to one another. And it was nice that Sam thought up April's name. Then later we would fly at one another over things like Sam wanting to come and go as she pleased and come home at all hours. We tried to give them their own space: we turned the whole top floor in our Holland Park home into a self-contained flat, with its own kitchenette. But if someone is living with you, you can't help being concerned for them and wonder where they are.

'It was a wonderful time when Gerry eased off at Compass, because he was painting and wasn't pressured, and had time for us all. But there was competition for his attention. I will admit to some feelings of jealousy if Gerry and I were sitting watching television and Sam would breeze in and snuggle up to Gerry and get cuddles from him. Richard was quite different. He wouldn't talk to me for two years, and could barely talk to Gerry in front of me. I just don't think he could cope with the changes at first. But now he's fine. We have all grown and matured together and I really value the relationship I have with them both.'

Robinson remembered, 'It was tough on Heather having Sam and Richard moving in, particularly with Richard being antagonistic in the early days. I'm sure Heather felt it was difficult, particularly with her own children coming along: April in 1991 and then Timothy in 1994. She had her problems with it, but she handled it brilliantly, especially with having another woman in the house – for that was what Sam effectively was. I think Richard and Sam developed a real bond with Heather and certainly a strong love for the younger children.'

By the time Robinson went to Granada in November 1991, Sam was at boarding school, St George's in Ascot, Berkshire, and came home to her father or mother at weekends, but Richard was still at home. Robinson recalled, 'I was just not around in the daytime, because for about a year my time was taken up as I got involved in Granada. But if you are sensible you get people in place so you can spend time with the family, so I did that and made sure I had a day off a week.' As a result of that adjustment, Robinson did develop a deep relationship with Richard and Sam. He and Richard played golf and watersports and went to rugby together, and with Heather and Samantha they would all go to the theatre.

He bought a seaside house in Ireland, which the family enjoy because it gives them a way of spending a lot of time together. It is a lived-in, homely holiday home where Robinson can exchange his boardroom suit for a wetsuit. Several of his own paintings hang on the walls of the sitting rooms, which are small but cosy and beautifully furnished. There is a big outhouse, where Robinson has a complete toolset hanging neatly on the wall in size order. Here he stores his motor mower, wetsuits, canoes and other outdoor gear. It has an Aga, which he sits around with family and friends chatting over a Coke or a cold beer. Ray Kennedy, his brother-in-law, goes out there to have a cigar, Robinson follows him for a chat, Heather goes to see where her husband has got to and Fiona follows the rest of them out. Before long, everyone is in the outhouse, or spilling into the surrounding garden, a lovely formal garden with a pond and a big tree in the corner that holds April and Timothy's tree house – built by Gerry. Solid, steep wooden steps go up to the platform at the first level. Then there is a short flight of steps up to the tree house itself, coming up through the floor. It looks like an ideal place to while away an afternoon in fantasyland. The little room is equipped with proper miniature windows, table, chairs, cushions and two real, live electric power points.

By that tree is a path leading down to a stone-pillared gate, which opens out on to a rough field sloping further down to the narrow, stony beach. There Robinson has had built a concrete jetty, and is constructing a breakwater from the stones and pebbles washed up on the beach. A white fibreglass speedboat lies tethered above the water line. It is the boat that sank under Gerry when he went out to sea in it in April 1998. It has an outboard motor and two white-cushioned bench seats, one in front of the other.

Robinson's sister, Fiona, said, 'He's like a pied piper there: they can have kids running around the place, some family, some just local kids who bring their friends. They have the run of the place. Gerry doesn't care – he just says, "Well, they're only young." One time he organised a treasure hunt for the children on an island out in the lough. He hid chocolate coins in gold foil all over this little wooded island and they had a great time hunting for them.'

7

Arriving at Granada

After five months of searching for a chief executive, troubled leisure group Granada has poached one of the best-regarded managers in the sector. Gerry Robinson of Compass, the contract catering and healthcare group, starts next month in the hot seat vacated by Derek Lewis in May.

Daily Mail, 22 October 1991

As Robinson's private life was beginning to settle down, he had to get to grips with the daunting job he had taken on at Granada. As is so often the case, the seeds of its problems were sown when its founder, Sidney Bernstein, stepped down as chairman in 1979. (For Bernstein's career and the origins of Granada, see Appendices I and II.) He was succeeded by his nephew, Alexander, a gentle academic man with none of his uncle's domineering drive. He was none the worse for that, and delivered respectable results in his first decade at the helm, driving up pre-tax profits by more than four times, and more than tripling the annual dividend. But it was a measure of the stock market's doubts about his stewardship that the share price responded to these gains by itself rising only two and a half times by 1989.

Alex left Cambridge University with an economics degree in 1959 to manage not even a Granada cinema but one of the humbler chain of Century cinemas at Northcote Road, between Wandsworth and Clapham Commons in south London. He recalled, 'One moment I was reading economics amid disciples of Keynes and the next minute I was trying to persuade kids to enjoy the Saturday matinée in Clapham. It was quite a culture shock.' He moved from there to be a television producer in Manchester, before transferring to the management side of Granada, as the first managing director of its TV Rentals operation.

Most important of all from the point of the public's perception of Granada, Alex twice successfully retained the group's vital northwest television franchise, the second time for only £9 million a year. He also expanded the declining but highly profitable rentals business and persuaded the rest of the board to make the historic and ultimately spectacular investment in satellite television. But he admitted that when he succeeded Sidney it was not easy to see where to take Granada. Would-be predators noticed the lack of direction, and within a few months in 1985 and 1986 Alex had to see off two takeover approaches. One was from Ladbroke Group, the gambling concern, and the other would-be bidder was the Rank Organisation, which operated the rival Gaumont cinema chain and had itself been a major British film-maker in the early postwar years. The Rank bid might have been successful had the Independent Broadcasting Authority not refused to accept the transfer of Granada's television franchise to a new owner. Bernstein agreed to hold talks with Cyril Stein, the then head of Ladbroke, but news of the first meeting leaked and Bernstein called the talks off less than a week later.

After those episodes, Bernstein was very much on trial with Granada's institutional shareholders, who pressed for more aggressive leadership. The tension increased with the appointment of Derek Lewis as first managing director and then chief executive. After Cambridge University and London Business School, Lewis had joined Ford Motor Company, becoming finance director for Ford of Europe in 1978, when he was only thirty-two. He had a brief spell in the planning department of Imperial Group, the tobacco company, before becoming Granada's finance director in 1984. In 1988 he was made managing director, and two years later chief executive.

Anyone promoted that quickly is liable to make enemies, but Lewis had more than his fair share. One said, 'He was a very able finance director, but he moved into general management without any general experience. I argued he should have line experience first, such as running a division. Then Alex Bernstein promoted him far too fast, from managing director to chief executive. I was concerned that, whenever there was a problem, he invented a financial engineering solution rather than try to deal with it operationally. And there was too much use of management consultants.'

Lewis, who subsequently became a not entirely successful director-general of Her Majesty's Prison Service, had been

Granada's chief executive for only a matter of months when the snipers began circling. In December 1990 Granada announced a 26 per cent drop in pre-tax profits to £120.6 million for the year to the previous September. By January 1991 the institutions were said to be criticising the acquisitions for which Derek Lewis was apparently responsible, including Lasky's, the electrical retailer, and several computer maintenance companies. He was also vilified for investing £35 million in Rupert Murdoch's fledgling Sky satellite television venture – even though the decision was made on Bernstein's initiative. That later turned into a gold mine, but its early years were fraught. One institutional shareholder reportedly said, 'It is widely recognised now that Granada has made a number of disastrous acquisitions. In our view the company has been badly run.'

None of this might have mattered too much if the company could have won a breathing space. But its shares were sliding disastrously, from a 1990 high of 357p to a mere 161p in early 1991, and this would affect its ability to raise money. The signs were gathering that Granada would need to raise as much as £300 million pretty quickly, to cut borrowings and maintain its shareholding in Sky, which at that stage was eating cash at a horrendous rate.

By the spring there was no doubt that the price of Granada's being allowed to raise the £300 million was Lewis's head. Derek Higgs, then head of corporate finance at the merchant bank S.G. Warburg, adviser to Granada, said, 'Granada has lots of good businesses and it isn't in desperate talks with its bankers. But that's not actually the same thing as one hundred per cent success for the strategy.'

Lewis quit in May, but only after Bernstein had asked the nonexecutive directors if he himself should be the one to go. Understandably, then, Bernstein took extreme care in choosing a new chief executive. The headhunter Miles Broadbent put a string of people in touch with Bernstein, but none fitted the bill. It reached the point where Bernstein warned Broadbent that he would have to turn to another headhunter, but then he suddenly came up with Robinson. 'I instantly took to him,' said Bernstein, 'he was in a different class from the others. It worked straight away: within a few minutes I knew he was the right man for the job. I introduced him to one of our nonexecutive directors, who agreed with my opinion, and it just went from there.'

Nevertheless, Bernstein insisted on half a dozen interviews with Robinson before finally making up his mind, as well as following up numerous references – particularly with Lord Sheppard, Sir Anthony Tennant and Eric Walters, all of whom had nurtured Robinson at Coca-Cola and Grand Metropolitan.

Robinson was initially reluctant to cut himself off completely from Compass, because of his emotional ties with that company. He wanted to stay on as nonexecutive deputy chairman, but Bernstein was not keen on that because it would look as if he were not totally committed to Granada. They agreed that he could simply be a nonexecutive director of Compass, but after discussing it with Francis Mackay, the Compass chief, he decided to make a clean break after all.

Bernstein recalled, 'At the request of a nonexecutive director, to avoid any misunderstandings after our experience with Derek Lewis, Gerry and I defined our relationship in writing, and it was presented to the board – but then never looked at again. What Gerry brought to us was a very, very clear view of the main issues and what they were. He will work out what the most important issues are and push on these. He is very clear and very demanding of the chief executives of the divisional companies. Things seemed much simpler once he was involved. He cut through a lot of the bureaucracy we had in the company at that time. He said to the chief executives, "This is what you should be doing, and this is how much profit you should be making." But he has not the slightest trace of pomposity, and he worked largely with the people who were already here: Charles Allen was the only person he brought with him.'

So expectations were high and reputations were on the line when Robinson arrived at Granada's then London head office in Soho's Golden Square in November 1991. 'I very quickly became absorbed in what was going on at Granada,' said Robinson. 'You become very busy and your mind gets very clogged up with the detail. I read everything. I thought I had to do one main thing, which was to concentrate on the mainstream businesses. Granada was already deep into computer services and at that time we were looking at a number of other projects, including an upmarket holiday-camp operation. I had to put these plans to one side for the time being. It was very much a question of looking at what the numbers were showing us, and every single business had been slowly declining.

'We were shedding £100 million cash in 1991, the year I arrived. Yet I had an early sense that this was something you could do a lot with very quickly. Our merchant bank adviser,

John Nelson, has a very good nose for what the City wants, and he also felt that things could be done.' Nelson and Robinson had known each other well since the stock market flotation of Compass, and Bernstein had become disenchanted with Warburg as Granada's merchant bank advisers. So in 1992 Nelson's firm, Lazard Brothers, took over as Granada's main adviser.

Soon after his arrival Robinson called for the group's main financial files and spent a fortnight going through the accounts, getting a feel for where the problems lay. Despite his accountancy background, Robinson is not a great lover of figures in themselves, but he does admit to a weakness for the investigative side of the numbers game, finding out the secret victories and defeats hidden in movements of cash, debts, assets, liabilities, stocks and profits. 'I had a lot of huge folded sheets with all the numbers spread across them,' Robinson explained, 'and they made a lot of sense to me. Basically, volumes were dropping and costs rising. We had to do something quickly.'

On 12 December 1991, Robinson met the financial press for the first time in his new guise, when he presented Granada's results for the year to 30 September. He had had nothing to do with them, as he made perfectly plain. The *Daily Mail* reported,

> His expression said 'don't blame me' as Granada reported an awful year. Profits before tax crashed by 53 per cent to £57 million and the final dividend is slashed from 7.9p to 4.5p, making 7p for the year, a 43 per cent fall. Granada has sold lossmakers – like its Canadian rental business – and cut jobs in its computer maintenance division. But more

action is needed – so the future of fringe leisure interests, such as night clubs and theme parks, must be doubtful. Also expect surgery at its much-loved television company – however painful that might be for chairman Alex Bernstein. There are no signs of a pick-up in TV advertising, the rental market is too mature for rapid growth, and motorways and bowling depend on recovery in consumer spending.

But the wheels were already in motion. Before revealing those dismal figures, Robinson had sent his fellow directors his initial review of the group's operations. This was to become a key guide to the tasks confronting the board in 1992. (See Appendix III.)

Said Nelson, 'When Gerry arrived at Granada he did a whistle-stop tour of the company. He wrote a review and then asked me and a colleague to go round and do the same thing, without seeing what he had written. It was quite uncanny how the two papers coincided. Bar computer services, it was the same theme everywhere: good businesses being managed strategically rather than operationally. They all have a consumer element and they needed hands-on, detailed, hard-driving management and they were not getting it because they were run by senior and rather general management from on high. Television, with David Plowright, was typical.'

But, though Robinson used the veiled language of someone who is new to an organisation, there was no mistaking his intent. He says in that review,

It is worth perhaps clarifying that I see my own initial task as one of settling the Group down to concentrating on running the main businesses that we now have ... in a much tighter and more profit/cost conscious way. This will inevitably involve a rather more hands-on approach than has been the case in the past which may, at least initially, lead to some discomfort in some areas.

The question of which areas was to become utterly clear.

The main points of the review were:

- UK TV Rental: 'I believe that we have an excellent business here which is capable of giving strong profits and cash flows long into the future.'
- Television: 'Strategically I believe we have a powerful profit and cash producer in this division, and that that is not at all inconsistent with our wish to be the highest quality operator in the network.'
- Leisure: 'We need to enhance greatly the returns we make from Motorway services. I am deeply unimpressed by the senior management in Ten Pin Bowling. Nightclubs look similar. There seems little doubt that our purchases in Theme Parks were a mistake. We should get out of Travel at the earliest possible opportunity.'
- Computer Services: 'Although this has been nothing short of a disaster for the Group, it is a delight to see the extent of the turnaround under John Curran's management.'
- International (US and Canadian hospitals, Telerent in Germany and Kapy, electrical retailer, in Spain): 'All of these businesses are for sale in either the short or medium term.'

Nelson remarked, 'Gerry made it clear that Granada was not going to buy or sell anything for quite a while, until the housekeeping had been sorted out. He said there was no point in buying anything until the management had been sorted out and the existing businesses were in order, and there was no point in selling anything until we had sorted it out because they wouldn't get the full price for it. Then, as time developed, they began to make disposals.'

But it did not take a degree in business studies to see which part of the group was going to feel Robinson's 'discomfort' first. Some of the harshest strictures in his review are reserved for what many inside and outside the organisation regarded as the jewel in the crown: Granada Television, the Manchester independent television producer and broadcaster responsible for *Coronation Street*, *World In Action* and the lavish drama series *Brideshead Revisited* and, yes, *Jewel in the Crown*.

The review states (author's italics),

There is little doubt, perhaps sadly, that the old, more comfortable, era of ever increasing advertising revenues, of selling at fixed prices to the network, of sharing often rapidly increasing network costs and of having a virtual monopoly in which to operate is over. The high prices paid for their franchises by a number of operators, together with the emergence of new operators, particularly Carlton in London, will change the face and pace of the industry. Increasingly too, the appearance of satellite in more and more homes will begin to eat into the monopoly advertising position. Tightly controlled budgets, particularly on the production side, with an increase in the use of independent producers for new material, will be the order of the day. Granada Television has a proud history of being a quality player as a producer/broadcaster, and its reputation and standing were undoubtedly key factors in winning its franchise on such favourable terms. *Ironically, in the new scenario, that tradition may make it more difficult to adapt to the new commercial reality.* [There follows a three-year profit record and budget for 1991/2, which shows slowing rising turnover, steadily rising costs and plunging profits.]

Here … is a downward trend that cannot be allowed to continue … Together with the rest of the industry, we increased our programme expenditure in the run-up to the new franchise awards … It is clear that we need now to tackle our own cost base firmly, and to contribute where we can to achieving an overall cost reduction in the network schedule costs … As might be anticipated, there are conflicting views on this. The debate has begun – but clearly, we must get past that stage quickly if we are to make a worthwhile impact on this year's numbers.'

That was a direct challenge to the authority of David Plowright, brother of the actress Joan Plowright and guiding hand behind *Coronation Street*, *World In Action* and *Brideshead*, and latterly chairman of Granada Television. He declined to be interviewed for this book, therefore what follows is inevitably a partial account of the events leading up to his sacking on 3 February 1992.

Plowright succeeded Sir Denis Forman as chairman of Granada Television in 1987. Probably the high point of his five-year reign was winning the 1991 franchise round. All the contenders found this round very difficult because, as Prime Minister Margaret Thatcher had insisted on a blind auction subject to a quality threshold, Plowright had had the confidence to bid only £9 million, £26 million less than the rival bid from a vastly less experienced consortium led by Phil Redmond, creator of *Brookside*, the Channel Four soap opera.

Plowright was unstoppably triumphant when Granada was yet again awarded the licence for northwest England. The red carpet was laid out – literally – up the steps of the Quay Street studios and headquarters near Manchester Ship Canal. But Plowright and his supporters did not leave matters there. Every time someone walked on the carpet it played Cliff Richard's recording of the song 'Congratulations'. A visitor who needed to visit a lavatory in the building was regaled with the same song. When staff at Granada's television outposts in Chester, Blackburn and Lancaster opened celebratory boxes of champagne – yes, Cliff Richard's frenetic tones assailed them then, too. In case the Quay Street troops were not feeling sufficiently buoyed up, a large video screen showed a doctored compilation of the Queen, President Bush, Margaret Thatcher, John Major and Neil Kinnock adding their good wishes to the company. The partying was long and lavish. The Granada TV staff were each sent a bottle of Laurent Perrier champagne to their homes.

That was just a fortnight before Robinson arrived at Granada's head office. He recalled, 'I had this early feeling that David was going to be a problem. They ran their own affairs at Granada Television and saw the group head office as a minor irritant, an encumbrance. I could not understand that. It may have sprung from the history of the company, but Granada Television's financial performance made it only a small contributor to the group, not the most important part any more. TV Rentals made far more money.'

That attitude was precisely what infuriated Plowright and his colleagues in Television's curiously dated 1960s Manchester office block, which houses the main studios and is topped by a splendid penthouse flat built for Sidney Bernstein and still used by important visitors. As far as any of the top echelons of the Television management were concerned, what mattered was programme quality – and never mind the bottom line. Indeed, there was an inclination to sneer at the bottom line, keeping spending up to ensure that profits did not become too significant in the overall scheme.

There was, and still is, a very strong corporate ethos at Manchester. Many have worked there for more than twenty years, and are rightly proud of *Coronation Street* and *World In Action*, and still look back longingly to *Brideshead Revisited* and *Jewel in the Crown*. But Robinson, coming to Granada with a fresh pair of eyes, was worried by the speed at which the climate was changing, both commercially and technically. Satellite and digital broadcasting would soon remove the old certainties, forcing television companies to be more flexible and innovative about how they generated revenues and managed costs.

According to Robinson, Plowright was angered by the very idea that he had to compromise. He was part of a great tradition that stretched back to the days when he had joined Granada as a news editor soon after the company won its first ITV franchise in the 1950s. As far as he was concerned Granada Television's reputation was built on the quality of its programmes, and that if he did not maintain standards Granada's franchise pledges might be broken. Advertising revenue might fall – at the end of 1991 Britain was in the teeth of a recession – but the company had weathered such setbacks before and would do so again.

'I had a very clear picture very quickly,' Robinson recalled. 'I knew Plowright was going to be difficult because it was well known that he was his own man. He always left me with the impression that he felt the group was lucky to have him. He had obviously decided to take a fairly bombastic stance, which was naïve because he was not in a strong position. I had a rock-solid contract and I had just been brought in to do a job, so I was always going to have the main board behind me at that stage. He had been used to years when he had had Sidney Bernstein's ear, and when the Granada TV board had been virtually identical to the main board. I really did try to move things forward with him, and I found him both likable and engaging. We had half a dozen meetings, but he would turn up half an hour late as a protest, agree things, and then nothing would happen.'

The breakdown in the working relationship between Plowright and Robinson was agony for Alex Bernstein, who had known and got on with Plowright for many years. Lewis had complained that Plowright was impossible to deal with, but Bernstein had mistakenly dismissed this – until he found out for himself how difficult Plowright had become.

'David had done a tremendous job in building up Granada Television in Manchester, which was important for our franchise application,' said Bernstein. 'He had done this by a tremendous effort at public relations and a lot of it was promoting himself, which is not a bad idea if you are the chairman of the company. He thought that he was totally irreplaceable and really didn't listen to anyone else. It was as if there was a frontier outside Manchester for any group executive coming up from London. All heads of operating companies are a bit like that, but he took it to extremes. I think he and Gerry liked each other personally, but David didn't take to Gerry telling him what to do, and he didn't even want to give Gerry the information on which to take a view. I could see they were going to come to blows.'

In a forlorn effort to patch things up, Bernstein took his rebellious television chief to lunch. It did not help. Bernstein told Plowright, 'Come on, Gerry is chief executive and I have to support him. He is a very experienced and very tough businessman – don't underestimate him.' According to Bernstein, Plowright was clearly in no mood to be conciliatory, and replied, 'If he can be tough, I can be tough.' As a last throw, Bernstein contacted Granada's nonexecutive directors and got them together with Sir Denis Forman to talk through the problem. But it became apparent that the collision could not be resolved.

Robinson picked up the story: 'Following one perfectly amicable meeting, he wrote me a memo saying he did not agree any of what had just been agreed. That was it as far as I was concerned. You couldn't go on like that: it was just a nonsense. I phoned him and said we had better get together very quickly for a talk. He said he couldn't do that because he had an urgent business trip to the United States. I told him he should cancel it, but he refused and went off.

'While he was there I think it dawned on him how serious the situation had become. He tried to organise all sorts of cost-saving plans in a hurry, but it was past the point of no return. He came back and we finally met. There was no personal animosity, not like some situations where you can personally loathe each other. I always found David personally very pleasant and affable. He said, "Are you firing me?" and I told him, "Yes I am, David." I think he was genuinely shocked and surprised that it was actually happening. I don't think it was possible for David to envisage that I could even contemplate this. When he realised I was serious I think he had a sort of panic.'

After Plowright left, Robinson issued a statement saying, 'Granada owes an enormous debt to David and I very much regret that we have been unable to reach a working agreement for the future.' Plowright, more acerbically, said, 'There is a fundamental disagreement between myself and the board about how to manage the change into the new broadcasting environment of the next decade. I wish my colleagues all the success they deserve.'

With his past knowledge of the television industry, Bernstein warned Robinson that there was going to be a tremendous fuss about Plowright's departure, but neither realised it was going to be as much of a row as it turned out to be. 'It was a public-relations disaster,' Bernstein admitted. 'I can understand David being very bitter about it. It was the worst possible way for him to go. Gerry wanted him to stay on as nonexecutive chairman, but he wouldn't have done that.'

Robinson admitted he was unprepared for the media explosion that followed his ousting of Plowright. It was his first taste of a high-profile row that was splashed over the national newspapers, and incidentally earned him the unwanted soubriquet of 'an upstart caterer'. Robinson recalled with a wince, 'I thought the David Plowright business would be a one-day wonder. I was completely surprised at the reaction.' TV stars from Jeremy Brett to Julie Goodyear lined up to express their fears for Granada's future. The staff in Manchester signed a petition demanding Plowright be reinstated. As a silent but eloquent protest, his name was added to the screen credits for every Granada programme that night. Sir Paul Fox, late of the BBC and Thames TV, said Plowright's departure 'sounded the death knell for ITV', although it somehow managed to survive such a dire warning. Newspapers carried lengthy articles with such headlines as 'DON'T LET THE MONEY MEN RUIN TV.'

Peter Paterson, the *Daily Mail's* TV reviewer, wrote,

Actors, programme-makers and everyone else concerned with commercial TV production know that in having lost a major fight with the accountants now in charge of the Granada group – with interests covering television rental, ten-pin bowling, motorway cafés, and computer servicing, as well as its television station - Plowright has lost their battle too. No one outside the industry complained when in the 1980s Mrs Thatcher turned her attention on the bloated fat cats of ITV, shored up by their licence to print money, grossly overmanned, resistant to technological change, and apparently immune from the abrupt dismantling of trade union power she had accomplished elsewhere in the economy. There were new groups waiting in the wings, with new plans and new ideas, eager to challenge the near-monopolies in their regional strongholds. Granada, unlike Thames, TV-am, and TVS, survived the protracted and unsettling auction process, with Plowright richly rewarded and praised for achieving a near-miracle - holding onto his company's licence with a bid of only £9 million, against a rival bid of £35 million by Brookside creator Phil Redmond's consortium. The key to his success was his passionate commitment to quality programming. Other bidders may have paid lip service to the idea of public service broadcasting, and included grandiose pledges to make wonderful programmes, if only they were granted a franchise. But everyone in the industry knew that when

Plowright – responsible for such programmes as Coronation Street, Brideshead Revisited, The Jewel In The Crown and World In Action – said it, he meant it.

And, while Robinson was digesting all this and more, the millionaire actor John Cleese sent him a fax urging him, 'Why don't you fuck off, you upstart caterer?' Robinson had the poise to remark, 'I obviously admire him more than he admires me,' and the two later had a friendly lunch at the Connaught Hotel in Mayfair. More seriously, Robinson and Bernstein were summoned to see Sir George Russell and David Glencross, respectively chairman and director-general of the Independent Broadcasting Authority, to reassure them that standards would be maintained after Plowright's departure. Luckily Russell was sympathetic, because he had had similar trouble with his divisional heads at one of the companies he had run. But it was a formality that the Granada pair could have done without. Within Granada, though, the dust gradually settled.

'There was an awful lot of noise when David left,' Robinson recalled, 'but not a single resignation. I spent two or three days with each of the members of the Granada Television board and other senior people. Some were angry, some reasonable, but throughout these discussions we didn't lose a day's production. It was a tremendous lesson for me, but it never changed my basic belief that if you have got to do something you might as well get on with it. I might have done it differently if I had known what the reaction would be, perhaps moved him away more gradually. But he had no intention of retiring. He had seen Sidney Bernstein and Sir Denis Forman go on well past retirement age, and he would have done the same. He couldn't accept that things had to improve.

'My perception was that we were miles away from what we could do. The franchise system had changed. We had up to twenty years — ten renewable for another ten — compared with the previous franchise periods of five or seven years. But, in the old system, quality was the one differentiator. Everyone paid a levy based on the same percentage of advertising revenue, so it was all about what you could promise in terms of quality. And, as there was no satellite or cable television, and for much of the time no commercial radio either, the ITV companies together had a virtual monopoly of mass-market broadcast advertising.

'But then Margaret Thatcher changed the rules in the 1990 Broadcasting Act. Quality was taken out of the equation, apart from ensuring some minimum standards. Otherwise, it was just a matter of who put in the highest bid. David obviously contributed hugely to Granada Television. He was part of a long line of quality people who had taken quality seriously. But things had moved on, sadly perhaps, and it wasn't that simple any more. Nevertheless, there remained a fortress mentality at Granada Television. *World In Action* was in a world of its own, and there were other departments like that. It took three weeks for me to get to visit the Manchester operation, before the showdown with David. Even then the visit was highly orchestrated, twenty minutes with this executive, ten minutes with that one — and then dinner in Sidney Bernstein's former flat. David Plowright was the grand squire at the head of the table, and they all took it in turns to tell what were clearly very well-worn stories and anecdotes about the TV operation, none of which was designed to give me any real insight into how the business worked, or what the problems were. As far as they were concerned there were no problems, although the declining profits told a different story.

'The whole exercise had the wrong feel to it from the very beginning: it was as if I was a visitor from outside being given the glossy presentation. There was no sense of openness about it. They didn't seem to be bringing me into what was really going on. If they had done that I wouldn't have had any difficulty with it. David was not really managing the business in any way. He was making speeches and sitting in his office in the stratosphere, offering advice and encouragement, talking endlessly about the TV business. Andrew Quinn was really running the business. After David left, Andrew happily took over and I began to get a very different picture. Sure, you always get a bit of "We won't tell him everything", but you learn to make allowances for that and I was certainly now being given a much better feel for the business. Andrew did a very good job in a short period. His style helped generally in terms of opening up the operation.'

Only seven months after Quinn succeeded Plowright, he became chief executive of the whole ITV network. Enter Charles Allen.

Robinson and Allen have become one of the great double acts of British business, dating back to when they were both working for Compass. It has been widely assumed that Robinson pulled his former colleague across to Granada with him at the first opportunity. But the partnership was resumed only by chance. When Robinson left Compass he agreed with Francis Mackay not to poach. So originally Robinson had a former colleague called Chris Bucknall lined up to come to Granada and take over the Leisure division. Bucknall had run a business called Rosser and Russell at Compass, but that had been sold to Generale des Eaux, meaning he was no longer part of Compass. So Robinson was free to bring him to Granada.

However, it meanwhile turned out that Mackay and Allen did not see eye to eye. Allen recalled, 'When Gerry went to Granada, the opportunities were for me to run Compass or go to Granada. I was not comfortable with Francis's style, which was going to get much more involved in the detail. That wasn't my style. The cultural values at Compass changed. Francis is a very good negotiator and good at dealing with people. But he is not as good a communicator as Gerry, and the Granada canvas was much bigger.' So Mackay waived his 'no poaching' rule but in return asked Robinson if he would do a switch – take Allen instead of Bucknall. Both men agreed, but Robinson and Bucknall remained good friends and in due course Bucknall subsequently joined Granada too. In characteristic style, Robinson's charm enabled him to have his cake and eat it.

Allen joined Granada to run the Leisure division, which included motorway services, bowling, nightclubs, bingo and theme parks. But that was being reduced, because Robinson did not want to keep the nightclubs or bowling alleys. And he cancelled plans for a £130 million updated holiday-camp-type operation. Said Allen, 'It was really a question of putting a stop to a lot of things. Gerry was starting to concentrate on other issues and he left me to it. We had spent a lot of money on ten pin bowling, which I thought was just a fad. And we had a business in America, an Indian reservation which was a legacy from the bingo operation. I went across before the Christmas break in 1991, to discover it was a bit crooked. This was Louisiana. We were ordered to pay $500,000 in fines and I wanted to fight it, but it was such a small community that I discovered we would be up against the same judge who had made the order. So we just got out.'

Allen took the train to Granada's legendary Manchester television headquarters in September 1992, after Quinn moved on to run the ITV network. Allen initially wanted to run both TV and Leisure together, but Robinson was not keen on that because he felt Television demanded Allen's whole attention. They reached a compromise whereby Allen would publicly concentrate on television, but within the group would still have responsibility for Leisure. 'He found Television stimulating,' said Robinson, 'and he liked the whole artistic end of it. In no time at all he was fully accepted as a member of the team by his new colleagues in Manchester.'

Well, not quite in no time. Allen admitted that his first hurdle was the layer of people there who thought they should have got the job. He said, 'The brief going into Granada Television was that it could do more. All the given wisdom in the industry turned out to be completely wrong. Carlton Communications and United News and Media, the Meridian and Anglia group, said production was a waste of time: you should be a publisher-broadcaster. Now they have changed. Production is a cost centre, but instead of it being simply a service department I turned it into a business, generating revenue.

'It was a strange culture at the Manchester office. There were barons there that effectively owned parts of it but were not responsible for it. This was a business that needed a lot of attention, which we had to change quite dramatically. I initially had thirteen directors reporting to me, and that was too many. I took them down to five. And it was quite inappropriate for what was a division of a larger group to have its own nonexecutive directors, something which had arisen partly because of the requirements of the TV licence. There was no control culture. In broadcasting we were grandiose Granada, but we had made only £5 million a year.'

So Allen set about making the operation far more commercial than it had been. He decided that the key point was to underline the link between the Television company and the group. As Robinson had found, the people at head office in London were seen as little more than bankers who decided how much money to give to Television, so the Manchester management had to be nice to them, but that was about it. Allen made it clear that Manchester was merely a part of the wider operation, and not a particularly profitable part at that, and had to fit in with that bigger picture. A swathe of redundancies helped to put the message across.

'We were making some of the best programmes in Britain,' he pointed out, 'but we weren't making any money out of it. My challenge was to bring creativity and commercialism together. *Coronation Street* was earning less per episode than Yorkshire's *Emmerdale* or Carlton's *The Bill*. But I had the advantage of being the new boy. I could ask the simple questions and brought no baggage with me. I wasn't part of the club. That was the only way to drive pricing and demand better deals. The other way of making more of *Coronation Street* was to make more episodes, so it went three times a week, plus a Sunday omnibus, and then to four episodes a week. When they were planning *Cracker*, the controversial detective series starring Robbie Coltrane, I said I wanted some really challenging stuff, violent if need be.'

Then Allen turned his attention to another pillar of the Granada television empire: factual programmes. As with *Coronation Street*, the entrance to the *World in Action* offices is dominated by a large sign bearing the programme title. It does not quite say 'Strangers Keep Out', but the message is unmistakable: you are entering a private domain. '*World In Action* had a £3 million budget,' Allen discovered, 'but no one knew where it was being spent. I told them I wanted to know their plans. I said I wasn't going to interfere: I just wanted to know where the money was being spent. There was no strategic direction. So I said I wanted five heavy investigative episodes a year, five lighter episodes and thirty bread-and-butter.'

Allen's mission to commercialise Granada Television was considerably helped by the advent of ITV's Network Centre, which meant that the production companies had to start selling on an open-market basis, instead of carving up the schedules in a smoke-filled room. Human nature being what it is, at first the ITV companies naturally tried to carry on with what amounted to a modified version of the old arrangements, carving up the network through a cosy series of tit-for-tat deals. But, as someone coming to television relatively fresh, Allen had other ideas – like the previously unheard-of notion of selling programmes to organisations other than ITV.

'Basically,' he explained, 'if I have a programme and ITV don't like it, I want to sell it elsewhere: if it's a real business, you can't have only one customer. We were told we would undermine the business, but now ITV are more responsive because they know we can and will sell elsewhere. We made *The Mrs Merton Show* – ITV didn't want it, but it became a kitsch cult for BBC. That tended to concentrate minds a little.'

Meanwhile, Robinson's changes elsewhere at Granada were also beginning to pay off. Profits for the year to September 1992 recovered to £163 million, with the help of the £310 million raised just as soon as Lewis left, from issuing new shares and selling seventy-three bingo clubs to Bass for £147 million. With the decks beginning to clear, Robinson began looking for his first takeover – in catering. In line with Cleese's jibe, Robinson was comfortable with catering as a business and felt it gave Granada a solid underpinning of cash flow and profit. He said at the time, 'For most people, catering is a pain in the backside. They just want to give it to someone else to do. Contract catering's great attraction is its quietness. You can just get on with making money in a field no one really looks at and in a business where both the client and caterer benefit. They save money and we make it by catering more efficiently.'

Building on Granada's existing motorway services and roadside eateries, Robinson went for Sutcliffe Group, a catering and linen-hire company owned by Peninsular and Oriental Steam Navigation, which is best known for its cruise liners and cross-Channel ferries. There was no question of Robinson's becoming involved in the uncertainties of a takeover bid: it was a straightforward trade deal between two public companies. Granada paid P&O £360 million for Sutcliffe – a high price at the time, but Robinson knew enough about the industry to know he could make it work for Granada. He did. With that success under his belt, he later tried to buy Gardner Merchant from Forte, but got nowhere.

His strategy at that stage was to trim Granada's reliance on the declining market of television rentals, which dropped below 50 per cent of the group's total revenue after the Sutcliffe deal. As he expanded, he was hoping to leave the individual businesses to run themselves. 'The argument that we are too widely spread is nonsense,' he said. 'There is no stifling centre to the group. Each business has different requirements and people are given enormous freedom to operate, so long as they do it well.'

The Robinson formula was beginning to work. But the Sutcliffe deal was merely the appetiser for the battle that followed later in 1993 – for London Weekend Television.

8

The Television Game Show

Robinson joined Granada near the beginning of one of the television industry's periodic spasms, when the companies would have to decide whether to swallow or be swallowed. It meant that he was effectively running two businesses: the rest of Granada, where the usual commercial considerations applied, and Television, which for several years would have to be played like a game of lightning chess.

When Robinson arrived at Granada in November 1991 the new franchises under the 1990 Broadcasting Act had just been awarded. As expected, Granada had retained the northwest England territory it had held since ITV started in 1955 (see Appendix II). From that moment of birth the rules governing ITV had fractured every ten years or so, first as a result of official investigations led by Lords Pilkington and Annan and Professor Alan Peacock, then less formally by ministers coming to their own conclusions in the light of rapidly changing moral, technological and commercial climates. The old philosophy of the BBC's founder, Lord Reith, that the public should be given the broadcasting that was good for it, was no longer feasible when viewers and listeners increasingly demanded the right to receive the material they chose for themselves. More channels and, latterly, the proliferation of video, cable, satellite and Internet delivery routes, were making it increasingly impractical for governments to dictate what the public received.

These developments also made it less tenable for Whitehall to operate and levy huge fees from a franchise system. Scarce wavebands, for politicians to allocate like so much largesse, were becoming as much a thing of the past as handwritten books had been after the invention of the printing press.

In what will probably turn out to have been one of the last drinks from the franchise trough, Margaret Thatcher's 1990 Act had imposed a far more free-market environment, where franchises went to the highest bidders in a one-shot blind auction, subject only to a quality threshold. This was loathed by the television establishment, which had grown used to the old system with its backstairs dealings, mutual backscratchings and exchanges of favours to give the programme-makers the freedom to make programmes of which they could be justifiably proud. This had worked well while there was a coterie of the old guard like Sir Denis Forman, Sir Paul Fox and David Plowright to maintain their concept of proper standards. Their natural fear was that, now crude cash was to be allowed a much greater say, standards would fall alarmingly.

The auction played into the hands of streetwise intruders like Robinson and Michael Green, the highly ambitious head of Carlton Communications, which won the London mid-week franchise under the new system. In doing so it ousted the highly respected Thames TV, where there had been doubts about the intentions of one of its principal shareholders, Thorn EMI.

Advances in technology and the growth of satellite television convinced Peter Brooke, Stephen Dorrell and Virginia Bottomley, John Major's successive Heritage Secretaries with responsibility for broadcasting, that they each had to relax the rules governing the extent to which one organisation could control a mixture of newspapers, radio and television, and how large a share of those markets they could have. By January 1993, when the new franchise periods began, Brooke accepted the case for change and he was being lobbied intensively by the different ITV companies to give them this or that extra leeway. He eventually held a meeting of the industry's chairmen that June, which confirmed what he had heard many times by then – that the big companies wanted to get bigger, while the smaller ones wanted a contin-ued ban on more takeovers. But Brooke left the impression that he was going to change the rules to allow one company to own two stations instead of just one.

By this stage Robinson was getting into his stride at Granada. Since he had arrived the group's stock market value had risen from £775 million to £1.4 billion. But 1,800 staff had lost their jobs in Robinson's relentless search for cost cuts. He had also taken personal satisfaction, after the Plowright episode, that the biggest improvement had come from

Granada's ITV subsidiary, which reported a 50 per cent increase in operating profits to £33 million. That included a £6 million reduction in the Exchequer levy, thanks to the low bid Plowright had put in before Robinson arrived.

Robinson was also getting to grips with the arcane politics of commercial television. After swiftly removing Plowright and a brief reign by Andrew Quinn, he had installed his trusted lieutenant Charles Allen to run the Manchester operation. But Robinson realised this was not going to be enough on its own. He said, 'It seemed Manchester was not a sensible place to have all our television interests: it was as unsophisticated as that. We had to go for LWT first because London has a big influence on what goes on air, and we had to bid for that as soon as the rules allowed. The stock market went mad, and share prices just roared away, whether it was Central, LWT, Anglia or HTV.'

Brooke's expected changes would have let Granada buy Yorkshire Tyne-Tees Television, the deal many commentators were forecasting, as Yorkshire's franchise territory adjoined Granada's and in the early days of commercial television Granada had held both territories. Robinson was popularly supposed to be playing a waiting game before buying into Yorkshire, but in May 1993 LWT (Holdings), owner of the London Weekend Television station, pounced to buy 14.9 per cent of the Leeds-based TV station.

'I don't know why everyone's surprised,' said Robinson at the time. 'It doesn't matter where you make a TV programme. Our *Prime Suspect* is shot in London. Everyone already sells their advertising space from London.' That in itself virtually ensured the end of LWT's independence, for it had made itself irresistibly attractive with a key London franchise and a launchpad stake in another big ITV company.

Such were the complexities of the rules at that time that it was vital to manoeuvre in the correct tactical sequence. Had Granada bought Yorkshire in December 1993, it would not then have been able to buy anything else until the rules changed yet again. It would have been barred from competing for any other ITV station that came on the market. Robinson's first priority was to carve out a route into London, both because of the huge pool of production expertise there, and the steady drift of advertising spending to London and the southeast. And, while Granada's main strengths lay in drama and factual programmes, LWT had an unrivalled record in light entertainment with such shows as *Blind Date* and *Gladiators*.

Michael Green decided the LWT price was too high, which was true for Carlton because share prices by this point reflected takeover values and Carlton would probably still not have been allowed to hold both the London midweek and weekend franchises. Said Robinson, 'We naturally looked at Carlton, but we thought it would be unlikely that we could get it. It was not a pure television company, and in any case we didn't think anyone would be allowed to have both London franchises so it would be difficult for Green to make a competing bid for LWT – which, of course, was why he was furious at us for making our bid.'

Green denied that he was other than totally relaxed about Granada barging in. He said, 'Granada's bid for LWT didn't bother me in the slightest. There wasn't the slightest chance of anyone being allowed to have both the London midweek and weekend franchises, and ITV needed to be consolidated.'

But there is no doubt that Sir Christopher Bland and Greg Dyke, respectively LWT's chairman and managing director, were greatly put out at Robinson's approach. They were an unlikely but powerful pair: Bland, the Oxford-educated Olympic fencer, who after the Granada takeover went on to become chairman of the BBC, and Dyke, a former Marks & Spencer trainee and south London community-relations worker who rose from research assistant to director of progammes at LWT in just ten years. Despite their different backgrounds and different political views – Dyke stood as a Labour candidate for the old Greater London Council; Bland was elected to the GLC as a left-wing Conservative – both have famously short fuses and point-blank refusals to put up with what they regard as nonsense. When Dyke became managing director of LWT under Bland's chairmanship they formed a formidable partnership that was never really threatened until Robinson turned his attention to them.

They had more than a purely emotional interest in LWT's fate. In 1989 Bland, in tandem with the merchant banker Sir Martin Jacomb, had worked out an ingenious scheme to improve LWT's chances of retaining its hold on the London weekend brief when the ITV franchises came up for renewal in 1991. The company borrowed £100 million and drew £35 million out of reserves to repay shareholders 130p a share. The effect was to shrink LWT's equity and increase its debt.

At the time Bland explained, 'The more equity you have, the less you are able to hand over in a franchise bid. Our equity is about five per cent more expensive to service than debt is. By doing this we have freed about £5–6 million we can use to bid for the franchise.'

Reasonable as the plan may have sounded, some institutional shareholders fought hard against it. They were unhappy because the plan also involved letting more than forty top executives – including Bland – buy a total of up to 15 per cent of LWT's shares at preferential prices. Ernie McKnight, then head of UK Equities at Scottish Amicable, an LWT investor, remarked, 'LWT executives are carving a nice little deal for themselves. I'm all in favour of executive option schemes, but the board here simply wants fifteen per cent of the company upfront, which seems excessive.' Ironically in view of its pivotal role in the Granada bid, Mercury Asset Management was the main supporter of the scheme and LWT would not have managed to get it through without them.

Bland replied, 'You don't need only a few million quid to bid [for a franchise]. You also need a director of programming, a finance director, people to run the studios and so on. We have locked our key people in [with this scheme], and won't need to worry for a few years. We had no idea we would be so successful: we took out costs and paid off our debts faster than we thought possible. I can remember three or four months after our deal had gone through, LWT's share price was below where we had started and there were some worried people around. I got some sideways looks in the lift.'

Nevertheless, the effect was that LWT had some of the best-motivated and potentially wealthiest executives in Britain. By 1993 they were sitting on handsome profits and there were at least sixteen paper millionaires in the company, among them Bland, Dyke and the arts controller Melvyn Bragg, later Lord Bragg. But they could see that the increasing liberalisation of Britain's independent television industry could make what had been achieved up to then merely an appetiser. They wanted to stay independent so they could reap the full rewards.

The original idea for Granada to go for LWT came from Steve Morrison in Manchester – who later unsuccessfully urged Robinson to take over Manchester United Football Club. But Robinson bought the LWT plan and won board approval a few weeks before they bought the first block of LWT shares on the stock market, on 29 June 1993. Although everyone in the industry expected a further relaxation to come soon, in the summer of 1993 Granada could hold no more than 20 per cent of another television company through a deadlocked company over which it had no direct legal control. This was achieved by the device of using a special company to hold the shares, one of those off-the-shelf companies that banks and lawyers keep handy for such occasions. Ownership of that company was split 50–50 between Granada and its merchant bank adviser, Lazard Brothers. It was a legal fiction: as Lazards were acting for Granada, they would hardly suggest doing anything with the LWT shares that was against Granada's wishes.

But the device got round the rules, and there was little objection as the rules were anyway ripe for change. So Granada's stockbrokers, Hoare Govett and Barclays de Zoete Wedd, went into the stock market and bought 14.9 per cent of LWT (Holdings). Under the Code of the City Takeover Panel, anyone buying as much as 15 per cent of the shares in a quoted company in one swoop then had to make a full takeover bid. So 14.9 per cent of LWT was the most Granada could buy without triggering a bid that the government would have blocked under its then rules on the ownership of television stations. As they were offering 500p a share, about a third more than LWT shares had been fetching the day before, it was not difficult to find takers.

Mercury Asset Management locked in some easy profits by selling Granada about a quarter of its 21 per cent stake in LWT. In retrospect that might have told Sir Christopher Bland that he could not rely on MAM's loyalty when his shareholders would finally have to decide the company's fate. In the end, he was bitterly disappointed that MAM let him down. MAM took the position that it was compelled to act rationally in the interests of its clients, no matter how emotive the situation became. As soon as his brokers told Robinson that they had acquired the 14.9 per cent of LWT he wanted, he telephoned Bland to break the news. Bland wasted few words. 'Congratulations,' he replied drily. There had to be a pause before Granada could buy any more LWT shares, so that the public had a chance to buy and existing investors could decide whether to sell.

The following week Granada took its stake up to the maximum it was allowed by the government. 'We were remarkably upfront about it,' said Robinson. 'We bought twenty per cent and everyone knew we were going to make a full bid for LWT if and when the rules permitted. Our buying sent the shares soaring, and that was the first time we had a conversation with Christopher and Greg. We thought – correctly – that they wouldn't want to be taken over, so there was no point in warning them. We were right: they were very unhappy about it, made their feelings very plain, and said they very much wanted to paddle their own canoe. But we were also taking quite a risk. If the rules hadn't changed we would have been stuck with twenty per cent of something we had paid a high price for and had no control over, because Greg and Christopher were not about to give us a seat on their board!'

Bland told me, 'Yes, there was an initial shock about Granada emerging with fifteen per cent of LWT. We knew somebody had the stake. We weren't sure who, but Granada was one possibility of two or three. It was clear that at the moment he was able to bid he would bid. There was no nonsense about it being a strategic stake for investment purposes. He would bid and we would have to be fighting him off.'

On 23 November 1993, Brooke announced that from 1 January 1994 he would let one company own two regional television franchises – excluding the two London franchises – as well as 20 per cent of a third licence-holder and 5 per cent of any further licences. By then LWT had talked to Anglia and Yorkshire about trying to do a deal. This was designed, apart from anything else, to put pressure on Granada. The three would not at that stage have been allowed to come together as one, because they would have owned too many franchises. One proposal was for LWT to take Yorkshire but hive off the Tyne-Tees TV licence to Anglia. If LWT had bought Yorkshire, Granada would not have been able to buy LWT, as the combined group would then have four stations, taking Yorkshire and Tyne-Tees as separate stations. On the other hand, LWT was all too well aware that Granada could buy it, complete with LWT's 14.9 per cent of Yorkshire, ready to be used if the rules were relaxed further. In any case, Anglia threw in its lot with Lord Hollick's MAI, which owned Meridian Television on the south coast – the bid in which Lord Archer became famously involved in allegations surrounding a share purchase.

A few days after Brooke's announcement, Robinson made a last-ditch attempt to persuade Bland to agree to a takeover, which might have saved millions of pounds. But there was no incentive for Bland to cave in so quickly. Understandably, therefore, he rejected Robinson's overtures.

Bland recalled, 'He invited us to his house in Holland Park and we met him and Alex Bernstein because he wanted to explore the possibility of an agreed bid. I said there was no chance: I thought he had pitched his bid far too low. We left feeling unanimous that Greg Dyke and I would reject the bid and we would have no difficulty in persuading our board to agree.'

So Granada launched its bid on the Monday morning, 6 December 1993, after a meeting of the full board on the Sunday night. Although the government's new rules would not take effect for nearly a month, under the City Takeover Code the bid would take at least sixty days to complete. Those fund managers who had sold to Granada at 500p a share in June may have been cursing, for the opening shot was pitched at the equivalent of 580.5p a share, or £595 million. The offer was not in actual cash, partly because that was more expensive, and partly because it would have given some LWT investors a big bill for capital gains tax. Instead, the offer was six Granada shares for every five LWT shares. This also had the possible advantage of giving LWT shareholders a continuing interest in their business, along with the rest of Granada.

Robinson said, 'LWT shareholders are being offered the opportunity to participate in a substantial business which will be a major force in the changing television market.' Bland snorted that the bid had little to offer LWT shareholders, but Robinson was impressed that his opponent refused to suggest either that any of LWT's stars, such as Cilla Black, Michael Barrymore or Michael Aspel, would walk out if Granada won, or that programme standards would drop.

'I genuinely believe that Christopher and Greg didn't want to be taken over,' said Robinson, 'despite the fact that they were going to make millions out of it from their share options. Unlike Forte, LWT was well managed. Our bid was driven by the fact that in our view television companies were going to have to be programme-makers to survive, and LWT dominated the light-entertainment end of programme-making. I have a huge regard for Christopher and Greg: they were running a terrific company, making great programmes, and they had a team which was well motivated and was very good at motivating the people under them. They behaved impeccably throughout the bid.'

Apart from the routine mudslinging and disparaging of one another's claims, the only time the battle became at all brittle was when LWT produced a profits estimate of £43.8 million for 1993. Robinson said that figure required 'careful scrutiny' and had been 'generated in the heat of the takeover', adding, 'We will not be using those numbers for internal purposes.' He argued that the television business was unusually transparent in accounting terms, in that profits were normally reflected in cash generated. But this had not happened at LWT in 1993, with reported profits significantly outstripping actual cash earned. In public, Bland said Bernstein and Robinson 'should put up or shut up'. And he wrote to Alex Bernstein:

> Following Granada's press conference on January 27, its chief executive, Mr Gerry Robinson, was widely quoted as casting doubt on LWT's 1993 profit estimate. His comments were reported in The Daily Telegraph the next day under the headline 'Robinson scorns LWT figures' ... Let me reassure you – and Mr Robinson – about LWT's 1993 figures. They are rock-solid ... The numbers were reviewed by our Audit Committee, which consists of two non-executive directors; approved by the full board of LWT (Holdings) plc; and reported on by our auditors, KPMG, and by our merchant bankers, Samuel Montagu. The question is a simple one. Does Granada accept LWT's 1993 profits estimate, and withdraw the remarks made by Mr Robinson on January 27? Or, if not, why not?

Robinson admitted, 'We had said in advance that of course they would throw in everything they could to make their profits look as good as possible, so we pointed out that the increase in profits wasn't matched by the increase in cash and argued that they had raided reserves to make the figures look good. After Bland wrote "These figures are rock-solid" we drafted a joke letter saying "Oh yes, and San Francisco was rock-solid before the earthquake," but it was just as well we didn't send it – I think Christopher would have exploded!'

Bland insisted in 1998, 'He came close to slandering us and gave us a half-withdrawal, half-apology. I think he behaved badly at that point. He couldn't substantiate his allegations, and he was quite lucky we didn't sue him. Pouring cold water on our figures was one thing, but he was going too far. I didn't know about the San Francisco letter at the time; I don't think that was very funny.'

But, while Robinson refused to retract his suggestion that LWT had massaged the figures, the Takeover Panel did force him to withdraw a claim that less than half of LWT's operating profit was converted into cash. LWT told the Panel that it generated cash of £23.8 million, not £22.9 million, as stated in Granada's document, and this was the equivalent of 51 per cent, rather than less than half. The Panel also made Granada correct a chart that indicated a 26.8 per cent fall in cash inflow since 1992. The correct figure was 23.9 per cent. As if that were not enough, Granada was forced to admit that LWT had received three Bafta awards, not two, as it had stated, and clarify a graph of share prices. Bland made the most of the opportunity to get back at Robinson, saying it showed 'a slapdash attitude to putting out circulars'.

Despite that clash, less than a week later, on Monday, 7 February 1994, Robinson and Bernstein made one last attempt to agree a price with Bland and Dyke. But the LWT pair held out for nearly 900p a share, while Bernstein and Robinson had in mind something around 750p. That left the two sides too far apart, so the following day Granada went public with a final offer of thirteen of its own shares plus £1 cash for every ten LWT shares. With Granada shares priced in the stock market at 568p, that valued each LWT share at 748p, or £774 million for the whole company. Any LWT investor who preferred cash could have 686p a share. Bland insisted that this was still inadequate and failed to reflect the true value of LWT, so it was up to his shareholders to decide. By this stage LWT executives owned a combined 10 per cent of the company.

'We decided in advance the price we would pay,' Robinson admitted. 'You have to, don't you? You get one chance to raise your bid, so you knock ten per cent off to start with and raise it later to the amount you originally had in mind. LWT was not a steal. You don't get a steal in this market because it is so sophisticated. But there is something to be said for a hostile bid, because someone has to run a company. You can't have two or three people running it. In a friendly deal you get a stitching up of the top jobs to ensure no one loses out, and you keep people's pet projects running, and that simply delays the benefit. ITV was going to come down to two or three players. If you were not going to be one of those two or three you were not going to survive, however well run you were. We knew a hell of a lot about LWT. We knew their advertising revenue, and what they were getting for their programmes, because we were paying our share of that. The ITV companies shared a hell of a lot of information because they were trading with one another all the time, and it was by pooling information that they decided who paid what.'

So Robinson was able to pitch the LWT price pretty accurately, and duly won control on 26 February – but not by much. On the night before the deadline they had their hands on just 56 per cent of LWT's shares. That was enough, though Robinson did not realise how close Bland and Dyke were to staging a spectacular coup, the sort that is possible only when the directors of a target company are independently wealthy.

Bland revealed, 'There was a moment when Greg Dyke and I thought acceptances were hovering around 47 per cent and we could buy enough to stop Granada winning if we borrowed £30 million from Samuel Montagu. They agreed to lend us the money, but the arbitrageurs didn't have enough to make the difference. Granada got 56 per cent, so the loan wasn't required. I regret that we didn't launch an attack on the incompetence of their chairman [Alex Bernstein] and the inexperience of their chief executive [Robinson].'

John Nelson, Robinson's closest City adviser, said, 'LWT was a quite extraordinary battle. Gerry and Granada were much more confident of winning than we were. LWT was a well run company with good prospects and a management the City liked. We got it at a lower price than we thought, and it was in better shape than we thought. But they mishandled their defence and mismanaged the institutions. Bland kept on using intemperate language, being quoted in the papers saying bollocks to everything, which didn't go down well with the institutions.'

Bland quickly conceded defeat, saying at the time, 'I have congratulated them on acquiring a great company at what I believe will prove a great price. We are obviously disappointed not to have retained our independence.' His shares fetched £14 million, while Greg Dyke picked up £9 million and Melvyn Bragg more than £4 million. This was not lost on those LWT employees who had missed out on the incentive scheme. That night there was a party for the staff at LWT's office and studio complex on the South Bank of the Thames. When Dyke handed the microphone to Bland saying, 'And now over to the only man who knows he will definitely be out of a job next week,' some of the audience could not resist pointing out that their chairman hardly needed to work any more. Given Robinson's reputation as a cutter of costs and jobs, quite a few at LWT feared that they might be out on the street. Indeed, two hundred at LWT and Granada lost their jobs, mainly among the administration staff.

Bland recalled: 'We had a rather gloomy party that night. My abiding regret is that it was the breakup of a brilliant management team. ITV is still suffering from that. Greg Dyke wouldn't have worked for Charles Allen. If Robinson had been bolder, he would have given Allen something else to do. The LWT executives were rich enough to be able to go, so it would have taken sensitive handling to keep them. The Manchester people turned up the next day and started throwing their weight about, and got kicked out because the bid had not yet gone unconditional – so Granada did not yet strictly own LWT. But on the whole they were pretty fair in their treatment of our people.'

'When we took them over,' said Robinson, 'I think they thought people with cloth caps were going to leave their pigeons behind for a day and come down from Manchester to sort them out, but it wasn't like that. Greg Dyke invited me down to the morning meeting they held each week and introduced me to everyone, and I sat in on the meeting. There was no daftness. There was never any great problem in putting LWT in place. It was not antagonistic; people didn't fight it. There was Day One acceptance and because we knew a lot about it already we had a pretty clear picture about what we wanted to do before we went in. Because it was a business that fitted with what we had, I personally was not terribly involved in the merger after the first two or three weeks.'

Robinson was keen that Greg Dyke stay to run LWT, but Dyke preferred to go. Ron Miller on the sales side was another possibility but he, too, moved on. In the end, nearly all those who had made serious money went – apart from Melvyn Bragg – and that allowed others to come through. Charles Allen based himself at LWT for about a year and a half. He set in motion the process of how they should work together and of bringing together the mechanics of accounting and deciding artists' rights. Steve Morrison eventually went down from Manchester to run it.

There were certain requirements to keep LWT as a separate entity for franchise reasons and at the time of writing they are still separate entities. Granada decided not to go the route of Carlton, which brought all its production centres together as Carlton Productions. Robinson explained, 'The main commercial reason for not bringing Granada TV and LWT together is that if you stay separate you get two cracks of the whip at programme bidding. The same is true of Yorkshire – that later gave us a third crack. They have all got a chance of pitching for programmes. And it does seem to have worked. There may have been other scope for economies, but that would have been outweighed by keeping production separate.'

However, Ward Thomas, the chairman of Yorkshire Tyne-Tees Television Holdings until it was taken over by Granada, claimed that it was only a matter of time before the TV companies each brought their production under one roof. He told me, 'It's silly for Granada to have three production centres. It may make sense at the moment, to pitch for airtime, but you can't go on on the basis of selling programmes to one another. With satellite, cable and the other media, it is becoming a free market.'

The LWT takeover helped to establish Robinson's place as a chief executive who was prepared to be aggressive to get the company he ran in the shape he wanted. And it also made the television establishment take notice. Granada had almost been written off as a big player before the bid, because many in the industry and beyond still associated the group with the Derek Lewis interlude and the Bernstein era. People had lost sight of the fact that Granada had had eighteen months of good results, and so was a lot stronger. This was partly because Granada had not for some time been a member of the inner club of ITV companies, consisting mainly of LWT, Central and Carlton. As it was, Michael Green had rushed to make a conditional takeover of the Midlands-based Central as soon as Peter Brooke announced he would be relaxing the rules.

Robinson said, 'We bought a stake in two franchises and we could have come to some sort of deal with Michael over Central. It was a chip you could play with. We could have got our money back, even though it was not what we wanted. The price of LWT would have gone through the roof if Michael had been able to bid. As it was, you had to be in ITV already to make the bid for LWT work at the price we were offering. In the end it really only made sense to either ourselves, Michael or Clive Hollick at United News and Media. Clive seemed content to pick up Anglia, and LWT never got its act together with Yorkshire or Anglia.'

But the LWT bid was not only a first test of Robinson's standing in the television industry. For the first time since he had led Compass's failed bid for Sketchley, it was an opportu-

nity to check how he affected the pulse rates of City fund
managers – notably the forbidding Carol Galley of Mercury
Asset Management. It was the first bid by Granada where
people thought Galley had decided to put a deal together,
because at the time of the bid MAM held 15 per cent of LWT
and 17 per cent of Granada.

'Carol is very well informed,' said Robinson. 'If you go
to see her, you had better know the answers because she
comes up with all the questions. We always felt when we were
dealing with MAM that they were going to make the right
decision, so you had to think in terms of what was good for
them. But there was absolutely no prearrangement in terms of
them asking us to bid for LWT – in fact, the very suggestion
annoyed them. At the end of the LWT bid they phoned to say
they were going to accept. But that was on the last morning,
and it had been a very nerve-racking time because we didn't
win by a big margin.

'The MAM votes were crucial. We had thought Fidelity
were going to go our way because they seemed to be traders
who would simply accept the highest price. When they didn't
accept the final bid I thought, Jesus, we're going to struggle.
Greg and Christopher made a lot of the fact that they had
been sold down the river by their institutional shareholders,
who had shown no faith in their claim that they had the
ability to manage LWT for the long term. But, if some
American company came along and bid enough for Granada,
MAM and most of the others would probably go for it – and I
wouldn't blame them. It's their job after all, to make the right
decision on behalf of their investors.'

Bland, however, still feels MAM gave him and LWT a

raw deal. Four years after the bid was over he said, 'In the end it all hinged really on what MAM did, because it was a close contest and we knew we would win if they voted for us and we would have a hard time if they didn't. I still think it was a poor decision badly taken on the part of MAM. I have little respect for Carol Galley, but we took it on the chin. Galley wouldn't tell me in person what had been decided. Instead she phoned from her holiday home in France. She said she would support me in whatever we did in the future and I said, "You and I have a different idea of what constitutes support, because we want your support now." They knew a good deal less about the industry than we did. On the closing date Granada got 56 per cent, but 15 per cent of that was MAM's holding. I suspect the critical decision was not on the essentials of the case, but the fact that they had more by value in Granada than in LWT. If it had failed, Granada shares would have fallen. In the end the weight of money counted.'

MAM argued that, at the time, the markets clearly recognised that the price being paid by Granada was a full one and MAM points out that it took its decision as a result of its normal rigorous procedures. MAM does not accept that it was influenced by the value of its holding in Granada, as its investment clients who held Granada shares were not necessarily the same as the clients who held LWT. In most cases they were not the same. A MAM adviser added, 'Not only was the price a full one but it was widely acknowledged at the time, including by the government, that consolidation in the industry was necessary if ITV companies were to have a viable future.'

•

Within a year, the television industry was contending with a new Heritage Secretary, the urbane Stephen Dorrell, who took the deregulation process a step further. Like Peter Brooke, he refused to sanction a free-for-all. But like Brooke, he saw that technology was moving on. 'Convergence' was the buzz word of 1995 – convergence of television, telephone and computer. To confuse the regulators even more, newspapers were bursting into electronic form on the Internet, where the audience was doubling every year. So he went for market share. He allowed newspaper groups with less than 20 per cent of UK readership to buy up to two ITV stations, provided they did not end up with more than 15 per cent of viewers, while television companies could buy newspapers, and naturally could also own more than one TV station provided their total market share did not exceed the magic 20 per cent.

'I want British companies to be able to compete on a world scale,' said Dorrell. 'The way you do that is by creating a much more open marketplace.'

The new rules left scope for Granada to buy a third franchise, as long as its market share was not too big. Yorkshire Tyne-Tees, encompassing an adjoining region which Granada had held until 1967, was the obvious target – and both the stock market and Yorkshire's wily veteran chairman, Ward Thomas, were well aware of how well they fitted together. To add to the 13 per cent stake in Yorkshire which Granada had gained through taking over LWT, Henry Staunton, Granada's finance director, tried to buy either W.H. Smith's or Pearson's investments in Yorkshire, each of which stood at around 15 per cent. They both wanted too much money, though, for Robinson's taste. 'Thereafter it became a kind of game,' said Robinson.

Thomas, who had started in the television industry as an advertising salesman for Granada in the pioneering days, had been Yorkshire's first chairman when it was awarded the franchise in 1967. He was brought back from retirement in 1993 at the age of sixty-nine to rescue what had become a dire situation. Yorkshire had become heavily overstaffed, and the management had divisionalised the company to make every operation into a profit centre. That has the advantage of making it easier to see where strengths and weaknesses lie, but in this case it created huge inefficiencies. The most conspicuous mess was selling more advertising airtime than they had minutes to sell.

'The morale of the employees had fallen considerably,' said Thomas, 'and it became clear to me that there were significant concerns regarding the company's longer-term survival.'

Over the next couple of years Thomas reduced the staff from 2400 to 1092, sorted the advertising sales problem and continued to develop hit programmes such as *Emmerdale*, *A Touch of Frost* and *Heartbeat*. Consequently the group turned round from making losses to making profits of £28 million for 1996.

In February of that year, though, Granada topped up its existing holding by picking up another 10 per cent on the stock market, taking its total stake to just under 24 per cent. To comply with the government's rules, a slice of these were put into Allquiet Investments, the deadlocked company owned 50–50 by Granada and Lazard Brothers. In September Granada and Allquiet exercised a block of warrants in Yorkshire shares, taking their combined stake up to 27 per cent. Charles Allen said at the time, 'We are still weighing up our options in relation to Yorkshire.' But by March 1997 speculation was boiling over, especially as Thomas had let it be known that he wanted £17 a share compared with the humble 156p they had been fetching on the stock market when he had returned to the company three years earlier. Some investment institutions took Thomas seriously, driving the market price up to £13, way above what Robinson had in mind, so he had to dampen the fever. He put out a statement that 'reports of the possibility of Granada making an offer for Yorkshire at or above the current market share price are misplaced: Granada confirms that, unless there is a material change in Yorkshire's circumstances (including an offer from a third party), it has no current intention of making an offer for Yorkshire.' Three months later they announced they were talking about a takeover bid at £11.75 a share – leaving some unhappy fund managers nursing Yorkshire shares they had bought at up to £1 or so dearer.

'We agreed with Ward Thomas that we would come to a deal,' said Robinson. 'The price we paid for Yorkshire wasn't cheap. It was doable, but a lot of the potential was already built into the price, and that was mainly on the programme-making side. They had strong programmes, and the rights to make current programming are very valuable. A three-week-old episode of *Blind Date* has a limited value, but the right to produce new episodes is very valuable. The big payoff was to sell advertising as one block for the whole of the north of England. We already had a joint airtime-selling operation with Yorkshire, but now the revenue would stay with us. That has begun to pay off for us. It means the advertiser only has to do one deal for the whole region, and we can offer special terms for that.

'The other benefit of buying Yorkshire, for us as an existing franchise holder, was that we could make structural savings such as closing their head office. We were hoping Ward Thomas would be chairman of our television division, but within months it was clear that there were going to be clashes between Ward and the Granada and LWT people. I liked Ward a lot, but in terms of a modern management approach it was not going to work. We had to take a longer-term approach and give opportunities to younger people who were coming through. It was the final bit of ITV, really. There was nothing of any size left, and we are not now trying to take one another over.'

From his BBC chairman's suite overlooking Portland Place in central London, Sir Christopher Bland claimed that there were fundamental flaws in ITV after the reshuffles of the mid-1990s. He said, 'The question is whether ITV can really prosper when you have three major companies, like Granada, Carlton and United News and Media, all jealous of one another. Granada likes making money out of making programmes, while Carlton is interested in driving programme prices down. There is general conflict of interest that prevents ITV from acting as one.'

Sir Christopher, refused to succumb to the Robinson charm. 'Is he any more than a deal-maker and a cost-cutter?' he asked rhetorically. 'I sat on the board of ITV with him. He was bright, engaging, but in business terms curiously unimaginative. All I heard him talking about was driving costs down.'

9

Forte

If Robinson's acquisitions of LWT and YTTTV had been the prizes in a helter-skelter game of lightning chess, his takeover of the Forte hotels and catering group in 1996 was more in the nature of big-game hunting. A long period of stalking culminated in a galloping chase and a ruthless kill, which left victor and vanquished totally spent for months afterwards. Heather Robinson told me, 'Gerry said after the Forte bid he was never going to do another one like that, because he found it so exhausting.' And John Nelson, Robinson's close adviser, confirmed, 'Forte was a nightmare of a deal. It took a lot out of people on both sides. Whereas LWT was hysterical, Forte was emotional. Gerry took quite a while to recover physically.'

The Forte story is one of the business legends of the twentieth century: how Charles Forte, a poor Scottish-Italian, made his way from Glasgow to London in 1934 and opened a

milk bar which eventually turned into Britain's biggest catering empire. He began quietly but moved into restaurants after
World War Two and in 1958 bought his first hotel, the Waldorf
in London's Aldwych. He was a great networker who very
quickly appreciated the importance of shrewd property deals
to a catering business, especially in somewhere as expensive as
London. In 1970 he merged his company with the 200-hotel
Trust Houses group, making him the country's leading
hotelier and caterer. That year he was knighted and became a
life peer twelve years later. He finally handed over to his only
son, Rocco, in 1993.

Robinson had been fascinated by the Forte company for
years, partly because it was the industry leader, but also
because he claimed he had always found it an easy competitor
in motorway services or contract catering. He said, 'They
were always whingeing about how difficult it was to make
profits, but at Compass we found it dead easy. There was
always a lot of knocking of the centre, of head office, an
underlying negativity by their executives whenever we met
them. Yet they were *the* catering company in the UK – you
couldn't avoid them. You couldn't do anything in catering and
not come across Charlie Forte in some way. He was incredibly
well liked, highly regarded and thought of in warm terms.
When I was at Compass, Charlie was just beginning to hand
over the reins to Rocco. I remember meeting Charlie and
Rocco at some presentation and there was that feeling of
Charlie's warmth and Rocco's discomfort.'

In the late 1980s Compass was too small and too recently
arrived on the stock market to contemplate a full-scale
takeover bid for the mighty Forte. But the Gardner Merchant

contract-catering subsidiary was another matter. It was a big and direct competitor of Compass, and its pedigree and parentage should have made it a real thorn in Robinson's side. Instead, though, Robinson felt 'it always looked a bit gentle. There was no pressure, no sense that it was going anywhere.'

It would be a gross exaggeration to suggest that the multibillion-pound bid for Forte was conceived at this point. But the bell rang after Robinson reached Granada and bought Sutcliffe Catering from P&O. In 1993 word went around the industry that Forte was willing to sell Gardner Merchant.

Robinson recalled, 'We kept hearing these noises that they had been talking to the management and Compass as potential buyers, among others. If you wanted to get the best price as the seller you would surely have come to us. You might have wanted it to go to the management, but you would still use us as a stalking horse. In the end the deal didn't happen. Not only did they not come to us, Rocco wouldn't even answer my phone calls. I wrote as well, but we got nowhere. We tried Ken Costa, Forte's adviser at their merchant bank, S.G.Warburg, but he said there's no point you bothering because they are so far down the road to a deal and have an exclusivity agreement with the management. And we thought, Christ, what a way to run a sale! Let's have a look at the whole thing, let's see what's going on here.'

That began a tireless process of going round to every Forte outlet in the UK, and many abroad. The Granada team pored over all the published information on Forte, including its annual reports and press cuttings, and looked at how much they made from the various hotel chains, like Post House and

Crest, relative to comparable competitors. All told a similar story of low profit margins and not being very competitive. They claimed only fifty people worked at the London head office, but Granada reckoned it was really seven hundred because Forte simply regarded the other six hundred and fifty working there as belonging to the individual divisions. That was to give Robinson a huge bonus in terms of extra savings when the takeover succeeded. Granada also looked at Forte's motorway service stations, even though they knew they would not be allowed to keep them after a takeover because they would own so many that the Monopolies and Mergers Commission – now the Competition Commission – would certainly order a large proportion to be sold.

Nevertheless, the Forte motorway outlets gave Granada a straight comparison with their own motorway operation. Both were trading under the same conditions laid down by the government, they each had the same number of outlets and they were charging the same prices. The difference was that Granada's apparently made one-and-a-half times as much money as Forte's. On the A roads, according to Robinson, many of the Little Chef snack restaurants were opening later than scheduled in the morning, they looked run down, and some of their electric signs weren't working.

'It was terribly bitty,' he said. 'Some were very good if they had a good manager or manageress, but service was generally slow, to the extent that it almost stopped you buying anything more. Everything we touched left us with the feeling that this was not a well-run affair.'

John Nelson noted, 'There were relatively few under-managed big UK companies at that time, but after the

Gardner Merchant episode I said to Gerry, "This is one for later." That episode gave me the feeling that Forte was a soft company. It was just badly managed. Gerry and Charles Allen made sure they were touching Forte at every point commercially, competing with them, and every time they just felt soft. But the Forte share price stayed quite high, despite the underlying decline. They made some bad deals, bought things far too expensively.'

By this time Granada was caught up in the bid for LWT, which was very time-pressured because of the sudden change at the end of 1993 in the rules governing how many TV stations anyone could own. In that situation Granada had to move fast, so the plans for Forte had to take a back seat. At about the same time Forte announced it had replaced seventy-five of its top hundred executives. Robinson thought that maybe his quarry was going to get its act together, that the share price would surge ahead and it would simply become too expensive for Granada. But as Forte's results came out, half-year by half-year, there was little sign of its position improving.

The hotel industry was struggling to recover from the deadening effects of the Gulf War against Iraq. Millions of people postponed or cancelled business and holiday trips after the war for fear that Saddam Hussein's fanatics would blow up a plane or hotel in reprisal. Forte's pre-tax profits tumbled from £215 million in 1990 to £61 million and it had to cut its dividend the following year.

Meanwhile the Granada share price started to rise, reflecting Robinson's changes and the benefits flowing from the LWT takeover, making it easier for Granada to offer its own shares in making a bid. There was a moment of panic in the would-be predators' camp in September 1994, when Forte bought the Meridian hotel chain at a knockdown price of £230 million – but the stock market had become sceptical of Forte and instinctively assumed it had overpaid. Meridian was not making money, and analysts wrongly calculated that the deal would dilute Forte's earnings. Its shares slipped. All the same, its profits were recovering, reaching £127 million in the year to March 1995 and continuing to rise beyond that.

In the summer of 1995 Granada and its merchant bank, Lazard Brothers, secretly took the Forte companies apart, analysing every aspect. By the time that exercise was completed they hoped they knew almost as much about their intended victim as Sir Rocco Forte did, if not more. But Robinson and Allen knew they were going into what would be an all-in wrestling match on a huge scale, where defeat would be a career setback from which neither might recover. Their doubts nagged at them right up until the minute they decided to go ahead. Robinson admitted, 'The final decision to bid was what Charles and I call a "51/49er". It was that close.'

They had three big worries:

- The Council of Forte. This body had less than one-tenth of 1 per cent of the company's shares, but held the right to wield half Forte's votes if it chose to use them in a takeover, so it could effectively block Granada. The depth of concern on this point by Robinson and Allen – and, for that matter, by John Nelson at Lazard Brothers – was well hidden during the bid. The business press tended to dismiss it as a highly unlikely eventuality, on the grounds that if the Council did try to block a bid they could face law suits both by Granada and by Forte shareholders angry at being denied the opportunity to accept a lucrative offer. But it nagged at the Granada team.

- The potential difficulty Granada might face in trying to sell a large number of Forte's hotels. Robinson reckoned ahead of the bid that he could have to raise anything from £600 million to £1.6 billion, nearly half the value of the initial bid, to bring debt down quickly.

- The City might take a dim view of something as ambitious as a bid for Forte, and possibly ask whether Robinson and Allen had succumbed to the all-consuming megalomania that so often grips successful chairmen and chief executives. It is the sort of reputation that, once conferred, is hard to shake off, and an early criticism of the bid was that there was no obvious fit between the two companies. That this was regarded as such a major potential pitfall showed how conscious the Granada pair were about their standing in the financial world.

But, misgivings or no, they pressed the button and decided to launch the £3.3 billion bid simultaneously with Granada's annual results on Wednesday, 22 November 1995. Nelson said, 'We held a press conference out of the blue at the City Presentation Centre in Chiswell Street, and decided to keep firing ammunition at them day after day.' The initial offer looked generous: four Granada shares plus £23.25 in cash for every fifteen Forte shares. With Granada shares down that day from 697p to 649p, the package valued each Forte share at

328p, 62p higher than the price they had been trading at in the market the previous day. On the day of the announcement they soared to 347p on hopes of an even better offer. Robinson kept Granada's own shares buoyant by simultane-ously announcing a one-third rise in pre-tax profits to £351 million for the year to the end of September. Lazard's raised the billions of debt finance through four banks in five days just before launching the bid. The one snag in the run-up was that one of the banks dropped out at the last minute because of a conflict of interest and had to be replaced.

It was a well-kept secret, but the inevitable need to let more people into the plan may have enabled the City's always well-informed traded-options market to get wind of what was happening at the start of the week of the announcement. The price of options on Forte shares started to rise, and Granada was strongly rumoured to be the bidder.

But Sir Rocco Forte waved away such speculation. He said in 1998, 'I wasn't expecting an offer at all. Obviously the question of whether the company might be bid for was always at the back of my mind. We had discussed with our bankers and amongst ourselves, but no one thought we were a likely target or that anybody would be prepared to make the financial leap because they would have to pay a substantial premium to get us. Certainly we felt no one in the hotel industry at that time would be likely to make a bid. On the face of it, Granada was a very unlikely purchaser. They were not in the hotel business in any way, and I believe they looked at three or four targets before deciding on us because they thought it might be easier.'

Just as Robinson had been scathing about Forte's

apparent unwillingness to see Granada as a realistic player at the time of the Gardner Merchant sale, so he was less than impressed by the hotel group's reluctance to take precautions against a takeover bid. 'You would have thought they would have reasoned that, as Granada's name was being mentioned and we had results coming up in a few days, they had better be on the alert just in case,' he pointed out. 'After all, we had launched the bid for LWT on the day of our results two years earlier. I was amazed that the Forte bid plan was so public for so long within Granada, and yet it didn't leak. I suppose it acquired an air of unreality. We look at lots of things, and most simply don't happen. The first question was, should we approach them to try to obtain an agreed deal? We thought, after Gardner Merchant, there was not a chance of that and, by surrendering the element of surprise, the Forte share price would have gone shooting through the roof.'

As it turned out, 'shooting' was a slightly unfortunate word. When a takeover bid is being launched the normal procedure is for the aggressor's chairman to make a telephone courtesy call to the chairman of the target company at about 7.30 on the morning of the bid, fifteen minutes before the public announcement, to say something like, 'Sorry about this, but we're making a bid for your company.' In line with that custom, Robinson called Rocco Forte's home number, only to be told by a member of the domestic staff that he had gone shooting. So a bemused Robinson phoned Keith Hamill, Forte's finance director, and said he had heard Rocco was out shooting: Hamill innocently confirmed the tale. It later emerged that, without a mobile phone, the stranded chairman missed the first train back to London because he was preoccupied with making a string of anguished calls from a public telephone box, and had to kick his heels on a Yorkshire station platform until the next train arrived.

Robinson recounted, 'I told Henry Staunton, our finance director, about Rocco being away shooting and in a lovely piece of understatement he said, "I think he's going to regret doing that." But it was nonsense to suggest that we had planned to announce the deal when Rocco was away. It was all terribly unfair. As I've always made very plain, I don't believe doing this sort of job well is about how much time you put in. Sir Maxwell Joseph, the late chairman of Grand Metropolitan, used to do three half-days a week. So it was completely unfair – but what a story! It created an image, and Rocco compounded it by saying, "Well, I really work six days a week; this was a rare day off." I don't object to people shooting, though I couldn't do it myself, and I have no sense that he should have been at his desk – except that, with the rumours going round, I would have made bloody sure that I was either at my desk or reachable on a mobile phone, especially the day our results were coming out.'

Sir Anthony Tennant, Forte's urbane deputy chairman and Robinson's former boss at Grand Metropolitan, said, 'The shooting story seemed a cheap trick, but it caught on. The bid was impeccably well timed. It was not too long after Rocco had started running the thing, so he hadn't had quite as much time as he should have had to show he could do well. Rocco suffered from being the son of Lord Forte, who had left the company very overborrowed. Rocco did a lot about that. Rocco was officially chief executive for years when in fact he wasn't, because his father was still running the business. Once

Rocco got his chance, he was pretty good at streamlining the business and getting rid of non-core assets.

'But the hotel upswing had not begun to show through. That's a double benefit when it happens, because as you get occupancy up you get room rates up too. So it's very much a cyclical business. Once you begin to get into a seller's market you can stoke the prices up and stop doing discount deals to fill rooms. So, two years later, it would have been very difficult to take over Forte. We were advised on the bid by Warburg, UBS, Cazenove, Morgan Stanley and a friend of Rocco from J.P. Morgan. We had quite a robust strategy, but we were not expecting a bid. We should have been prepared, and we were not.'

Whether or not it was a cheap trick, the image of Rocco Forte having to hurry back to London to deal with an unexpected takeover bid got the Granada campaign off to a flying start. While Forte regrouped, the early public relations victories went Granada's way and Robinson's team basked in an unreal air of euphoria for a while. Jonathan Clare, Granada's public relations adviser at Citigate Communications, said, 'Gerry had been very good to Granada's big shareholders, in the sense of explaining strategy to them, so they understood why we were doing the bid. The strategy was to get away from the distractions like computers and theme parks, but that really left TV and motorway services. The strategy was to build a much clearer company, based on TV and hotels and catering. TV rental was not growing, but its value was that it was a big cash generator. Gerry made all that clear to the institutional shareholders.'

Meanwhile, Sir Rocco had to make up lost time with his own institutional shareholders, in the City of London and around the country. Sir Anthony Tennant admitted, 'While Gerry Robinson was always very good at building institutional confidence, Rocco didn't spend enough time with the big shareholders. You have got to keep steady contact with your key shareholders.' Sir Rocco received a frosty reception from the notoriously touchy financial community in Edinburgh. Standard Life reportedly told him, 'You haven't been up here for three years. Now you have got this little spot of bother, what do you expect us to do?'

Sir Rocco was also forced into the unhappy position of having to disown his father's management record. 'I inherited a conglomerate,' he said at the time, 'and I have gone through a process of giving the group greater focus. I have dramatically improved the business, which has been rebranded and now has a strategic framework. I think I have sold businesses well and on the whole got more money than the City expected. Not bad for a supposedly poor manager.'

In the previous two years he had sold Gardner Merchant, the Harvester pub-restaurant chain, the UK franchise for Kentucky Fried Chicken and 75 per cent of Alpha Airports, the airport caterer. But Sir Rocco reserved his most bitter attack for Robinson's assault on the Forte hotels. 'We have been spending a lot of money refurbishing our hotels,' he said, 'and he wants to take advantage of our higher room and occupancy rates. We bought three hotels from Granada this year and we have already improved their occupancy rate by seventy per cent. He just doesn't understand the business.'

Robinson brushed aside such criticism. 'It's not a complicated business,' he insisted. 'It's a straightforward, repetitive, manageable business that is about filling the rooms at the best price you can get. People's perception of Forte was often that it is an international and upmarket hotelier. In reality it had strong mid-market hotel chains and a good roadside catering business. Most of the profits still came from Britain. It was a perfect fit for Granada.'

He intended to sell Lillywhites, the Piccadilly Circus sporting goods store, the stake in the Savoy Hotel chain, the remaining 25 per cent of Alpha Airports, and Forte's motorway service stations. Granada also planned to sell some of the 'trophy' hotels such as London's Hyde Park and Grosvenor House hotels and the George V in Paris if they could get the right prices, while tidying up the mid-market hotel brands under the Post House and Travelodge brands, bringing the upmarket hotels under the Meridian name, and promoting Little Chef and Burger King.

Within a week of the bid being announced, the City's analysts reportedly began to swing behind Robinson. But there were still plenty of doubters. Bruce Jones, the leisure industry analyst at the giant Merrill Lynch US securities house, said, 'We have great faith in Robinson's skill at cutting costs, but top hotels are bad news when the economy takes a dive. It's easy for good managers like him to say that someone else's business isn't complicated – wait and see.'

Meanwhile, Sir Rocco carried on selling hotels, and the Council of Forte sought a legal ruling on the circumstances under which it could legitimately block the Granada bid. Robinson was assiduously touring the institutional investors and continuing to hear polite noises, but he admitted, 'You get no real indication from the big shareholders as to how they are thinking. It's important to meet them, but they are very dispassionate: pleased if they are Forte shareholders and the shares are going up, unhappy if they are Granada shareholders and the share price is being knocked. There were big decisions to make and no way are the institutions ever going to say what they are going to do until the last minute. You don't really get to serious Forte shareholders, other than those who have shares in both companies, until much later. It's a very phoney war. But it makes for good press stories!'

Nevertheless, there is no doubt that the pressure was getting to Robinson, despite the relaxed, jovial front he presented to the outside world. He admitted, 'What surprised me was the weight of opposition that was brought to bear, with Alan Parker of Brunswick Associates, the City PR firm, advising Forte. Our approach, through the excellent Jonathan Clare and Citigate, was to be pretty straight about it. I think we did lack some capacity to put the right twist on stories. It's quite hard in the midst of that sort of battle not to be frightened by the turns it's taking and these things do have an impact, certainly internally. But I have a naïve belief that the truth will out. The important thing is to be calm, though that can be very difficult.'

Alex Bernstein knew all about being on the receiving end of a predator's attention, because in earlier years he had had to rebuff takeover approaches from Ladbroke, Rank and Carlton. He joked to Robinson, 'Whichever way round it is, a takeover bid does take it out of you, but let me tell you, it's better being an aggressor than a defender!' Bernstein, a cautious man with more experience than Robinson of how business ventures can go wrong, was nervous about the Forte bid. Because he was not sure his chief executive could pull off such an ambitious deal, he played devil's advocate behind closed doors, closely questioning Robinson to make sure he had all the answers and had thought of as many potential pitfalls as possible. 'But at one stage he thought we wouldn't make it,' Bernstein remembered.

Nevertheless Robinson took his advice to heart, resisting the City's frenzy during a bid, and instead merely listening politely before making up his own mind. Lazard's had a team of seven, and there were six from Granada, as well as Dan Mace of the lawyers Lovell White Durrant, Nigel Mills of ABN Amro Hoare Govett, the stockbrokers, Jonathan Clare from Citigate and Simon de Zoete, the corporate financier of what was then BZW, part of Barclays Bank. There was also a team working exclusively on producing propaganda, including Granada's Roger Mavity and Chris Hopson. Working to a general plan, they drafted a stream of press releases, each written three days before releasing them so they could be cleared by the lawyers.

In the midst of all this hectic activity, and to the surprise of these highly paid advisers, Robinson did away with the tra-ditional, daily early-morning team meeting in favour of infor-mal gatherings as and when he felt they were needed. He said, 'Advisers want you to win because they have worked with you and of course their fees are tied to success. They want to show you that they really do earn those large fees, but these morning meetings are a waste of time. Most of the time we had nothing to discuss – it was just everyone psyching one another up.'

The psyching up reached near-crisis proportions in

December, when Forte delivered two blows that had the Granada camp wondering for the first time how much of a chance they really had. First, Sir Rocco said he wanted to split Forte into two separate businesses, one for hotels and the other for catering, each with its own share quote. Alternatively, someone else could simply buy Forte's catering operations – Granada, they coolly let it be known, was welcome to apply. Robinson derided this as an admission of defeat by his prey, declaring it was 'like the captain of the *Titanic* saying he meant to hit the iceberg'. The beauty of the manoeuvre, though, was that it took the initiative away from Granada and made it look as if Forte was brimming with proactive ideas. Shareholder sentiment swung towards Sir Rocco.

The tit-for-tat battle kept going right up to Christmas. Granada claimed that it could improve profits by £100 million a year more than the Forte management could, without going so far as to say quite how this would be achieved. Forte unsuccessfully complained to the City Takeover Panel that this was unfair. Said Sir Anthony Tennant, 'We thought it should never have been allowed, but it was.' But a few days later Forte hit back, selling its Travelodge US motel chain for £108 million.

Robinson flew to Ireland to spend a family Christmas away from it all in Donegal. But the second major blow to Granada's bid fell on Christmas Eve, when the *Mail on Sunday* disclosed that Whitbread, the beer and restaurants group, was willing to pay £1 billion for Forte's restaurants: the 420 Little Chef and Happy Eater roadside snackeries, the motorway-based Welcome Breaks, the Wheelers fish eateries, and the 112

UK Travelodge hotels. This put firm flesh on Forte's promise to demerge the catering side of the group, and put a definite figure on it.

The plan was warmly welcomed by the big fund managers, though John Nelson at Lazard's insisted it had played into Granada's hands by tacitly admitting that the shape of the group was wrong and that Forte did not want to run the bread-and-butter end of the business that actually made a large and dependable slice of the group's profits. That point of view was lost in the excitement sparked by such a radical deal, however. So, to some extent, was the fact that Whitbread would hand over the money only if the Granada bid was defeated – and Sir Rocco was hoping that would give the brewers enough of a carrot to help him out by buying enough Forte shares to thwart Robinson.

That was not the end of the bad news from Robinson's point of view. Granada had timed the original bid announcement so that Forte's official defence document would have to come out over Christmas or the New Year, when the City and business world are traditionally quiet. Nevertheless, when it was published on 2 January, the Granada camp had to concede that it was a tough, boldly worded piece of work.

The intended Whitbread deal gave credibility to Sir Rocco's claim in that document that he was in effect creating a 'new Forte'. It would be a focused hotel company that would take full advantage of the long-term upswing in the industry. Sir Rocco told his fellow shareholders:

> The new Forte will be a highly efficient and very valuable pure hotel company. It has scale, good quality assets, clearly defined brands and worldwide representation. By concen-

trating on one business activity, further significant cost effi-
ciencies can be achieved, starting with annual savings of
£24 million already identified from administrative costs.
The new Company will have a strong balance sheet and
the ability to finance growth.

He went on to predict that profits for the year ending at the
end of that month would be 50 per cent up on the previous
year, with a promise that dividends would rise by at least a fifth
for that year and each of the next three years. He offered to
buy back £800 million of Forte shares, and distribute to
shareholders Forte's stake in the Savoy Hotel group. And three
of Forte's more venerable directors would make way for
younger blood. Sir Rocco concluded his broadside ringingly:
'The board believes that the hostile bid totally fails to reflect
the outstanding prospects of Forte, let alone offer any
premium for control. Moreover, under the terms of the bid,
Forte shareholders stand to suffer a substantial decrease in
income. Your board strongly recommends shareholders to
reject the offer.'

Forte shares were in demand after that, rising from 330p
to 343p while Granada shares reeled back to 642p, more than
50p below their level before Robinson launched the bid. That
meant the share-exchange offer for Forte was now worth
only 326p a share. Robinson's bid was dead unless he raised his
price. He had just a week to act. 'Towards the end there was a
fury,' recalled John Nelson, 'with both sides issuing as many as
five press releases a day.' While the rest of the City feasted over
Christmas, the rival teams had been working continuously to
prepare more propaganda ammunition for the New Year
offensive. And Whitbread's intervention meant there were

now three companies touring the City to make their respective cases; Whitbread had its tale to tell, too. The Granada camp feared that this could mean their own arguments becoming lost in the crossfire.

But there was one little piece of unfinished business to attend to before the climax of the battle. The Council of Forte still theoretically had the right to block the deal, despite its tiny shareholding, by exercising as many votes as all the other shareholders put together. Robinson and Bernstein met the Council to present their case – no easy matter, as some of these venerable old gentlemen found the meeting apparently taxed their powers of concentration and one or two nodded off. Their position was made all the trickier because they had mainly been appointed by Charles Forte.

In the end, though, it came down to money. Sir Anthony Tennant said, 'We took the view that as a public company you cannot use an artificial lever like that to thwart the other shareholders. We tried to persuade them, like any other shareholder, to vote against the bid. They then tried to extract their own price. But it was up to them, not for Rocco to tell them what to do. Rocco didn't ask them to use their veto.'

The trouble was, there was no clear way of valuing their stake. It would have been absurd to value it at half the value of the entire £3.3 billion bid for Forte, as their shares were worth less than £3 million. Said John Nelson, 'They started talking about £250 million, but we made them put the lowest figure on the table that they would accept, once they had narrowed it down. They came up with £50 million. I told Anthony Beevor of Hambros Bank, who was acting for the Council, that I didn't think our guys were going to accept that, but said I would ring him over the weekend if there was any change. I rang him at lunchtime on the Saturday and he said, "Oh, I wasn't expecting you to say yes!" We were worried that they would go back on their word and hold out for more, but they didn't.'

That gave the Council a useful sum with which to extend its role as a general charity, which by 1999 was giving £2 million a year to a wide range of social causes – and had recruited Alex Bernstein to its ranks of old buffers! As part of the payoff, Robinson agreed to hold regular meetings with the Council to keep it informed. But that fell into disuse and Granada later paid another £750,000 to sever the connection entirely.

The Council issue settled, Robinson pressed on with his final thrust, despite suffering from an untimely toothache. He added another £500 million to the original £3.3 billion offer, in the form of a special dividend of 47p a share to be paid out of Forte's own coffers. While it was arranged that way mainly for tax reasons, Sir Rocco sniffed: 'Now we see this bid for what it's worth – a 1980s-style, highly leveraged asset-strip which has nothing to do with management skills.'

There was nothing left for either side to do, except spend the last two weeks sniping at one another. Lord Rees-Mogg, the former editor of *The Times*, loyally weighed in with a ponderous article supporting his old friend, Sir Rocco. He concluded, 'Perhaps Mr Robinson really is the star manager of his generation, but probably not. He would not be making such a muddled bid if he really were that good.' The City's fund managers either did not read Rees-Mogg, or ignored his sagacity. Instead, they gobbled up Forte shares by the million in the belief that Granada had done enough to win. Granada itself joined in, snapping up a tenth of Forte to give it a head start before the votes had to be counted.

Sir Rocco personally bought nearly £15 million of his company's shares in a last-ditch effort to stave off defeat. For he could see from the expressions on the fund managers' faces that they were deserting him. So strongly was the tide moving against Sir Rocco that the Granada camp feared he might fall on his sword to deny them right at the death. He had been urged to step down from running Forte, or at least to become nonexecutive chairman and appoint a new chief executive, and this could have been enough to deny Granada. John Nelson explained, 'If Rocco had become chairman and brought in someone else as chief executive, and done it earlier, it would have been much harder for us. Our biggest fear was that they would change their management by bringing in a new chief executive. It would have been difficult, during a bid, to bring in a top person who was already in a job, because of the risk of Forte losing and that person then being out of a job. But they could have made Anthony Tennant chairman and chief executive, and Rocco out, with a brief to recruit a new chief executive as soon as the bid was over. Or we thought they might have promoted Keith Hamill, the then finance director.'

Charles Allen was less sanguine about the chances of Forte snaring a big-name outsider. He recalled, 'Although it was difficult to recruit a top-level chief executive in the middle of a bid, if you give someone the right sum of money you can get someone in. Argos proved that in 1998 when it hired Stuart Rose during the bid by Great Universal Stores. The big question was getting someone that was credible.'

Any of those ploys could have swayed the floating voters, but the sacrifice was too much for Sir Rocco to bear. Instead, after a heated debate at one of his large family's regular Sunday lunches, he offered a compromise. He would remain chief executive, but allow Tennant to become chairman. It was far too little far too late, especially as Sir Rocco was let down at the last minute by Whitbread. They failed to buy a blocking stake in Forte to enable them to buy the restaurants side of the group – partly because, at a cost of £300 million, even a 10 per-cent stake would have been more than they could have comfortably afforded.

So Sir Rocco was at the mercy of the fund managers. And the investment group with the key 15 per cent stake in Forte was Mercury Asset Management, led by the redoubtable Carol Galley and Stephen Zimmerman. The Forte camp had feared MAM from the outset, as in similar circumstances two years earlier Forte believed that MAM had committed its shares in LWT to Granada at the outset. Despite vehement denials, suspicion that Galley had been behind the Granada bid all along hardened into outright accusation when MAM duly voted for Robinson. Even though Granada's first-day victory margin was greater than MAM's shareholding, Forte sympathisers claimed that without that they could have bought enough shares in the market to beat the bid. This claim was regarded by MAM as disingenuous, as the bid was initially accepted by holders of almost 70 per cent of Forte shares.

Three years on, the vanquished were still bitter. Sir Rocco told the magazine *Business Age* how he confronted Galley and her colleague, Stephen Zimmerman:

The excuse Carol Galley gave me was a lame one. She said they had to make the choice between two heavily indebted companies and they preferred the cash-generative abilities of Granada. I pointed out that Forte's £1.2 billion debt was small compared with the extra £3.2 billion Granada would saddle itself with because of the bid. Anthony Tennant interrupted me and suggested at this juncture there was no point in prolonging things. I then said: 'Well, you can't expect me to be happy about this decision.' We walked out to the lobby to the lift and then I could not contain myself: 'You know from the very beginning that everyone has been saying to me that you have been behind this whole deal.' They both jumped as if I'd let off a banger: 'Oh no, we are a very honourable institution and we wouldn't do a thing like this, etc, etc.' All the way down in the lift they carried on in this vein and this was the first time that Zimmerman had actually said anything. So I still think there was more to this than met the eye. I know that a number of the pension funds who had their money managed by Mercury had indicated that they did not want their shares voted in favour of the bid. And, since the bid, a number of them have said they will keep their money with Mercury as managers only if they have the right to take the decision on how their shares are voted in a bid situation. So, to some degree, this episode could stop this sort of thing happening again.'

MAM has since confirmed that only one letter was received from one of its clients, and the fact that it was written was leaked to the press. And that letter stopped short of asking MAM to vote against the bid, as MAM has a duty to act in its clients' best interests. MAM's clients were kept informed throughout the bid and MAM insists there was no pressure, written or oral, to vote in a particular way.

Sir Anthony Tennant added, 'I don't know that we shall

ever know the answer to whether MAM had wittingly or unwittingly done anything to encourage Granada's offer. They traded actively during the course of the bid, and it was widely suspected in the market place that they had made up their mind before the bid started. First-day acceptances were greater than their stake, but only by two per cent and holders of seven per cent were waiting for their decision. There was no question that they decided the outcome of the bid. The story they gave us was that the defence had been so strong that they had no option but to take the bid, because we had driven the price so high! But they didn't act to persuade Forte to make changes before the bid.'

Robinson replied, 'It was nonsense to suggest that Carol Galley encouraged us to bid for Forte. We made Galley and one or two other shareholders insiders the night before the bid. It's up to them in that sort of situation: we just tell them we've got an important announcement coming out, and they can hear it in advance as long as they agree to become insiders and therefore can't trade in our shares until the announcement is made public. Some prefer not to become insiders so that they are free to trade. But, when we went to see MAM, Carol said, "I hope this isn't going to be another LWT." She had no prior knowledge.' Bernstein confirmed this: 'We thought it would be in their interest to be in favour of the bid, but there was no question of them knowing about it in advance.' And Nelson said, 'When MAM were told about the deal, the night before the announcement, they were genuinely very shaken, because it was a surprise to everybody. They certainly didn't make up their mind until the end. They are people who back managements, and I was genuinely doubtful whether they would back Gerry.'

Back him they did, but the battle left Robinson drained. 'Winning the Forte bid was the biggest anticlimax I can remember,' he said. 'We had a lunch on the day the bid closed, with all the advisers and everyone who had been involved, but there was no sense of triumphalism. It was quite the opposite, because now we had to make it work: that was what lay ahead. I had a genuine sense of feeling sorry for Rocco and his father. They had lost the business they had built up, and I don't think anything you strive for in that frenetic way ever fulfils you.'

Nonetheless, however he felt inside himself, Robinson did not spoil it for others on the team who were in more of a mood to let their hair down. Nelson recalled, 'We had a hell of a party here at Lazard's the night we won, for everyone involved in the bid, and Gerry took us down to the Boot pub on Moorgate later on for a real Irish party. It was the Granada Annual General Meeting the next day, and there were some pretty pale faces on the platform!'

Then the work began. Apart from recruiting new management to run Forte, Robinson had to ensure that he sold enough of Forte's and Granada's assets to shrink the group's huge debt mountain. They sold the Welcome Break motorway service stations and the remaining shares in Alpha Airports, both for more than expected. Because several firms were interested in buying Welcome Break, an Arab investment group called Investcorp eventually paid Granada £476 million rather than the £330 million Whitbread had agreed to pay Forte for it. But there was a catch. Whitbread and Forte had come to an agreement that meant if the motorway services business was sold within a year Whitbread would have been entitled to share half of any surplus over Whitbread's £330 million offer. But as a condition of allowing the takeover of Forte, the Office of Fair Trading insisted Granada had to sell Welcome Break, as it already had a large slice of the motorway business under its own name. As the price Investcorp offered was £146 million higher than Whitbread's valuation, Whitbread would have been entitled to £73 million if the deal had gone through within a year. Once Granada spotted this clause it had to ask the OFT permission to wait beyond the year before selling – permission that was thankfully forthcoming. Meanwhile, Mohammed al Fayed bought the remaining 25 per cent of Alpha Airports for £52 million. Fayed was interested in Alpha because BAA was not keen on letting Harrods into Heathrow, and Fayed wanted to improve his negotiating position. The George V hotel in Paris went for £104 million after a literal royal battle between the Sultan of Brunei and Prince al Walid, which al Walid won.

But for a second time Robinson performed a handstand over the Meridian hotel chain, which Forte had bought from Air France and which mainly managed hotels for their owners. At the time of the original Forte bid, in November 1995, he said he would capitalise decisively on Meridian and use it as a springboard for expansion. By the time of the final offer in January 1996 it was to be sold. But, victory secured, Granada decided to keep the chain after all. 'Forte did a good deal when it bought Meridian, but, in a year, they had done nothing with it,' said Nelson.

Apart from selling some trophy properties such as London's Hyde Park Hotel, the really big headache was the Savoy Hotel group. Taking in the Connaught, Berkeley and

Claridge's hotels in central London, it had been fought over for more than forty years by a succession of property magnates and hoteliers. They had all been seen off by the late Sir Hugh Wontner, who in the 1950s had cleverly won shareholders' approval to create two classes of share: low-voting 'A' shares which the rank-and-file investors would have, and high-voting 'B' shares, to be held mainly by Wontner and his allies. This scheme was drawn up to thwart one of the earliest would-be bidders, the property magnate Sir Charles Clore. But it prevented any predator from wading into the market to buy the company, or even appealing to shareholders at large over the heads of the board.

The last suitor was Charles Forte, who painstakingly acquired two-thirds of the shares. But, because of Wontner's voting structure, these shares carried less than the 50 per cent necessary to win control. Forte tolerated what it saw as a stalemate, in the hope that eventually the Savoy would be forced to give all shares equal voting rights. The only concession Sir Rocco had been able to wring out of the Savoy board, after Wontner's death and his own father's retirement, had been the right to have two representatives on the board.

This was a situation that Robinson had to resolve, if only because through Forte Granada now had hundreds of millions of pounds tied up in its investment in the Savoy group, eating up bank interest but paying next to nothing in dividends. Robinson did not want a high-profile Savoy deal interfering with the sales of Forte's upmarket Exclusive Hotels. So, while that was going ahead, he and Alex Bernstein became directors of the Savoy and encouraged the board to take a long-term view. They could afford to do so because the Savoy had recruited a top-class hotel manager, Ramon Pajares from the Four Seasons group, to be the managing director. He was beginning to turn it round into good profits, and the Savoy share price was going up accordingly. This meant that the difference between the Savoy's stock market value and its asset value was narrowing. As it closed Granada began receiving unsolicited approaches from would-be buyers.

Meanwhile, however, Lazard's discovered that the Wontner camp no longer had control. Some holdings had been trimmed, a long-standing shareholder had died, the shares had gone into an independent trust, and the trustees were taking a more objective view of their obligations. They were more inclined to sell to the highest bidder rather than, like Granada, have their trust funds tied up in this way. Said John Nelson, 'We sat on that information, because we thought it would cause all sorts of mayhem if it came out at the wrong moment.'

Granada began to suspect that the board knew the game was up, and it was only a matter of time before control changed hands. But still they did not let on. Then in about September 1997 ING Barings, the Savoy's merchant bank adviser, was asked to explore sale possibilities with Granada. It was very low-key at first, but then a couple of offers came in and Robinson had some leverage. He started to act tougher and told them they didn't have control. 'Once they became aware of that,' said Nelson, 'it was extraordinary how quickly the objections fell away.' The deal was wrapped up with a very good price of £520 million – equal to £778,000 a room – from Blackstone, an American investment group.

I O

The TV World in Action

He did not fully realise it at the time, but when Robinson joined Granada and took ultimate responsibility for its television interests, he was entering one of the world's most ruthlessly political industries. The furore over his early sacking of David Plowright was merely a foretaste. And the manoeuvring in 1993, which ultimately brought Granada the London Weekend, Yorkshire and Tyne-Tees television licences, turned out to be little more than a beginners' class. Those acquisitions, combined with the long-standing Granada franchise and the more recent stake in British Sky Broadcasting, put Robinson at the heart of the UK television market and brought him up against such powerful figures as Rupert Murdoch, Michael Green, Sam Chisholm and many other lesser figures with even more fragile egos circling one another in the piranha tank.

Television is bound to be political, both in the parliamentary sense and in terms of how it is run, at least while there is a limited number of channels. Book publishing has its dramas, but the political steam has been taken out of it since it became technically and financially feasible to publish virtually any book of a reasonable quality. By the same token, newspapers retain their political status and colourful management flavour because the reading public will support only a limited number at either national or local level. Just as with radio, politicians feared television in the early days and sought to control it because of its apparent power to influence a mass audience. And, until the advent of digital broadcasting, there was room for only so many channels. The government, or one of its agencies, was the natural arbiter of such scarcity, a role the politicians grasped gratefully. Not only did it give them enormous patronage and scope to dictate standards, it was a ready source of tax revenue. Within the television organisations, whether commercial or public like the British Broadcasting Corporation, that same scarcity produced a correspondingly savage never-ending fight for decision-making power. Owners or senior executives of television stations were courted by politicians, while those further down the ladder feasted on the reflected glory and the crumbs of power they were allowed to wield. (For a more detailed discussion of how these forces shaped independent television in its formative years, see Appendix II.)

Thanks partly to the vacuum left by Sidney Bernstein's retirement, and the fact that Granada's franchise was so far from London, the company was isolated within the industry by the time Robinson became chief executive in 1991. A new generation of leaders had emerged as a result of the controversial 1990 franchise round. At the core was Michael Green of Carlton Communications, the London midweek franchise holder, Christopher Bland and Greg Dyke at London Weekend and Clive Hollick, whose Meridian station held the licence for the south of England. Granada, largely due to the efforts of the ill-fated Plowright, had effortlessly retained the northwest franchise. 'We were seen as arrogant and separatist,' said Robinson. 'Michael had Carlton and a share of Central, LWT was independent, and we were nowhere. It was important to get into the politics of that, to know who was doing what and where.'

Granada had been involved with satellite television ever since it had been a founder shareholder of British Satellite Broadcasting, the short-lived rival to Sky. BSB was the winning contender for a Direct Broadcasting Satellite licence, which the government awarded in 1986. Derek Lewis, Robinson's predecessor, had naturally been interested in satellite as an extension of Granada's terrestrial television operations, and saw it as a new avenue for the group's rental shops chain. The other investors were the *Financial Times* and Penguin Books group, Pearson; Richard Branson's Virgin Group; the Amstrad computer firm, led by Alan Sugar; and Anglia Television. The unsuccessful rival for the licence, DBS UK, had been backed by Michael Green, London Weekend Television and the advertising agency Saatchi & Saatchi. Soon after BSB won the contest, the British magazine publisher Reed International, the London-born Australian businessman Alan Bond and the French media group Chargeurs joined the consortium. Meanwhile, Amstrad dropped out. Sugar realised that it was going to be an expensive business and he would be better placed as a supplier of satellite dishes to whoever was broadcasting.

Sugar was right. The first round of financing was for £220 million, to put up two satellites, with no prospect of revenue for at least two or, as it turned out, three years. In any other business it would have been dismissed as a ludicrously hare-brained proposition. Incredible as it seemed in the light of subsequent events, the DBS licence was awarded just like the existing television franchises – by the Independent Broadcasting Authority, as a monopoly, subject to the usual quality standards. They did not seem to appreciate that a satellite broadcaster does not have to be *in* Britain to beam pictures to Britain. In 1988 Rupert Murdoch took space on the Luxembourg-based Astra satellite for his fledgling Sky venture. Battle was joined in what turned out to be one of the world's biggest games of poker. Granada, through first Alex Bernstein and David Lewis, and latterly under the aegis of Robinson and Charles Allen, gritted their teeth and hung on. But successive crises and relentless cash calls proved too much for Bond, Branson, Reed and most of the other investors. 'It took a lot of courage on Alex Bernstein's part,' said Robinson. 'He was convinced it would work and he kept putting money in, even though Granada was stretched.'

No one was more stretched than Murdoch was, though in the end he was rescued by the ineptitude of BSB's management. They were hampered by the fact that the DBS technology their licence committed them to was much more expensive than Sky's system. On top of that BSB launched in April 1990, nine months late and giving Sky a vital fourteen months' start. And, instead of the normal dish-shaped satellite receiver, BSB opted to go for an unusual square arial, or 'squarial', which was fraught with technical problems and became the butt of jokes.

Cost was no object from the start as far as BSB was concerned. Its headquarters were in a plush new building on the Thames by Battersea Power Station, and the company followed the traditional broadcasters' pattern of commissioning extensive production for itself, as opposed to Murdoch's preferred tactic of buying in old material as cheaply as possible. But both BSB and Sky were hampered by the fact that dish makers were unwilling to gear up production until they knew which was going to be the winning system, as it soon became apparent that there was going to be only one winner in this game. The question at the outset was, which one? That meant neither side could get quickly enough to the critical viewer mass it needed to generate sufficient subscription and advertising revenue. And, like the manufacturers, many of the would-be customers were also waiting to see which of the two satellite services would survive.

Within months Sky established a lead that it would never relinquish. BSB's investors went into crisis mode, setting up a four-man committee to keep a close eye on the day-to-day management. One or two of the investors, notably Pearson, were already beginning to think that a merger with Sky would be inevitable. But there was a big political hurdle, particularly for Granada. As a terrestrial licence holder – and the bids had to be in for a new round of licences in 1991 – it did not want to offend the authorities by throwing in its lot with Murdoch, who was close to Margaret Thatcher but mistrusted by the Whitehall establishment. But the financial pressures were too great for Bernstein to resist for long and a deal was struck in October 1990. To Bernstein's horror, the IBA chairman Sir George Russell did not learn of the deal until he read it in the following morning's papers. But, although it would bleed money for a while longer and ultimately wash off Reed as a shareholder, by the time Robinson arrived at Granada the following year the satellite television problem had stabilised and was rocketing towards profitability.

'Rupert needed to put the two satellite businesses together,' said Robinson, 'because Sky was sucking up cash at a phenomenal rate. Rupert brought in Sam Chisholm not long before I came on board. My management style is that if you have got someone good, support them because there are not many good people around. So with Sky I thought, I'm not getting involved, because it looks as if someone is sorting it out. Sam was exceptional, had a good feel for programmes that would work and he knocked it into shape. But it was not an accident that Sky was working well. It was the most amazing customer-led attitude that Sam imposed. Sky's telephone service in Scotland is a hugely slick, tightly driven affair.'

In the early stages of Robinson's tenure at Granada, once the reverberations of the Plowright affair had died down, the first big question to present itself was what to do about Independent Television News. While it had acquired a reputation that equalled and often excelled the BBC's news coverage, led by its flagship *News At Ten*, behind the scenes ITN was in a very rocky state. In the early 1990s it had been losing money and had become an unexpected victim of the controversial money-led franchising system created by the 1990 Broadcasting Act.

The quality requirements of successive Broadcasting Acts had always insisted that the fifteen ITV franchise holders must provide an adequate local, national and international news service. While this was easy enough to achieve in terms of local news, it would have been horrendously expensive for each of them to provide their own national news programmes: it could have led to the ludicrous situation of all fifteen having to send camera crews and reporters to cover every major national and international event, from a royal wedding to an African famine. So ITN had been set up by the original franchise holders, as a cheaper alternative. In time that gave ITN an independent life of its own, for it could play its shareholders off against one another. As long as it was not too extravagant, its costs would always be met – to the disgust of realists like Greg Dyke, then running LWT.

Robinson, at this stage watching quietly from the sidelines, agreed with Dyke. 'It was all over the place,' he said, 'always overrunning on its costs.' However, the 1990 franchise round brought a sudden end to that cosy climate. Thames, TVS and TSW lost their licences, so did not want to spend a penny more than they had to, while some of the 'winners' in the blind auctions had bid so high that they did not have much money to spare for any outside investments, even one as vital as ITN.

Unfortunately for ITN, this change in circumstance coincided with a drastic cash shortage. The company had moved from a shabby little office block near London's Oxford

Street to glittering new premises designed by Norman Foster Associates and built on the Grays Inn Road site of the former *Sunday Times* headquarters. There was far more space there than ITN needed, but the plan was to rent out the extra floors. However, just at that time there was an abundance of office space in London, so the news organisation collected nowhere near as much rent as it had hoped for, while still having to pay £5.5 million a year for its lease. To make matters worse, in early 1991 the incoming chief executive, Bob Phillis, found a £9.8 million deficit in the financial controls and had to contend with the one-off costs of covering the Gulf War.

By autumn 1992 there was not enough money to pay for the lease on Grays Inn Road, and the numbers were heading alarmingly into the red. Liquidation was unthinkable, but there was no immediate answer to the increasingly urgent question of where the money was going to come from. Luckily, though, there were also the makings of a new deal that could save ITN.

The 1990 Act that had contributed to ITN's problems also supplied the trigger for change. It insisted that by the beginning of 1995 at least half of ITN's shares had to be held by non-broadcasters. As commercial organisations, they would have to be persuaded that ITN was in a healthy financial shape before they would invest. Dyke and Carlton's Michael Green saw the opportunity to push through a radical reformation. But it was Green who squared the politicians and cajoled the other ITV companies to either come in or get out – with Green as chairman. The original plan was for Carlton, LWT and Central each to hold 20 per cent of ITN, with the Reuters news agency group and another nonbroad-caster to have the rest – Daily Mail and General Trust, as it turned out. That was not quite what the 1990 Act required, but Green was lobbying intensively at Westminster to have his way. He was also a friend of Stuart Lipton, whose Stanhope property company owned the freehold on the Grays Inn Road building, and so was ITN's landlord. Green was to per-suade Lipton to sell ITN the freehold, a key piece in the prop-erty jigsaw. Some of the other ITV companies took Green's scheme gratefully as a painless way out. Others, including Robinson, took the opposite view: if Green was sticking in there, it had to be worth staying in too. 'We kicked the door into it because we wanted our share of it,' said Robinson.

In April 1993 Green became chairman of ITN. But one significant bone of contention remained. While Green wanted to be chairman of ITN as long as possible, Robinson was adamant that the chairmanship should be rotated among the shareholders. 'It's a good protection for ITN that you don't have one person trying to dominate,' Robinson explained. 'I felt we were not doing something we said we would do, in allowing one person like Michael Green to stay as chairman. I wanted it discussed on the basis of a two-year rotation, as that was my understanding of how it was going to be. But it came out that the chairman was to be chairman until he resigned or was voted out.

'There was no doubt that Michael wanted to be chair-man of ITN for as long as possible – that was where he was coming from. I talked to all the other nonexecutive directors and we agreed that rotation was a sensible protection for ITN and all its interests. Michael tried to resist, and I had some sympathy with him because he had spotted that ITN could be organised in a different way to make it profitable. ITV was very messy at one time and Michael led the charge to sort it all out. Full marks to him for that. But it was absolutely clear to me that it was vital to rotate.'

Robinson's power and influence in the television world was accumulating. In 1994 he had completed the takeover of London Weekend Television, giving him a London base for Granada's television operations, and many observers calculated that before long he would be adding Yorkshire Tyne-Tees Television to his collection. The question of rotating the ITN chairmanship came to a head at a board meeting on 23 January 1995, when Green found himself isolated on the issue and conceded the point without putting it to a vote. He stepped down and was replaced by Robinson.

Green recalled, 'Gerry and I disagreed about the chairmanship of ITN. My first serious meeting with Gerry was about me persuading him to join the ITN board. He wanted Charles Allen to do it, but it consisted of all the chairmen of the ITV companies because I wanted ITN to be above the ITV frame. It also provided news for Channel Four then, and I had ambitions to take it further. Gerry and I got on very well at that stage. I had worked very hard at ITN, put in a lot of hours that I thoroughly enjoyed. I could see the change in that business. But I am a natural businessman. I don't believe in trophy chairmanships: in my view the buck must stop with the chairman, which it can't if it is constantly changing. The idea of a rotating chairmanship is completely alien to my thinking. I gave in in the end, with good grace, because I felt that for the sake of ITV it would be wrong for Carlton and

Granada to be at loggerheads over something like ITN. That was my only clash with Gerry. He is very able, very bright, charming, fun, we have had plenty of laughs. But I don't think he is ever going to collapse from overwork.'

Within a fortnight of manoeuvring Green out of the ITN chair, Robinson found himself in another key television post: chairman of BSkyB. Again, he was there as a result of the endemic industry politics. But this time, instead of moving the pieces, he was if not a pawn then little more than a side-flanking rook in the global chess game the mighty Rupert Murdoch was playing to achieve a dominant position in satellite broadcasting. While the Sky–BSB merger had set the UK business on track towards profitability, there was still much to be sorted out. The 1993 results had been good enough to justify paying the shareholders a special dividend, so that they could begin to see some reward for their years of hard slog. And in the summer of 1994, less than four years after the merger had been consummated, preparations began to float BSkyB on the London Stock Exchange. Robinson was a keen supporter of the project, which came to fruition in December 1994 and soon focused the spotlight of publicity on just how rapidly BSkyB's fortunes had recovered. It soon became one of the strongest shares in the media sector.

But the flotation brought to a head a discontent that had been simmering between the shareholders and Frank Barlow, the Pearson executive who was then BSkyB's chairman. He had suspected that Sam Chisholm, as a Murdoch man, was spending time on Murdoch business rather than working exclusively for BSkyB. 'Barlow was getting involved in the detail of every issue,' said Robinson, 'worrying about the days

Sam was working for News International as opposed to BSkyB. It didn't matter, when we were getting things sorted out.'

There was also a row, related to the point about how Chisholm spent his time, over a proposal to establish a £24 million bonus pool for directors and senior executives. Even Murdoch thought it was too generous, but it added to Barlow's isolation. At the start of 1995 Murdoch, Robinson and Jerome Seydoux of Chargeurs decided that Barlow would have to go before BSkyB was floated. At that stage Murdoch alone had 50 per cent of BSkyB's shares, and Granada and Chargeurs had another 30 per cent between them, so they had ample power to get rid of Barlow. 'It was decided that I should take over as chairman of Sky,' said Robinson. 'There was no competition issue because there was no conflict. It was ITV versus pay TV. Taking over from Frank Barlow was a doddle, because there was no great amount left to do as chairman. The questions were, as they usually are: Is the chief executive a good guy? Is he doing the right thing? If so, leave him to do it. And Sam Chisholm was doing a fabulous job.'

That for a short time put Robinson into a unique position in British television: he was simultaneously chief executive of Granada, one of the biggest ITV companies, and chairman of both ITN and BSkyB. He drew on his considerable Irish charm to disarm anyone who questioned such a concentration of power, but there was eventually bound to be a conflict of interest. ITV and Sky were operating rival news services, and Granada's long-term goals were strongly opposed to those of its satellite rival. Robinson served out his pre-set two-year term in the ITN chair, but the impossible clash arrived in the shape of digital television, when Granada and BSkyB ended up backing competing systems. Robinson duly stepped down as Sky chairman in spring 1998 and after a suitable interval that year he sold Granada's directly held BSkyB shares for £429 million.

By the time he bowed out, Robinson had proved something of a thorn in the side of Rupert Murdoch, who was not used to having his authority challenged. That appealed to the competitive aspect of Robinson's nature, for he likes to take a dig at people who lay claim to more power and influence than they may actually deserve. After the flotation, Murdoch's stake in BSkyB was cut to 40 per cent, denying him a controlling voice. At the same time Robinson and Chisholm, who struck up a happy partnership, were conscious that they were running a public company with a wide range of shareholders who expected their board to act in all their interests, not just Murdoch's. The great media tycoon found this occasionally hard to take.

The stamping ground for an early skirmish was provided in May 1995 by Murdoch's attempt to bring BSkyB into his proposed takeover of three Italian television stations owned by Silvio Berlusconi, that country's former prime minister. Murdoch would have liked BSkyB to have done the deal, and he was not pleased when Robinson and Chisholm came out against it. Robinson said, 'Sam took the view that Italy is a great place to eat pasta and have a holiday – but not to do business. You cannot always trust the numbers, and it takes a lot of work to decide whether you can rely on the numbers in any given case. I was dead against going into the Berlusconi deal. We had just floated and it was wrong to burden Sky with it, because it would have meant issuing a huge number of shares. In the end the deal was not done anyway.'

Murdoch told the media analyst Mathew Horsman, 'Sam was always frightened of the Italians, and in retrospect he may have been right. We looked at the books, and it looked like a God-awful mess, and probably was. Still, it was an opportunity we missed.'

Robinson had put his marker down, that he was not to be a pushover as chairman of Sky – contrary to the prediction of his predecessor, Frank Barlow, who said that Murdoch had seduced Robinson into taking the job. Murdoch apparently got his own way over the question of bidding for the contract to run Britain's Channel 5. Robinson and Chisholm were keen to win that contract, and agreed to make an offer of £25 million a year. Murdoch insisted that the Sky bid should be no higher than £2 million and the rest of the board backed down amid protestations that they were not that sold on the idea anyway. The contract went to a rival bid worth £22 million from a consortium of Pearson, the Thames Televison, Penguin Books and *Financial Times* group, and Lord Hollick's United News and Media.

That was a rare defeat. In 1996 Robinson won another trial of strength involving Chisholm and Michael Green, over digital television. The Independent Television Commission was due to issue digital terrestrial licences in the following year, and it would give the first major opportunity for ITV companies to get in on pay TV, where a large proportion of marketing and revenue are directed at generating subscriptions by viewers, who are offered at least thirty channels. Until satellite and cable television were launched in Britain, mass audiences had been used to receiving a handful of channels free at the point of switching on their sets. Revenue had been in the form of either the BBC licence fee or a charge for advertising.

Robinson had been slow to move on the digital licences, in contrast to Green. From early in 1996 researchers at Carlton had been looking into every aspect of digital, to see whether to bid and how much. In December that year every-thing changed very quickly. Chisholm asked if Sky could come in as a partner with Carlton. He was worried that Carlton might tie up with a big American partner that could be a threat to Sky, and he wanted to give Sky a stake in anoth-er pay-TV avenue, in addition to satellite and cable. Chisholm and Green signed a deal to form a jointly owned company, British Digital Broadcasting – whereupon Robinson got wind of what was going on, and immediately wanted in too.

Chisholm recalled, 'Gerry phoned me. He asked, "Are you doing a deal with Michael?" I didn't know what to say. There was a pause, and he said, "Stunned silence". So I had to admit it. I told Michael we had to do a deal with Gerry, but I told Gerry Michael wouldn't stand for diluting the shares down to a third each. He said, "I think he will." And he was right.'

Robinson explained disarmingly, 'There were all sorts of shenanigans between Sky, Carlton and us. The phones were hot for a week. People think things are worked out well in advance and thought through. In reality something comes up and you say, "How are we going to get out of this?" Either you're in or you're not. And things move quickly in television.

The whole episode epitomised the difference between what you read in management textbooks and what really happens. You need to be flexible. We had said we didn't want to be in it, but when there was a decent chance we went for it like a rat up a drainpipe. There was no question what was going to happen: we were going to have a third of BDB. The rest could take care of itself. I knew Sam was very keen to get some profit out of it too – and I was prepared to scupper it. I said I would be unhappy at anything other than an equal three-way split.

'Eventually we wangled a deal from nowhere. But the nice thing about Michael is that he has a logical mind, and he was persuaded that that would be more powerful than him having a larger share of a weaker grouping. That was how we went to the ITC.'

The Independent Television Commission duly awarded the franchise to BDB – but only on condition that Sky be not part of the consortium, because of its satellite interests. So they were out, Carlton went back to the 50 per cent stake it had previously settled for – and from nowhere Granada ended up with the other half and Sky was to be a deadly rival in the digital race that developed in 1998. But they were rivals that had to do business with one another, for BDB, or ONdigital as it became, realised that it had to have access to Sky's movie and sports rights to make a pay-TV system work.

'People say they want other things than movies and sport,' Robinson explained, 'but not enough of them do. In relation to buying content we are like cable, in that it is in Sky's interest to supply us. If they try to block us out we will bid against them for rights, driving their price up.'

But a year before digital came to a head, Chisholm said he wanted to quit Sky because of ill health. And that led to another face-off between Robinson and Murdoch, who wanted to settle all the arrangements for Chisholm's departure. However, Robinson said that as he was chairman he would do it. Said Chisholm, 'Rupert was incandescent, because he likes to do everything his way, even if he has only forty per cent of the shares. He protested at the next board meeting, but Gerry told him where to get off.'

Robinson, in more conciliatory mood, reflected, 'Rupert is incredibly influential, but wonderfully unpompous while at the same time being very competitive and aggressive. On the other hand, I had a friendly relationship with Sam. In the end Sam decided he had had enough. The doctor had said this is all very well you ignoring this septicemia, but if you don't stop you will have a serious problem. Then it all became terribly muddled, whether Sam did or didn't want to stay. Rupert is quite a hard taskmaster, but so is Sam. He worked weekends and God knows what else, and Rupert and Sam were obviously in contact a lot.

'My relationship with Sam was such that it was quite difficult for me to be seen as unbiased in the play over his departure. Because of BDB it was clear that my position was going to be uncomfortable, and I suspect Rupert saw me as a Chisholm man. There was no falling out. It was clear that I didn't want to go on as chairman of Sky, and Rupert didn't want me to do it.'

Chisholm told me, 'He's an amazing person, Gerry Robinson. At Sky you have got a number of dynamics at work. You've got guys like Rupert, who is very focused, tough, used to getting his own way. But Robinson is the sort of independent chairman chief executives dream of, because his great strength is his respect and his belief in management. I am a guy who makes his living assessing executives, and I can tell you he is one of the best. He stands out, and I think his greatest strength is his belief in management and the way he supports them. He has a good sense of humour and he is numerate, so he understands what's going on. He has been very successful at what he has done. He's got a lot of charm, but underneath it all he is tough. He doesn't like answering to people, and he doesn't scare easily. If he makes his mind up, Gerry is a man who will not be fobbed off.

I I

The Arts Council

Gerry Robinson walked into one of the private dining rooms at Claridge's Hotel in Brook Street, Mayfair, and looked around him. It was the November 1997 dinner of the Thirty Club, a high-powered group of media and show-business figures who meet regularly to exchange gossip and indulge in a little networking. He did not realise it at that moment, but Robinson was about to be networked.

'Hello, Gerry,' said a familiar voice with a slightly nasal London twang. It was David Puttnam, the bearded Oscar-winning former film director responsible for *Chariots of Fire*, *Midnight Express* and *Bugsy Malone*, among many other cinema hits. A Labour party sympathiser, Puttnam had been ennobled and now trod the red-carpeted corridors of the House of Lords, keeping the government in touch with what was going on in the arts. As it happened, a big job had just fallen vacant. The Eton- and Oxford-educated Earl of Gowrie had announced his resignation as chairman of the Arts Council, the prestige-laden body that for fifty years had helped governments decide the devilish question of how to spend public money on the arts in all its forms.

Lord Puttnam wanted to know if Robinson, a fellow Labour sympathiser who like himself had not been to university, would let his name be put forward for Gowrie's job. Robinson recalled that he told Puttnam, '"I'm not interested, no way, I've got other things to do with my time." Unfortunately, though, I made the mistake of agreeing to talk to him about it again. He said it could be done without taking up a lot of time, but it needed a sound business approach to something that had got out of hand. I could see that, because that is how these things tend to go, and I had a general interest in the arts, so I made further enquiries.'

Lord Puttnam remembered, 'I was instrumental in recruiting Gerry. We had several discussions about it and he never quite said no, and I caught him in a weak moment, at a Thirty Club dinner, and said, "You have never said no and you would be perfect for the job." I just felt very strongly it was vital that we had someone who would roll up his sleeves and get on with it. I am a big fan of his: failure isn't in his vocabulary. I remember the flak he got from the television people when he stepped into Granada, so I thought Gerry wouldn't duck when the shit hit the fan – and that was crucial.'

While Robinson was wavering Alex Bernstein, his former chairman at Granada, added his support to Puttnam's discreet campaign. Robinson was one of the growing band of businessmen who were keen to see Tony Blair succeed, and he had personally given £30,000 to the Labour party. That he was willing to consider such a departure from his business career was a sign both that his interests were broadening and that Granada appeared to be running smoothly under the growing influence of Charles Allen as chief executive. Robinson was already known in the arts world as a council member of the English Stage Company as well as chairing the development committee of the Royal Court Theatre in London. And he is a genuine enthusiast: he likes to paint local landscapes in Donegal, as well as going regularly to opera, ballet and theatre.

The Arts Council started advertising the chairmanship. Then, prompted by Puttnam, Chris Smith, the Secretary of State for Culture, Media and Sport, approached Robinson, who also went to see Hayden Phillips, then Smith's permanent secretary, whom he knew already because the department regulates television. 'I started to gather information on the job,' said Robinson, 'and how it could be sorted out relatively quickly. I was hugely impressed with Chris Smith, still am. He has a clear picture of where he wants to go, and as clear a picture about how to get there. London's South Bank, museums around the country and the Arts Council have all changed because he was determined that we should make a better fist of the public money we give to the arts. That has been his policy all the way through. The Arts Council was a shambles, and the government wanted it sorted out. I believe that this governed the choice of me. They were caught with their own financial restrictions of sticking to the budget for a year.'

From the outset the government expected Robinson to preside over a major shake-up of the Arts Council. This he did with a vigour that inevitably caused a furore in the arts world. While Lord Gowrie, a former Tory minister, diplomatically welcomed him by saying, 'Gerry Robinson is a brilliant man and no stranger to the management of change,' the arts establishment's apprehension was better summed up by John Tusa, the managing director of the Barbican Centre in the City of London: 'If Robinson's appointment reflects a feeling that arts institutions need more managerial kicking rather than financial support, we are in trouble.'

Robinson officially became chairman of the Arts Council in May 1998, although he was effectively in control from the moment his appointment was announced in January of that year. So much antagonism did he stir up that within a year Tusa had become one of the leaders of the unprecedented opposition coalition of actors, writers and directors who were to call themselves the Shadow Arts Council.

The Arts Council of England, to give it its full title, is the national funding body for the arts. It was originally founded in 1946 under the chairmanship of the economist Lord Keynes as the Arts Council of Great Britain, itself a descendent of the wartime Committee for the Encouragement of Music and the Arts, which was formally set up by Royal Charter in January 1940 to encourage wider interests than mere survival during World War Two. In 1994 the Arts Council of Great Britain was divided into the Arts Council of England, the Scottish Arts Council and the Arts Council of Wales. There was already an Arts Council of Northern Ireland. The present-day Arts Council is responsible for fostering the arts by distributing public money from central government and revenue generated by the National Lottery. The

Council still operates under a Royal Charter, which sets out its constitution, describes its membership and gives it three objectives:

- to develop and improve the knowledge, understanding and practice of the arts
- to increase the accessibility of the arts to the public
- to advise and co-operate with departments of government, local authorities, the Arts Councils for Wales, Scotland and Northern Ireland and other bodies on matters concerned with the first two objects.

In practice, the Arts Council tries to help people enjoy the arts by supporting drama, music, dance and touring companies, contemporary art galleries and exhibitions, film and literature projects. Most of its money is devoted to regularly funded organisations ranging from the Royal Shakespeare Company and City of Birmingham Symphony Orchestra to the Poetry Book Society and the National Youth Jazz Orchestra. About a third of the annual government grant goes to the ten Regional Arts Boards, independent bodies responsible for supporting and developing the arts in their own areas, in partnership with local authorities.

On the face of it, the arts are in rude health in Britain. Around four out of five people attend an arts event every year, including nearly 10 million theatregoers, 5 million listening to classical concerts, 9 million visiting art galleries or exhibitions, about 2.5 million each going to opera, ballet and jazz, and nearly 2 million watching contemporary dance. That does not include cinemas and museums, which are administered separately. There are over 1200 performing arts venues,

over 700 performing arts companies, 2500 galleries and museums, and more than 550 festivals are held each year.

But Robinson had a very different impression from his
discussions with Smith, and from what he saw at the Arts
Council's London headquarters in Great Peter Street, not far
from the Houses of Parliament. He sat in on several meetings
of the Council, as a member, before taking his place as chairman. He said, 'It was not managed directly, and things that
aren't tend not to go well. All the time it was turning back in
on itself and reviewing issues again and again and again. But I
knew I was going into something where I would get a lot of
criticism. It was like entering a family row: everyone in the
family are rowing among themselves, but as soon as an outsider turns up they decide it's not so bad after all – and turn on
the outsider.'

It did not take long for the whispering to begin. One
opponent, who asked not to be named, told me, 'Take the
South Bank Centre. Lottery money was beginning to be tight
on cash and biased towards London. Robinson came into the
department for an important meeting on the South Bank
after about a week on the Council and said we'd got to ditch
it. He hadn't read the papers, hadn't talked to anyone. So
millions of pounds was wasted, and so was a huge amount of
work involving the architect Richard Rogers and others. In
my view he cannot behave like that. That sort of impulsive
decision-making might pass for decisiveness and clarity at
Granada, but the Arts Council is a very different world. He
doesn't employ the people that get the grants. He failed to
understand that these things work by persuasion in that
world. It's a voluntary sector, but he treated them as though

he was their employer. He doesn't listen, doesn't do his homework.'

However, others argued that the Arts Council was being asked to put up a substantial sum for a project that was no more than a refurbishment, and as such was unlikely to generate any significant new audience.

The South Bank row revolved round a £135 million undulating canopy which Lord Rogers had designed to cover the Queen Elizabeth Hall, Hayward Gallery and Festival Hall. Two years earlier Lord Rogers, then the Arts Council's vice-chairman, had won an Arts Council competition to revamp the area. Lord Rogers received a £1 million Arts Council feasibility grant for the scheme in 1995 and another £1 million in 1996. Although the publisher, Sir Paul Hamlyn, was paying £17 million and the Heritage Lottery Fund and South Bank Centre Foundation were contributing another £43 million, that still left another £75 million to be found, which the South Bank Board had asked the Arts Council for. However, timing is vital in these matters, and the Arts Council had come under fire for its Lottery grant of £78 million to the Royal Opera House, so it decided to impose a £50 million ceiling on all individual projects. That left the canopy project £25 million short.

Nevertheless, as Puttnam had predicted, Robinson braved the flak. He recalled, 'We had extraordinarily painful debates about the South Bank, and there wasn't the finance. I said, "That's it, good night, no money." There was a lot of flak, especially from people like Richard Rogers. I personally felt sorry for those who had put in considerable effort, but the plain fact was that the money simply wasn't there to do it.'

Or, as one Robinson supporter put it, 'Everyone that had any sense knew it was a mess and a muddle, and frankly they were all rescued from it by Gerry Robinson's decisiveness.' By then Robinson had lined up a key ally by choosing a new chief executive. He interviewed four or five candidates personally and, less than three weeks after he had been appointed chairman, chose Peter Hewitt, a former chief executive of Northern Arts and subsequently corporate affairs director of Tees Health Authority.

'He had made the Northern Arts Board probably the most respected regional board in the country,' said Robinson. 'He had a very high reputation. He came at it with a fairly northern feel, that anything south of the Wash needed sorting out — as, in this case, it did. And it was important to have someone coming in fresh, who hadn't been beaten by the system.'

With that vital role filled, in March 1998 Robinson decided to make two radical changes to the Council, both of which set off loud explosions of anger as they apparently confirmed the worst fears of the arts world that the Council was being taken over by a grey businessman. The first was to cut it down from the twenty-three members he inherited. Secondly, he wanted more people on the Council who were currently engaged in the arts. 'I was determined that the members of the Council shouldn't also be members of the specialist panels,' he explained. 'When I arrived we had ten councillors there who had an axe to grind, which meant that nothing could be debated with any width. The other members of the council were members of the Regional Arts Boards. So the council was very ineffective as a forum for debating issues and taking decisions.'

Like Robinson, the other councillors had three-year terms, and several had nearly three years still to run. But, instead of picking off the ones he wanted to get rid of, Robinson said he had to have a clean sheet, and so asked everyone to resign. 'I believe that some did so on the assumption that someone else would be going,' said Robinson. 'When it came down to just four of them staying, there was a reaction. But that was understandable, when you have emotional people who have good access to the media and are able to put their points across very effectively.'

When Robinson made the announcement to the media, he wrapped it in a package of 'managed change'. Hewitt tried to draw some of the sting from the news by claiming correctly that some of the decisions had predated the arrival of both himself and Robinson. He also deflected what turned out to be accurate speculation that there would be redundancies among the Arts Council's staff, then standing at more than three hundred.

In the end, about half went. Robinson's decision was formed by an episode from his early days there. He recalled 'I went round the offices, and a huge number of people just were not around on the day. It wasn't just that they were out of the office, seeing someone. No one seemed to know. We had an ancient computer system, and even simple things like the phones weren't being answered.'

Hewitt told me, 'This was a very unwell organisation, with no clear direction, and no ideas in terms of public relations. We were very clear from the start that this was a major-change exercise, and there was going to be a degree of pain and discomfort, and sure enough that is what we found. You can't do that without some people feeling they have lost out. Arts is made up of a very large number of vested interests. Those that already have a lot of support think they should continue to do so in perpetuity, and the others think they should have a place at the table.'

In April 1998 the old Council discovered exactly what Robinson had in mind for them. Advertisements for new members of the Council were placed in newspapers, despite claims from existing members that no vacancies existed. 'I don't want to sound unduly miffed about it,' said Charles Denton, who represented film on the Council, 'but the whole thing is being handled rather shabbily.'

That was a mere whimper compared with the response of the theatre lobby. In May all seventeen members of the Council's drama advisory panel resigned, led by their chairman, the West End producer and former actress, Thelma Holt, who also resigned from the Council itself. The best-known member of the walkout was the playwright Sir Alan Ayckbourn. Holt said, 'The drama panel has been castrated. The umbilical cord between the artist and the decision-maker will no longer work under the changes Gerry Robinson has introduced. They will lose all these names, handpicked by me, but they don't care. Their view is we're expendable, we can be replaced. Ironically, I was one of the architects of having a slimmed-down Council. But my intention was I and the others should resign when appropriate. What actually happened was I receive a phone call when I'm in the bath in Tokyo telling me I've been sacked. I said, "Oh, no I haven't." Then I get a call from Gerry, whom I hadn't even met, saying he agrees with everything I say, then he goes and castrates us.

The Robinson reforms may suit Granada, but they don't suit me. They are all about finance and not artistic merit.'

Within a week the walkout had turned into a nation-wide protest by senior figures in the theatre. Led by Sir Peter Hall and Sir Cameron Mackintosh, about sixty major theatre directors and producers signed a letter to Chris Smith complaining at the changes to the Council and declaring, 'We would not wish to serve on any Arts Council of England panel whose chair is not a full member of the council.' One signatory, Nicolas Kent, director of London's Tricycle Theatre, said, 'The government has completely undervalued the theatre. More producing theatres have gone to the wall under this government, including Greenwich, Farnham and Liverpool Playhouse, than in thirteen years of Tory rule. We are now seeing a situation where businessmen are being brought in to manage the Arts Council and not paying attention to the people who actually know something about the theatre they are supposed to be supporting.'

Robinson, the carpenter's son from Donegal, took the patrician route of replying through the Letters page of *The Times*. He told the editor:

Sir,

Recent days have seen much misrepresentation relating to the future role of the governing body (the council) of the Arts Council and its links with its advisory bodies. I have today written to all Arts Council panel members serving when I took up my appointment. My letter states that the position remains as follows.

The governing body will in future number about ten and those ten will not directly represent particular interests, reflecting widespread recognition that a slimmer and more effective governing body is needed. It will, however, include figures of stature in the arts world.

The chairman and chief executive of the Arts Council will meet each panel annually and will meet each panel chairman with the appropriate art-form director several times each year to air matters relating to that art form and to ensure that their specialist advice is properly understood.

Panel chairmen will also have the opportunity to attend and take part in council discussions of substantive matters of particular relevance to their art-form. Direct access to the governing body will be at whatever regularity is necessary to ensure good and well informed governance.

Needless to say, the above arrangements will apply to all art forms, not just drama.

Yours sincerely, GERRY ROBINSON

This was all of a piece with an interview he gave to the *Sunday Times* at about this time, when he said, 'It's important to remember that neither the council nor the chairman run anything. You get the worst of all possible worlds if you have somebody whose role is primarily strategic getting involved every day. But the thing is to distinguish this background noise, which is unstoppable, from the real guts of the feeling that is around.'

As he explained to me, 'I am not sure you necessarily need high-profile people on the Arts Council itself. It would have been easy to people it with big names who were not doing anything, but the immediate need was to clarify things, which in the short term often has a negative effect. To me the key people working for the Arts Council should feed things up the system to the Council. The Council should be deciding the key issues of strategy, not day-to-day nuts and bolts.

That is why it wasn't working before. So it was quite a difference in approach.'

The row over Robinson's sacking of David Plowright from Granada Television in 1992 was briefly replayed at the Arts Council, complete with the following lament from Norman Lebrecht, the *Daily Telegraph*'s arts correspondent:

> IF THE entire membership of the Arts Council of England were to dance naked round the studios of News at Ten singing Tudor madrigals, the event would excite little comment in the saloon bar of the Pig & Whistle. Such interest as exists in the Arts Council is largely self-interest. Those who feed off its grants-in-aid and lottery awards are fascinated by the writhings of this mysterious organism. To the rest of the world, a revolution at the Arts Council is about as riveting as a Cabinet reshuffle in Chile.
>
> But before you turn the page in search of weightier matters, let me warn you that what is going on this week at the Arts Council is a sign of dark things to come, an erosion of the decencies of public conduct and fair play for which this country has always stood.
>
> Given the paltry level of public interest, the Arts Council is a soft target for any point-scoring businessman who wants to get in with the party in power. Deride its lumbering ways, castigate its latest lunacies – a £4,977 grant, for instance, to 'research' a David Bailey exhibition, perhaps by flicking through girlie mags – and any mug can sound like a shining knight without harming any vital commercial interest.
>
> The Arts Council is the nation's Aunt Sally. To do a good job it needs to court unpopularity, reminding Government of an irksome responsibility and giving performing groups less than they need. Knock the Arts Council and you will raise a cheer from artists and philistines alike. Abolish it, and you won't lose the next

election. But tamper with it, and you open a Pandora's Box whose pent-up furies will rebound on those who can't leave well alone. When Tony Blair appointed Gerry Robinson of Granada to be chairman of the Arts Council of England, he cannot have given the matter a second thought. Robinson, a pioneering downgrader of television arts and documentary programming, was sent in to annoy the 'luvvies' and freeloaders of the subsisdised system.

He arrived with a package of changes that last week provoked the resignation of Thelma Holt and her drama panel, dance chairman Lady MacMillan, and some 15 others yet to declare. Just the sort of people New Labour wants to punish as it plays for a place in the *Sun*.

The cause of the mass departure is Robinson's decision to slim down the council to 10 members, shorten its deliberations and generally eliminate 'fudge', 'waffle' and 40-page documents (does he never read Granada contracts?). Heads of advisory panels will be removed from the council, which will thus be freed from the arm-twistings of special-interest lobbyists.

Rubbish, say departing members. The allocation of public funds is discussed by panels of experts in each art form. Their decisions are taken to the council by a chairman, and debated there before subsidy is granted. By silencing the panels, the council will take decisions in ignorance or – worse – prejudice.

Take the longest-running sore. Two orchestras in the deepest doldrums are located in Robinson's franchise area – the Halle in Manchester and the Royal Liverpool Philharmonic. Both are suffering the consequences of years of weak leadership, artistic and administrative. In the face of looming bankruptcy, the council's music panel responded with due caution, doling out small loans and advances until it becomes convinced – which is not yet the case – that steps have been taken to put both bands in order.

Under Robinson, the music panel will have no voice on Council, where the chairman and his new chief executive, Peter Hewitt, hold unchecked power. It would be heroically gratifying and not wholly unreasonable for Robinson to solve the musical problems of his region at a stroke - although anyone who cares for music in the North-West knows that money will only delay disaster. What is needed is reorganisation from the roots up.

Speed and efficiency are fine qualities for running a business, but other considerations come into play when handling public funds. No one would deny that the Arts Council made a mess of Covent Garden and the South Bank. The messes were no greater than Whitehall made of the British Library and lately of hospital waiting lists, but the Arts Council's were more visible because it is so transparent in its agonised deliberations.

When handling public money, openness is more important than efficiency. The Arts Council has survived because it is trusted to play fair. Autocracy, secrecy and the 'atmosphere of fear' that some felt in Robinson's first meeting will destroy its delicate fabric. Eight council members who sought a meeting with Chris Smith, the Culture Secretary, did not receive the courtesy of a reply. New Labour is out to eradicate the chaotic democracy of the Arts Council. What Smith and Blair have failed to grasp is that when they no longer have an Arts Council for us to kick around, there will be no one to blame for the state of the arts but themselves at the next election.

After that blast, most of the opposition folded their tents and appeared to steal away. Lady Macmillan's place on the Council was taken by the Royal Ballet dancer Deborah Bull, who had been a member of the dance panel. Within a year Thelma Holt, who continued to need Arts Council money, was inviting Robinson to her West End production of *Macbeth*.

And it did not take long for Robinson to find new recruits to replace the rebels. In June 1998 Robinson was able to submit to Chris Smith the names of his slimmed ten-person Council. The new members were Deborah Bull, the concert pianist Joanna MacGregor, Hilary Strong, director of the Edinburgh Festival Fringe, Derrick Anderson, chief executive of Wolverhampton council, and two sculptors – Anish Kapoor and Antony Gormley, famous for the £13 million *Angel of the North* erected by the A1 in Northumberland. Professor Christopher Frayling, rector of the Royal College of Art, was reappointed, along with the poet (now the Poet Laureate, no less) Andrew Motion and Prudence Skene, director of the Art Foundation. The former general manager of the Royal Shakespeare Company, David Brierley, was also reappointed, to represent the still-fraught drama department. And, if Robinson harboured any illusions that the Council's own administration was in no need of improvement, he would have been brought down to earth by Professor Frayling's disclosure to a newspaper that the letter inviting him to reapply had begun 'Dear Sir or Madam'. He remarked acidly, 'As I've been on the Arts Council for eleven years, you'd have thought they'd have known which I was by now.'

And the new Council should have been under no illusions either, for ringing unmistakably in their ears were the latest words of Chairman Robinson: 'There are no guarantees that what we supported in the past we will be able to support in the future. We are in a position where demands for funds exceed supply by ten to one. There is no question of cutting back on Lottery projects already approved by the

Council, but those awaiting support – and even those given encouraging noises – are not guaranteed.'

As he explained later, 'We sat down and examined the Council's overall financial position. It was a fairly simple matter of comparing revenue with the projects that we were committed to, to a greater or lesser degree, and those that were just a nod and a wink. Inevitably, the total number of projects would have cost vastly more than we had money for. And the projects kept piling in: we had to put a stop to that. It was rather cruel, because time and money was being spent on things that weren't going to happen. But there are no rewards for telling people that. We had to give people big disappointments, but I think you just have to go through that period.'

Such hand-wringing had its effect, though, for in July the government announced a £125 million increase in the Arts Council Grant-in-Aid over the following three years, consisting of £40 million in the first year, £40 million in the second and £45 million in the third. That was a useful increase over the previous annual grant of £184 million, which had actually been cut by £1.5 million the year before. The Arts Council also distributes £250 million a year of National Lottery money to the arts in England. Conveniently, the Lottery rules were changing to widen spending on other than purely capital projects. This meant that that money could be used to finance a new play, for example, rather than being confined to helping build a new theatre.

However, the Lottery arts grant was cut because the government had identified a sixth good cause, education and health. So a few weeks later Robinson announced one major award and cancelled more than a hundred others, saying the

Arts Council no longer had the funds for building schemes above £15 million except in exceptional circumstances. There was indeed £15 million to develop the Brighton Dome complex, but the Royal Shakespeare Company was denied a £2 million development grant towards renovation of its main theatre in Stratford-upon-Avon. And the Harbourside Centre in Bristol was told it could not have £58 million it had asked for, towards an estimated cost of £200 million.

Duncan Fraser, director of the Harbourside Centre, said, 'We are all completely shocked by the Arts Council's decision. This is a complete devastation for the region.' Harbourside had already received nearly £5 million from the Lottery for design and initial construction work on a car park. But Peter Hewitt insisted that Bristol had received no firm promises and the scheme was 'flawed'. Robinson explained, 'There was a lobby that argued that Bristol deserved a project of some sort, so let's pour the money into this one. It just didn't make sense.'

But Harbourside was a mere pinprick compared with the rumbling furore over the Royal Opera House in London's Covent Garden. A world-class opera house, it had suffered more than its counterparts in other countries from the fact that opera, and for that matter ballet, are so expensive that they can never cover their costs through ticket sales alone. The ROH is as alive as most such organisations to the potential for raising revenue through advertising, sponsorship, corporate hospitality and offering special facilities through various grades of club membership. But that is still not enough, so inevitably the ROH is a constant visitor to whichever government agencies distribute money to the arts – in this case the

Department for Culture, Media and Sport and the Arts Council.

The first Theatre Royal, Covent Garden, opened on 7 December 1732. There has been a permanent presence at the Royal Opera House since 1946 when the Royal Ballet and the Royal Opera were established as the theatre's resident companies. At the same time the Sadler's Wells Theatre Ballet, now Birmingham Royal Ballet, was founded.

Politically, the ROH was close to no-win. It is easy to agree that it is a national asset that must be preserved in good condition, as an affirmation to the world of Britain's status as a civilised and sophisticated society. In that sense, it is the equivalent of an emerging country's airport or radio station. But, particularly for a Labour government committed to raising the lot of the poorest sections of the community, it does not do to be lavishing too much public money on something that is only ever going to be enjoyed by a tiny minority, and arguably a well-heeled, elitist minority at that. Were it otherwise, the financial problem would not exist. Hence the periodic agonising over the scale of the ROH's losses and whether anything resembling a rational system can be devised to decide exactly how much public assistance it should receive – not to mention what should be done if such a system produced an answer that still left the opera house off-key, financially.

When Robinson was appointed chairman of the Arts Council it was suffering through being linked by association with the problems and feuding over the management of the Royal Opera House. He said, 'The potential for flak was just enormous, for the ROH had come to epitomise all that was wrong with arts funding. If you want world-class opera, you have to subsidise it, but there is a difference between being subsidised and being profligate. So we had to get a grip financially, with a combination of Lottery money and Grant-in-Aid. The Lottery money was committed far too far in advance. The ROH took the view that the Lottery money would be available come what may. And we said, "That's not the way it's going to be." The Arts Council had made the classic assumption that everything was going to come in to budget – but nothing ever does. We just had to get a much clearer feel for what was going to happen in the next two to three years, what the productions were going to be, what they were going to cost, how it was going to be financed.

'I had been on the other side of this process with the Royal Court Theatre, where we asked for £14 million, and I couldn't believe how easy it was to get it! So I understand the attitude of ROH and others. But from the Arts Council point of view it has to be very different. On the other hand, the Paris and Milan opera houses are more heavily subsidised than London. We are doing a lot to see what happens across the rest of Europe. Some Italian opera houses have very little subsidy, because they can fill an open-air amphitheatre with two thousand people for several nights, with the same opera. But, in the round, Italian opera is well subsidised by the state.'

In October, Robinson used the annual Arts Council lecture at the Royal Society of Arts to warn the ROH that it would have to smarten its act. He said, 'We shouldn't fear taking the arts to a wider audience or crossing art-form boundaries to challenge those audiences. Exposure enriches our art. It doesn't cheapen it. The Royal Opera House will not only have to demonstrate its willingness to widen access through cheaper ticket prices and to develop significantly its educational programmes if we are to carry through its rescue plan. It will also have to demonstrate that it is soundly managed.'

To underline the point, Robinson said that the regions would receive more aid and praised the initiative of the actor and director, Sir Ian McKellen, in moving to the West Yorkshire Playhouse in Leeds. He pointed out, 'Too often artists and performers have continued to ply their trade to the same white, middle-class audiences. In the back of their minds lurks the vague hope that one day enlightenment might descend semi-miraculously upon the rest. Ian McKellen's example in quitting London for Leeds may be a strong sign that this is an attitude that just won't do any longer.'

The reference to 'white, middle-class audiences' generated the predictable storm of criticism, but by December 1998 Robinson was sufficiently satisfied with the change in attitude by the new management at the Royal Opera House for him to increase its annual grant by more than a tenth to £16 million for 1999 and then to £20 million for 2000 and 2001. In return, the ROH promised to raise £100 million from private money, to cut the price of many seats by a fifth, and to offer more access to its educational programmes and workshop performances. Robinson said the increase was based on a 'genuine turnaround in their attitude'.

At about the same time, however, Robinson was hinting that the chairmanship of the Arts Council was a very demanding affair. He told the London *Evening Standard*, 'I didn't really want this job. It has a lose-lose quality: whatever you do is likely to be wrong for many people. If something was tagged onto my gravestone, I would want it to say "made an impact on the arts", not "sorted out the Arts Council".'

Unfortunately that impact was not always the sort he wished. There was just enough truth in the image of the businessman cost-cutter to give the arts lobbies a plausible platform from which to launch another attack. In the early part of 1999 a group led by the director Sir Peter Hall set up a Shadow Arts Council as a standing focus for discontent.

He launched the pressure group with a rally at the Old Vic theatre in London, telling Dame Judi Dench, Sir Tom Stoppard, Simon Callow, Harold Pinter, Sir Alan Ayckbourn, Sir Harrison Birtwhistle, Sir Richard Eyre, Sir Michael Gambon, Sir Jeremy Isaacs, Sir Simon Rattle and a hundred other supporters, 'We are not whingeing luvvies, as the government appears to think. We are eminent individuals who bring in millions of pounds for the economy. But we still live in a country where the term "intellectual" is perjorative and even "artist" is suspect. Instead of being made to feel valuable, the arts have been told to get better access and better management, when the real need is for resources. You cannot expect something to spring back to life after fifteen years of Thatcherism unless you give it medicine.' Robinson tartly accused the new group of 'organised whingeing'.

Sir Peter explained to me, 'We will comment on each development and get the artists who know about it to comment. There are two or three artists on the Arts Council now, and seven or eight bureaucrats. When I was on the Arts Council we had Henry Moore, Sir Michael Tippet, and C.P. Snow there too. There's no one like that there now. Gerry

Robinson is a terribly nice man, but I don't think the arts respond to business rationalisation. What he is doing is saying the small projects don't cost a lot of money, but they don't have very big audiences so let's kill them so we can look after the big projects. That is stupid, because small projects become big projects. It's a much more spontaneous and organic and unexpected process than he realises. It think it's a terribly grave situation. He sent away so many of the artists from the Arts Council so he could get on with the rationalisation, which was a big mistake. The only weapon the arts have is noise, and that is why I am making a noise. It's essential for people to speak up. I think if Gerry Robinson looked at arts across the board, he would have to spend a lot more.'

But not everyone agreed with the arts funding debate being couched in terms of more v. less. Some, such as John Keiffer, director of performing arts at the British Council, which promotes British culture abroad, saw the Shadow Council as trying to rebuild a fence between the so-called arts and popular culture. 'It seems to me,' he said, 'that the Shadow Arts Council would do better encouraging the Arts Council to make some really radical decisions rather than heckling from the wings.'

It will not be possible to judge Robinson's tenure at the Arts Council until after he has stepped down. But it is clear that there is more to his policy than simply cutting costs.

He believes the Council has a four-fold role. It must be:

1 A friend to the artist, helping people in the arts whenever you possibly can. Advice, tax issues, helping them to do what they want to do.

2 The most aggressive collector of funds for the arts.
3 The point of call for anything to do with the arts, keeping good statistics and information about what is going on and who can help with any project ideas.
4 An effective administrator of the funds.

Robinson said, 'Why haven't we got, say, a million members chipping £50 a year each, in return for privilege and access?' Are we getting all we can from European sources, or from corporates?' What are we doing to make the tax case to the government, for concessions to the arts?' Why aren't we persuading government to contribute three times as much as they do, because that is the general level of contributions to the arts by European governments? My first year or so was mind-blowingly frustrating, but I was anxious to make it work. You are never going to be loved: for this role the best you are going to get is an underlying acknowledgement that this organisation is doing all right. We want to help to bring art into more ethnic areas, and to a wider audience generally. We want to get to younger people through the education system. My job is to enable artistic knowledge and passion and commitment to be genuinely useful without shooting off in different directions. I don't care if it means playing opera before a football match. Making art more widely available, is not dumbing down. Before, the Arts Council was just picking up the money and deciding where it went.'

That remark has strange echoes of the very thing that the Shadow campaign was complaining about. One of its leading lights, John Tusa, managing director of the Barbican Arts Centre, asserted that the Arts Council had become increasingly concerned with 'allocating, monitoring and managing funds' – precisely what Robinson appeared to want to escape from. Oddly for a managing director, Tusa also complained that dialogue between the Arts Council and its clients was being determined more and more by 'managerial criteria'.

Robinson, as an accountant and former company chief executive, certainly pays homage to numbers as a measure of success, in the sense of wanting to see more people attending artistic events. Perhaps Hall and Tusa would not approve of supporting an English National Ballet tour by having sponsored coaches to collect people from the outlying areas and on the coach explaining what the ballet was about, the plot, the main characters and so on, so that people could understand what they were going to see. Or maybe they *would* approve of that approach, but it is plainly some way away from a dry question of counting numbers. 'We greatly underestimate people's fears and apprehensions about going to see something like that for the first time' says Robinson.

He also insists on something that many arts supporters find anathema: having proper, practical assessments of projects. He said, 'I genuinely think there are a lot of people who feel more rounded, feel better, through art and you can only do that through a series of practical things that you set out to do, with arts people plus businesspeople to see projects through to fruition. It's important that that combination really, really works. It's better to tell someone right at the beginning that something isn't going to work, rather than give them exploratory money and then say "Sorry, there's no more money." There is a constituency in the arts that is pretty tricky. They feel sullied that they have to deal with the financials.

They need money, but they hate it. There are many exceptions to this, but many have this attitude that if it's good, not many people can like it, and the corollary is that if a lot of people like it, it can't be good.

'It's been very different from any business problem I have had before, because of the political dimension. You can care passionately about the arts, how a lot of money can be wasted. We don't even have the numbers to tell us whether various arts events are becoming more or less popular. It's not difficult to get a database and then we can compare ourselves with other countries and measure the trends. Who are attending the arts? Young, old, men, women? Are they attending more or less often? We just don't know.

'Should some of it be free' A part of me says it should be, because that affects audience levels hugely. But the dominant part of me says if you pay for something you appreciate it more. We don't have the feeling in Britain that art is important, and that it's important to have good-quality art. In Paris the choice is enormous, and it's beautifully done. We haven't managed to make the man or woman in the street feel that way about art here. I think it must start in the classroom.

'Everything that succeeds in bringing in more people can only be helpful. If you increase it by even a small percentage it's worth it. Look at the National Theatre. That has been a tremendous success. So has Chichester, Glyndebourne, the Royal Court. The Albert Hall has been tremendously successful: it makes money which is ploughed back. More subsidy isn't the only solution.'

At the time of writing the Arts Council is still in transition, but there is no doubt that Robinson has already done much to clear away the muddle that was engulfing it. Whether he is able to do so in a way that leaves a lasting legacy remains to be seen. Experience suggests that, once a radical reformer such as Robinson departs, it is very difficult for what is essentially a spending organisation to resist the never-ending flood of demands on its resources. But he can hardly be blamed for what comes after his reign is over. It simply raises the question of whether the Arts Council can be managed on rational business lines or, as John Tusa argues, the arts 'need to cost money rather than earn it, and … a society that turns its back on them risks losing the capacity to understand itself.' That is ultimately a matter for government – but successive governments have found it impossible to stick to a consistent policy, however much they are urged by the Treasury to curb public spending on the arts.

I 2

Conclusion

The picture that I hope emerges from this biography is of a man who has had the intelligence and ambition to make the most of a poor beginning and take advantage of the opportunities that have come his way. There is little doubt that a beguiling Irish charm has opened doors. Nevertheless, he would not have got as far as he has without impressing some shrewd judges such as Eric Walters, who brought him from Lex Service to Grand Metropolitan, as well as Allen Sheppard and Anthony Tennant at the highest level of Grand Met. Alex Bernstein, too, took a very close look at Robinson before appointing him chief executive of Granada, and checked him out with many other people who knew him. Robinson would not have survived that degree of scrutiny had he not been able to deliver.

His biggest opportunity, and arguably the biggest slice of

luck, was the Compass buyout and subsequent stock market flotation, which earned Robinson a fortune worth at least £20 million, certainly many times more than he would need to be independently wealthy. That gave him the means to choose what he wanted to do, and he took the Granada job, knowing that it was a solid company with a good name, but which had fallen to a low ebb. That gave him a ready-made role as a corporate reviver, applying the managerial equivalent of smelling salts and a new coat of paint. By 1998, after the takeovers of Sutcliffe, LWT, Yorkshire Television and Forte, that had been largely achieved and Charles Allen was establishing himself as chief executive and a possible successor to Robinson in the chairmanship. As Robinson was becoming more of a part-timer he added the part-time, unpaid role of heading the Arts Council.

John Nelson, who worked on Robinson's biggest deals when he was advising Granada on behalf of the City merchant bank Lazard Brothers, pointed out, 'Part of Gerry's secret is to get on with people well, because then they work better for him in that sort of mood.' This suggests an element of deliberateness in Robinson's apparently easy-going manner that is not immediately apparent. We like people to fit into nice, neat categories and there is still a tendency for the English, particularly in the allegedly sophisticated southeast, to fit the Irish into one of a handful of cartoon stereotypes – of which the smiling charmer, with a glint in his eye, a pint in his hand and a way with the ladies, is a prime example. But real life is rarely like that, so those who have met Robinson quickly go serious and, with a knowing look, add something to the effect of, 'But don't be deceived. Beneath that blarney is a mind like a razor and a heart of pure steel.' Up to a point, of course this is true. Robinson has, after all, climbed to the top of the pole in British business, and nowadays that is hard to do without considerable skill, ambition and intelligence. He can analyse a business problem and cut to the key issue with impressive speed.

Robinson says the biggest single influence on him was Alan Costin, the financial controller at Lex Service who recruited him from Lesney. 'If you told Alan you were going to do something,' Robinson recalled, 'he would put it in a little file and he would ask you whether you had done it. Believe me, you didn't leave things undone for very long once he had tripped you up once or twice. I think my mother is a bit like that, in the sense that she follows up something until she gets what she wants. Dad was quite the opposite: he would prom-ise the moon and never deliver it. I have always been good at separating the idea of making something happen from just watching it. Business is a serious affair. And the only way you can run a business is at first hand.

'I don't see a simple divide in my character. You would get the genial side of me, even in a serious meeting. To have a sense of the ridiculous and have a laugh is important, but it must not be confused with the understanding that "we must get this done". Nothing happens accidentally – you must make it happen, and I can be a hard taskmaster. I wouldn't like to be on the receiving end of me if I weren't delivering. I am not prepared to say everything is all right if it isn't. I am always very, very irritated by sloppiness. The most difficult management problem is when the person is trying his or her damndest and it's not working. There's no point leaving them in the role, because that can be even worse. Instead you have to say, "We are going to find something else for you to do." If you leave that decision for too long, people start saying, "He's hopeless." But if you catch it early you can find something else for them to do while they still have their self-respect. I don't think it's kind to have someone in a senior job who can't do it, and just hope they'll be successful.

'At Granada, although we don't lose many people we do push hard because I don't believe that you can run anything and just be nice: you have got to have a hard edge. It's the equivalent of conditional love. If I don't come out of a meeting with something done, then the meeting has been a waste of time. I think that was very clearly there in the Arts Council, that lack of a clear view that what they do is important. Part of that is not knowing what success is, and knowing the goal to go for. There is a useful technique – to separate whether someone is right or not from what you are going to do about it. Is George doing a good job, or are the problems such that I have really got to think about it? If you get at it early enough, either it corrects itself and people sort it out, or at least you have started a process and it's no great shock to him to discover that you think things should be changed. It can work if you haven't talked to everyone about how awful he is.

'It's amazing how it can get to the point where you can change things without aggro. You should definitely be generous to people who have been with the company a long time and are trying their best. Many, many people try very hard and can't make it. They are owed their dignity in the process, but you must not keep them on in a role in which they're failing. When it comes to the crunch there is no messing. Wanting something to work well is a very good way of getting it to work well. I think that part of it comes from my dad. He hated to see anyone in the family idle. The important thing was not to be spotted doing nothing! He couldn't resist finding you a job, whether it was weeding the potatoes or cutting the grass.'

Robinson has translated this sense of orderliness to the way Granada is run at the management level. It revolves around a Medium-Term Review held between April and July each year, in which the people running every part of the business look at what they had been doing right or wrong in the previous year, and what they expect to do the following year.

'We do one division a week,' Robinson explained, 'then the numbers that flow from those decisions are hotly debated, with group management saying you have got to do this and the divisional people saying we want to do that. There has got to be enough give and take in the process to allow for that. If a guy isn't strong enough to fight for his position he probably shouldn't be in the job in the first place. The results of that process become refined into a set of budgets for the year beginning October 1, which is when our financial year starts. Then we sit down with them once a month during the year and that is it – no more argument. It's a very good process because it means you are not constantly bickering.

'I have a file for everyone that reports to me and if I have an idea I put it in the file and once a month we go through it, unless it's urgent. It controls the amount of time you spend. Most of it is yes or no. If you don't sit down once a month, formally, dates set a year in advance, things tend to drift. Acquisitions are added to the budget numbers, according to what you have said is the justification for buying the business.

And there are no bonuses, so we don't get the wrangle where we want to keep targets high and divisional managers want to keep them low. If there is a problem I'll get at it pretty early – it will not be allowed to fester. And if you want to make £100 million you had better have a plan to make £110 million in case things go wrong. Things very rarely come right by surprise. One time at Coca-Cola I had a good year for soft drinks because it was a hot summer, otherwise I would have been in trouble, but that was an exception. There are mature markets, but I don't believe there is such a thing as a mature business. It usually means there have been cock-ups some-where along the line.'

Robinson concedes that he chose Granada well. It is a nationally known company, for its television, its rentals or its hotels and catering, all of which have the business virtue of being reasonably predictable at a time when economic conditions have been helpful.

Robinson recalled, 'The feeling at Granada Television when I arrived was "advertising revenue is down, so what can we do?" And after we took over Forte they used to say, "Volume's down, what can we do? It's raining, there are road-works on the M4, there's nothing we can do about it." But it is vital at Forte or anywhere else that management can see they are not at the mercy of what God sends them. That is the difference between companies that work and companies that don't. You affect what happens. Small problems become big problems because people do nothing. You've got to ask, "Who's doing better and why?"

'At Little Chef we have been trying to tighten up what it offers, making it more akin to the other big brands like

McDonald's and Burger King. We are getting real growth out of Little Chef for the first time in years, but we have a lot to do in the detail of menus, what the waitresses wear, what the customer should hear when he or she enters the restaurant. It's paying off – sales volumes and profits are rising – but we need more fanaticism. You never get it right, and that still annoys me. It's difficult to get people to feel passionately about what they do. If you are the waiter or waitress in a Little Chef, you have to want to be turned out right and say "good morning". We have to work away at that and do the proper training. Heather hates it whenever we go in a Little Chef, because she knows I'll be tearing my hair out about this or that. I am always disappointed at it, but maybe that is me. I am always impressed when they do get it right, but I'm afraid I tend to concentrate on the negative rather than the positive.

'If we go into someone else's service station, though, I don't care. The whole motorway service business was hugely underexploited – it had become very tired. You get the right manager in the same service station and you can influence it hugely. Like making sure there aren't fifteen people waiting to be served. Now, if there are more than three people waiting we open another till. It's that attention to detail that makes things work. You have to have everyone greeted when they arrive. It's not anything to do with cost-cutting. It's basic stuff: what do the customers want?' And what they want is to be sat down, made to feel they matter, and given what they ask for in a reasonable time.

'People will pay quite a lot if you get it right but they will hate it if you get it wrong, even if it is cheap. We are passionate about trying to get it better. Little Chef outlets can still drive me mad, the way they can keep you waiting. And there were silly things to get right, like a lot of the branches had equipment that couldn't cook everything on the menu: that was sorted for about £750 a time.

'Little Chef serves fresh food and has a reasonably wide-ranging menu. Burger King is easier to manage because it's much more mechanised. But, as we have so many Little Chefs, we can easily experiment with four or five branches, and I don't think we have been innovative enough. One of the things you can bring to a business like that is giving it that big thought about where it should be going and how it should position itself. We are taking that approach in a better way in the Travelodge hotels. We get very few complaints there. We have a very mechanised approach to it and I genuinely believe we have got that right. It's about presenting something to the public that is really first-class relative to what you are doing and relative to the competition. People can choose: they don't have to have any particular brand. The hotels are the same: it's about incentivising and encouraging staff. It's also important that the reservations people come out to try out the hotels, so they can talk knowledgeably to customers on the phone and say "that room is at the end of a corridor" or "this one over-looks the lily pond". So often these simple things give customers confidence and make the difference between making a sale and not making a sale. It's the human interaction.'

But increasingly Robinson is looking to the future, to the time when he is no longer Mr Granada, no longer John Cleese's upstart caterer, no longer quaffing stage pints behind the bar of the Rover's Return on the *Coronation Street* set for the benefit of corporate photo calls.

In reflective mood as we shared a pot of tea in his elegant first-floor office overlooking London's Green Park, he said, 'I often think of the philosophy expressed in Milan Kundera's book, *The Unbearable Lightness of Being*, which says that nothing matters very much and yet, because it is all we have, everything matters greatly. I have never taken life that seriously, because I have the sense of it not mattering that much. But whatever you do, you must really go for it. No half measures. If that's what we are going to do, let's have a crack at it. You are going to do a couple of big things in your life and you had just better get them right.

'I am not saying don't try, for you must have the courage to try something. When we won Forte, I had a tremendous feeling. It had been the pinnacle of our existence for two months, then there was a huge anticlimax because now we had to pick it up and run it. I don't think anything you strive for in a frenetic way ever fulfils you. The principal thing you realise is that you can't simply choose contentment for yourself. You often say to yourself, "I won't do that again," and then of course you do repeat it. The important thing is to be yourself, to decide for yourself, "This makes me angry," "I am enjoying this and I'm not enjoying that." There is a hard balance between nihilism and "everything matters". I hate pomposity, and most people I have met and that have succeeded are not pompous – people like Rupert Murdoch, Sam Chisholm, Anthony Tennant or Allen Sheppard.

'Time is important. It's often in your quieter moments that you think, That's not quite right or, Let's do that. It's almost always in the quiet times that you decide something is important. Then you have to organise it, plan it. When you take up something new you have to be very, very careful about planning it and make sure you don't get swamped by it. I worked long hours for six to eight weeks when I came to Granada, meeting people, deciding who the key people and issues were. You have a peculiar clarity in the early weeks.'

By 1999, though, Robinson was conscious that one of his key remaining roles was to sort out the succession to himself as chairman before he quits around 2003, when he is 55. 'I don't think you can stay in one role for too long,' he pointed out. 'After a while, I don't think you are giving your best to it. If you haven't got a clear idea of who is going to succeed you, you probably haven't done your job properly, made sure that there are people in key jobs to carry on. At any one time the organisation is stronger than the individual – *Coronation Street* has lasted more than thirty-five years because it has never depended on one person. You need a good collection of people across the main skills. I am a genuine delegator anyway. Charles Allen runs Granada. When there is a genuine issue to consider, we bounce ideas off one another, and in the end we almost always do whatever is his choice. But I think about leaving things in safe hands. If you choose the right person, the company will prosper, and in ways you can't anticipate. I believe Charles is that person. In a way you cannot genuinely test someone unless you give them the chance to run things. I couldn't find out how Charles would react to management issues if I was checking on his every move. Give Charles Allen a problem and he will think of fifteen things he might do about it. He has a very unusual combination of qualities, both the imagination to see something and then the managerial capacity to make it happen.

'Charles wants to be in control, to be the one who runs the thing, and I have always allowed for that. He has wanted me to be there, and not to be there. It must often have been hugely irritating for him, but we have usually kicked around most things that matter. It's handy for him to have me taking the flak sometimes, and taking a reading on what will work and what won't.'

At the other end of Granada's head office corridor, by 1999 the Scots-born Allen was taking a comfortable view of his working relationship with Robinson. 'In my mind Gerry has always been chairman,' he said, 'even when he was chief executive. His approach has been to choose the right people and let them run it. That hasn't really changed. We have had a close relationship, and in the last five years it's got much closer. Both socially and in the business sense, I am sure it will carry on. In the end we both have the same philosophy: business is a game we play to win, but don't take it too seriously.'

That is why it is not difficult to believe Robinson when he insists that he wants to walk away from it all. 'I have no doubt at all that I will not get sucked back into industry in some way,' he said. 'It's getting easier and easier to stay away. I love being away from London and walking out in the garden, and I find it genuinely difficult to come back. I want to do my own thing in Donegal, working on the house and the land. That feels right to me and the more time I give to that the more important it seems. In Ireland the people are much more caught up in their daily lives and the lives of their families. I recognise that in me, that Donegal thing of "getting by". Heather and I have moved into a 330-year-old house, and I want to leave it behind in good shape. That is something when you have got an old house, to restore it and pass it on to the next generation. Compared to that, all the scurrying around in London doesn't seem vital. Although it matters to me, I often have an acute sense of its nonimportance. The older I get, the clearer I feel about that.'

So, although the boy may have left Donegal more than forty years ago, Donegal has never left the man. Gerry Robinson is neither as coldly calculating as some of his enemies might like to believe, nor as hail-fellow-well-met as you might imagine on shaking his hand at a party. Indeed, as one of his admirers remarked to me, if you do happen to shake his hand it is not a bad rule to count your fingers afterwards. Mind you, I have done so many times and am happy to report that I have always come away with the same four fingers and a thumb.

APPENDIX I

Granada's beginnings

A flickering, grainy, black-and-white moving image of King Edward VII's 1910 funeral cortège was the genesis of the Granada cinema and television empire. That, to the best of his memory, was the first film that the eleven-year-old Sidney Bernstein saw, in a converted shop in Ilford, east London. An anonymous but kindly woman may have unwittingly burned the moment in his mind. She gave him a box of chocolates for doffing his cap at the solemn scene in the darkened little room, imitating the adult custom of those days when a hearse passed in the street.

Bernstein's early exposure to what is now called media did much to determine his approach to the distinctive content of Granada's television output, with its balance of the social realism of *Coronation Street* with the gritty journalism of *World In Action*. While the first piece of film Bernstein remembered in his later years was that news report of Edward VII's funeral, by that time the family had been regular theatregoers for many years and his father owned a fledgling chain of music halls. As soon as Sidney Bernstein was old enough, he ventured beyond such familiar family haunts as the

Ilford Hippodrome to the Coliseum in London's West End and he became a stage-door fan at the Royal Opera House, Covent Garden. The pattern was already set for what is still recognisably the modern Granada TV business.

Sidney's father, Alexander Bernstein, went into cinemas through a combination of accident and necessity, although as he sat enjoying the shows with his family his business brain had been noticing how rising affluence was giving people the spare cash with which to enjoy themselves. Music hall was booming, helped by the advent of electric light in 1905. Pubs, then still largely male haunts in most of Britain, were losing ground to music halls, where customers of both genders could drink in more congenial surroundings. At the same time, of course, there was no radio or television to divert them. The elder Bernstein realised that there was money to be made behind the bright lights and the greasepaint.

Alexander was a naturalised Latvian who had migrated to Ilford in the 1880s with his mother and sister. A portly man with rimless glasses, a salt-and-pepper moustache and a silk top hat, he had tried various business ventures from trading to quarrying before he settled down as a property developer with an office in Finsbury Square, in the City of London. In 1906 he bought a former rubbish dump opposite Lower Edmonton railway station, about seven miles northwest of the family home in Ilford. It seemed best suited to having shops on it, but, unless he incorporated some sort of attraction to encourage people to make the trip, he was not going to extract much of a rent from the shopkeepers. Nowadays the stock answer would be to install a cinema, but that was still a few years away. So Bernstein built a music hall, his family's first. He was a property man, so his plan was to hand the management and any profits to an impresario while he collected a rent. But, if shopkeepers had doubts about opening in Lower Edmonton, so did music-hall impresarios. The first Bernstein approached, George Adney Payne, pulled out after Bernstein had committed himself to the extent of hiring an architect and builders. In the sort of towering rage that his son Sidney would echo in the future he told Payne to go to hell and bravely promised to run the theatre himself. But, when he calmed down, he changed his mind and instead poached Payne's assistant, Harry Bawn.

The Edmonton Empire opened on Boxing Day 1908, yielding Bernstein £900 a year rent. The Bernstein children were dressed in sailor suits and nine-year-old Sidney was ashamed to be made to stand in the gallery and hand out sweets to the local kids. But before long the new theatre was joining the rush to film, at first by cautiously including one-minute shorts as a break during the live performance. The standard of those early efforts was so poor that they relied almost entirely on their novelty value – but their impact on the public was obvious. Alexander Bernstein built four cinemas in the next five years after the Edmonton Empire opened.

Sidney was the middle child of nine, born five years after Alexander had married Jane Lazarus, a Russian tailor's daughter, on 6 August 1893. Sidney had four brothers, Selim, Cecil, Max and Albert, and four sisters, Rae, Beatrice, Ida and Beryl. In the early years they lived in a terraced house with a garden that backed on to the River Roding and Ilford golf course beyond. It appears to have stood on part of what is now the South Woodford to Barking relief road, leading to the M11 motorway and northeast London.

Sidney was a bright child, in 1911 winning a scholarship to Coopers Company School in Bow, a few miles down Romford Road from Ilford. But he was soon faced with a much longer and more complicated journey to school, for Alexander's business was prospering sufficiently for him to move the family across London, to Cricklewood on the west side of Hampstead, into a recently built double-fronted, six-bedroom Edwardian villa with marble stairs and stained-glass windows. It had a small drive in front and a large garden behind, with a sauna by the garage.

Sidney had become taller and leaner than his brothers, with bright eyes and a pale skin, and was always neatly dressed. He was also extremely determined to get his own way, even at the cost of a mighty family row. At seventeen he quit school, despite showing every sign of being capable of continuing his education much further. He wanted to leave so that he could work for his father, but Alexander punished him by refusing to take him on. Instead, Sidney was sent to be an apprentice engineer at Simon Engineering, which belonged to family friends. There father and son might have remained deadlocked in one of those feuds that can become interminable. But Sidney suffered a personal setback that enabled his father to relent and give him a job in the family cinema business.

Sidney was desperate to join the army after his elder brother, Selim, had died at Gallipoli in September 1915 of wounds from a dumdum bullet. But on 24 September 1917, Sidney was finally told he was not fit for service because a kick in the face during a game of soccer had injured the septum in his nose and made breathing difficult. He had endured a two-hour operation without anaesthetic, as the surgeon tried to straighten his nose with a hammer and chisel. But that failed, leaving Sidney with a boxer's nose and permanent terror of pain to go with his breathing difficulties.

Wreathed in family sympathy, Sidney began working in a new part of the Bernstein cinema operation, a company called Film Agencies which rented out film prints and projection equipment. Sidney, still in his teens, quickly revealed his talent as a deal maker. Film Agencies and its offshoot, Kinematograph Equipment, had offices at 19 Cecil Court, off Soho's Wardour Street, which was already becoming the heart of the British film industry, as it was to be for many years. Every morning Sidney would go there from Cricklewood, half an hour or so away by bus, with sandwiches for his lunch. He would spend much of the day at trade shows or the new West End cinemas, seeking out the latest films to buy for the Bernstein theatres on the outskirts of north and east London. He even went into small-scale film production.

In 1920 he advertised in the trade paper, *Advertising Weekly*: 'Bring the success of Cinematography into your business'. The American-owned Phillips Petroleum asked Sidney to make a film about Phillips bringing petrol from the US. He took a cameraman to Barrow-in-Furness and filmed a Phillips tanker docking, the petrol being pumped out and taken to depots round the country, complete with the now familiar shot of a flare on top of a pipe burning off the excess. He followed that with another film promoting a smoke-free Phillips oil stove, the Valor Perfection. It was a silent film, as they all were then, with subtitles depicting a newly married man coming home to find his bride in tears because the gas cooker is belching smoke. He blames her and stomps off, in an echo of Sidney's own frequent exits from family rows. But, when the husband returns the next evening, everything is under control: his wife has bought a Valor Perfection. Phillips seemed pleased with both efforts, but Sidney did not make any more promotional films, possibly because his interests and activities were broadening and other possibilities were exciting him more.

Instead, he travelled extensively in Europe, and above all America, where the film industry had blossomed with its better weather and without the distractions of a world war on its doorstep. In June 1921, at the age of only twenty-two, Sidney paid his first visit to New York and saw for himself the marbled, mirrored, extravagantly lit cinemas there. In the midst of a Manhattan heatwave, cinema frontages were covered in frosting to advertise how cool they were inside. Doormen were dressed as gendarmes, Foreign Legionnaires or Keystone Kops to advertise the films they were running. Jazz bands and forty-piece orchestras performed four times a day to accompany the films. Ushers wore military-style uniforms with gold braid, showing customers to their seats with the aid of swagger sticks that lit up in the dark. Sidney recalled, 'It was like drinking champagne all day.' London had nothing like it.

Back in England, Sidney's influence was growing way beyond his years. Just three months after he returned from New York, he was asked to go to Scotland to entertain Lloyd George, then Prime Minister, who was touring the region. That he should be chosen for such a prestige assignment so young was a measure of Sidney's ambition and the ease with which he made important contacts. Sidney and a projectionist took the overnight train to Inverness, obtained an electricity generator and drove to Gairloch, which was still without electric power. Sidney Bernstein put on a Charlie Chaplin evening which Lloyd George was reportedly delighted with. That Christmas, Sidney went one better: he was asked to organise a royal film show at Sandringham. He drove there on 29 December with a print of Chaplin's *The Kid*. The Lord Chamberlain insisted on a preview, to vet the film, and fussily tried to get Bernstein to cut a scene showing a baby in nappies, on the grounds that this would not be suitable for delicate royal sensibilities. Bernstein refused, as the film was not his property, adding that surely even royal babies wore nappies. The Lord Chamberlain, having made the gesture, conceded but nevertheless surrounded the building with fire hoses in case the notoriously unstable flammable nitrate film caught fire.

The following year, 1922, Alexander Bernstein died, refusing surgery until it was too late and dying in a Harley Street clinic. Although an Alexander Bernstein Trust was set up and administered by his widow, Sidney was left in charge of the family business. In those days his sisters would not have been considered for a working role, and Sidney's only brother of working age was Cecil, then eighteen. Other plans were put to one side for the time being while Sidney and Cecil took control and ensured that the business was secure enough to maintain what was still a large though comfortably off family. In October that year the Edmonton Empire earned a footnote in variety history when the legendary Marie Lloyd gave her last performance there. Seriously ill, she insisted on going on and collapsed on stage. She died two days later and her dressing room, Room 108, was kept locked for over a decade.

Meanwhile, Sidney's film interests and social contacts were widening. In 1925 he became one of the founders of the Film Society, an avant-garde intellectual group dedicated to bringing the most adventurous and innovative foreign films to London.

Supporters included many of fashionable 1920s London, including H.G. Wells, George Bernard Shaw, John Maynard Keynes and Julian Huxley. The Society's credentials were firmly established by the opposition of the British Board of Film Censors and the London County Council licensing authority, egged on by hysterical allegations in the *Sunday Pictorial* and *Sunday Express* that this innocent exercise in raising the tone of the British cinema was some sort of communist plot. The Society defied its critics and continued until World War Two began in 1939.

In its early days the Film Society was a great vehicle for Bernstein to broaden his range of contacts at a time when his business was on the verge of becoming a major force in the cinema. The year the Society began, 1925, was also the year when the clearly wealthy Bernstein moved away from the family home in Cricklewood, while always returning on Friday nights for the traditional Jewish family dinner. For the rest of the week, though, he was a fully fledged man about town. He bought a house in Albemarle Street, in the heart of Mayfair and within walking distance of his office, now in Wardour Street itself. He rode in Hyde Park's Rotten Row first thing in the morning, returning to be greeted by a butler who had already run a bath and was waiting to remove Bernstein's riding boots. Once dressed in his handmade shirt and suit, he would light a Sullivan & Powell cigarette and contemplate a day that might involve lunching at the Savoy, dining at the Café Royal and dancing at Ciro's, The 400 or another fashionable nightclub. On Sunday he might visit the sculptor Jacob Epstein in his studio at Hyde Park Gate, meeting the likes of T.S. Eliot or Wyndham Lewis there. It was a world away from the mass appeal of the cinema, which was growing by leaps and bounds on both sides of the Atlantic.

Music hall wilted before the onslaught of the new medium, driven by the phenomenal output of Hollywood. The major European countries still thought they had the populations, expertise and cultural tradition to compete with the tidal flow of American imports, but despite sporadic resistance they have never yet regained the ground lost in those early days. American films and cinemas were bigger and, in the eyes of the broad public audience, better, with the huge platform of their domestic market to rely on. That made it possible to build more lavish cinemas and introduce technical innovations like sound and colour sooner than other countries. By 1927 only five in every hundred films shown in Britain had been made there: the vast bulk of the rest were American. The UK government made a feeble attempt to stem the tide by introducing the Cinematograph or Films Act, which made foreign films subject to a quota and forced cinemas to show a minimum number of British films. But it made little difference to the trend.

Bernstein realised how the entertainment industry was moving, so in 1927 he set about rebuilding his chain of north London theatres, converting them from mixed music hall and film into dedicated, purpose-built cinemas. He went back to the US in May that year and saw how sound was creeping in, at first only for shorts and newsreel items such as Charles Lindbergh's first solo flight across the Atlantic. Less than six months later, Al Jolson was bursting into song in *The Jazz Singer*: the talkies had truly arrived. But Bernstein at first held out against what is now agreed to have been the single most important development since moving pictures had been invented. He told a cinema trade conference, 'Full-length speaking films would necessarily be a great strain on an audience. I feel convinced that the human ear cannot stand long periods of mechanically produced music, sound or dialogue. As a permanent attraction I do not see that, at any rate for the moment, they in any way threaten silent films.'

That caveat, 'at any rate for the moment', suggests that Bernstein may not have really believed what he was saying, for if the human ear could not stand long periods of mechanically produced music, sound or dialogue in 1927, there is little reason to think that it could do so in 1937, or later for that matter. His caution may have stemmed from the more down-to-earth consideration of financial risk, for the new sound systems were relatively expensive and untested, and there were many different competing versions on the market. They cost around £100 extra per cinema per week to run, and talking films cost three times as much as the silents to rent, so there was plenty to think about, and Bernstein may not have wanted his competitors to steal a march on him while he made his mind up. But when *The Jazz Singer* came to the Piccadilly Theatre in London a year after its New York debut, Bernstein saw instantly that the game was up. Before long he was admitting, 'We can no more stop the revolution of talkies than anyone could stop the development of the wireless.'

Bernstein realised that he had to follow the American cinema in another way: the sheer grandeur of its picture palaces. He built the first of his new generation of New York lookalikes in Dover, a decent-sized town that still did not have a cinema. His new creation there had a huge entrance hall, with a carved stone balcony and Moorish arches that seemed to stretch into the distance. Spanish shawls were draped around, to offset cut-glass chandeliers and etchings of the Alhambra in Spain. But he also wanted an exotic name to give the public a taste of what they could expect. Bernstein got his inspiration from a walking tour of southern Spain: Granada. In the run-up to the grand opening in January 1930 he launched a teaser advertising campaign in the Dover area, instructing the local community to 'Start Saying Granada'. The second version, at Walthamstow in Bernstein's northeast London homeland, extended the Spanish theme with a metal canopy, Moorish wrought-iron columns, heavily patterned walls and masses of sweet-smelling pot plants.

But Bernstein's most impressive Granada was the one at Tooting in south London. To make way for it, he demolished twelve houses, six shops and four flats. At 7 p.m. on 5 September 1931, sixteen Life Guards trumpeters blew a fanfare on the steps of the Italianate façade to admit 4000 guests for yet another grand opening. The vast foyer was in the style of a medieval baronial hall with a minstrels' gallery, carved panelling and a heavily beamed ceiling. Heraldic Venetian lions stared down from high up the walls. To reach the auditorium, people had to walk through a 150-foot hall of mirrors with Italian Renaissance marble columns. The auditorium itself was in deep gold, with walls lined by cloistered arches and a ceiling embossed in rose and gold moulding. In the cloisters were murals of fifteenth-century troubadours and damsels. Stained-glass windows and wall paintings depicted illustrated manuscripts. The floors were covered in marble and deep carpets of rose and mauve. The proscenium arch was covered in rich drapes with a series of cusped Gothic pendants. A café served American-style snacks. There was a kennel and nursery for customers to leave their dogs and children while they watched the film, although the nursery later became abused by parents who did not bother to collect their children after the show.

At 7.30 on the opening night the curtains parted and a real car drove on to the stage in front of a set showing the outside of the theatre. Amid bowing flunkeys, a little girl got out of the car and declared the theatre open. So good were the acoustics that her tiny voice could be heard throughout the auditorium. Then everyone who had helped to build the theatre paraded across the stage, with the exception of Bernstein. Finally, the lights dimmed for a showing of *Monte Carlo*, Jack Buchanan's first talkie. At Tooting, as in most Granadas, Bernstein rounded off the grandiloquent effect with the American idea of installing Mighty Wurlitzer organs to take the place of the now redundant live orchestras. Invented by an eccentric Englishman, Robert Hope Jones, these magnificent machines could replicate any sound that an orchestra could make, and much more, to supplement the films' own sound.

Now that he had decided in which direction cinema had to go, Bernstein was tireless in promoting it and finding out what the public wanted. He encouraged his cinema managers to come up with stunts that played on public curiosity in the same way as a fairground or a circus did. He had twelve pianolas put on a Granada stage, wired to seem as if they were playing themselves and with a spotlight to pick out the keys as they moved. Inhabitants of East Ham in east London were startled to see a camel walking down the street wearing a placard saying, 'There's plenty of legroom at the Granada'. Bernstein went on radio to beat the drum for British film production, while conducting regular market research to discover what sort of films and which film stars people wanted to see, and why they went to the cinema in the first place. And he made genuine innovations. In 1928, two thousand children paid 3d (just over 1p) to see *Robinson Crusoe* at the Willesden Empire on a Saturday morning. It was the first showing exclusively for children, who had previously had to make do with short films during the evening performances that their parents took them to. This was the first move to segregate films among different types of audience, later reflected in the age-related certificates issued by film censors.

Bernstein also led the way for Sunday opening, after years of argument between the church and the police, keen to get young people off the streets. Bernstein persuaded the Labour MP, Herbert Morrison, to push a Bill on the subject through Parliament, but the resulting Act ordained no more than public meetings and local referenda. That was the cue for a sustained campaign round the country. One successful stunt had stooges in a cinema audience ask questions of an actor on film, with the answers carefully dovetailed. Bernstein arranged for every theatre and cinema in Dover to be opened and fully lit one Sunday only for the hopeful customers to be turned away with the explanation that their local council would not let them admit the public. That sparked enough of an outcry to overthrow the ban.

The ostentatious and publicity-grabbing Granadas, the Sunday-opening campaign and innovations like the children's shows, along with his highly placed social circle, marked Bernstein out as one of the leading figures in British cinema. Inevitably, he was at the forefront of the early consolidation of the industry into fewer, larger and more economical groupings. In 1928 he merged his family's business with Gaumont British Picture Corporation on terms that let him take £250,000 out in cash and still left him with a decisive 49 per cent share in the enlarged group, which was named Bernstein Theatres. Bernstein became managing director on a salary of £5000 a year, making him one of the highest-paid men in Britain. The controlling 51 per cent stake was later bought by the Rank Organisation, and this relationship continued until the 1960s, when Granada bought Rank's stake.

Sidney meanwhile developed Granada separately. To raise fresh capital, he set up each cinema as a separate company, with its own shareholders. All they had in common was the Granada name and Granada's management, not unlike some international hotel franchises today. This produced an extremely untidy organisation, which was not sorted out until the 1940s, when Sidney mopped up the outside shareholders by issuing them with Granada shares. In 1933, at the height of the Granada cinema-building boom, he moved his head office into an imposing block on the north side of Golden Square, still within walking distance of Wardour Street but apart from it. That remained the group's headquarters until 1996, when Gerry Robinson moved it to Stornaway House, the first Lord Beaverbrook's former London home near St James's Palace. So successful was the Granada name that Bernstein adopted it for his parent company, going public on the stock market in 1935 as Granada Theatres. By then there were twenty-one cinemas under the Granada name, thirty when war broke out in 1939.

In 1936 Bernstein was opening four cinemas a year under what was by then a well-refined formula. Sidney and his younger brother, Cecil, would identify a town or district without a cinema. Drawing on Sidney's early success with market research, they would send to the area a team of out-of-work documentary film-makers to elucidate the habits, tastes, expectations and even occupations of the local population. If that confirmed their initial hunch, they would arrange the finance, bid for a site and descend with their trusted team of architects, designers and builders. Cecil would withdraw to his office to deal with the business side and Sidney would be joined by another younger brother, Max, to supervise the early running in of the new cinema. Sidney would take a camp bed to the new site and supervise operations personally, provoking the workers to finish early by simply publicising an earlier opening night than anyone had expected. The Granada chain extended throughout much of England by this time, with stars such as Maureen O'Sullivan and Gracie Fields being invited to perform opening ceremonies and drawing the predictable crowds and newspaper column inches. The shows themselves were still often a mixture of film and live acts, publicised by increasingly outlandish stunts such as an aeroplane fly-past or bagatelle tables on wheels to keep the queue occupied.

All this came to an end with the war. At first the government kept all cinemas and theatres closed for fear of the expected German bombing. When that did not happen, at least outside central London, they were allowed to open and proved a great morale booster and source of escapism for the public. But the neon lights and potted plants were noticeably absent, and even posters had to go as paper was rationed. Publicity stunts were a thing of the past. But the public did not care: they flocked to the cinemas at the slightest excuse.

Bernstein's wartime experience at the Ministry of Information apparently gave him a taste for a broader canvas than simply running a cinema chain. He considered and rejected buying a newspaper or going into politics, although his later move into commercial television proved that he had the instincts of the classic newspaper proprietor in the Northcliffe or Beaverbrook mould. Instead, he returned to his early experiment with film production.

Bernstein had befriended the famous film director Alfred Hitchcock, who had been born in the same year, 1899, about five miles away in Leytonstone, east London. In 1945 Hitchcock, a notorious loner, asked Bernstein to come out to California and be his partner in the role of producer, handling the business side of affairs. The pair formed Transatlantic Films, but the venture was not a great success. The partnership made three films *Rope, Under Capricorn* and *I Confess*, which earned mixed reviews on both sides of the Atlantic. None ranks among Hitchcock's best, suggesting that, much as he resented it, he operated best as part of a big studio with all its demands. And Bernstein decided he was not cut out to be a movie mogul, so after a few years he returned to London and concentrated his attention on Granada once more.

The cinema chain he came back to was at once bigger and more rundown than it had been in 1939. The company had bought another fifteen cinemas from owners who wanted to get out of either Britain or the film industry. Bernstein added another ten immediately after the war. But wartime shortages of paint and materials had left many of the Granada chain in a sorry state. A Century chain of second-line cinemas was developed to give the group more than one presence in some towns. Bernstein took up the reins from his brother Cecil and returned to his prewar custom of making unannounced calls on cinemas. The managers were expected to run their staffs with a similarly strict dedication to detail. Until the 1960s they held a daily inspection of the staff on stage in their blue and gold uniforms with red piping, topped off with pillbox hats and capes. Ushers' white gloves had to be immaculate, usherettes' stockings ladder-free. But the big problem Granada and the other cinema operators faced was how to keep their audiences loyal despite the rising number of competing attractions: pubs and restaurants, the growth of travel by train and car, the desire for a change after the war years, with which ironically the cinemas had been so closely identified as an escapist retreat. But above all there was the looming threat of television. Bernstein responded to these threats with his characteristic combination of showmanship, high-mindedness and hard-nosed business sense.

First, he fell back on the prewar tactic of interspersing film at his cinemas with variety shows. He wrote in 1952.

I think one of the answers for some theatres … is occasionally to put on stage shows which, even though not staggeringly profitable, will do the theatre more good than showing the indifferent film … If Granada have live showmen, energetic, virile, aggressive men (and maybe women) who will go after whatever business is around, they will not only survive, but will remain an important independent group.

But he soon found that, unlike twenty or thirty years earlier, the audience for variety was a one-night phenomenon. People no longer returned for a second helping of the same bill, or at least not in sufficient numbers to make it worthwhile outside the West End. So Bernstein was forced to scrap touring shows and make do with one-off appearances by a pop or television star. In his more high-flown mood, Bernstein hired the Royal Ballet, complete with leading ballerinas such as Moirer Shearer and Margot Fonteyn, to tour his suburban cinemas. Like the rest of the industry, Bernstein briefly hoped that technical innovations such as 3D, Cinerama, Technicolor and CinemaScope would turn the tide. But he soon accepted that these were only temporary gimmicks. He wrote, 'We are all involved here in 3D, CinemaScope, Wide Screen and Narrow Screen and what you will … So far the results appear to be exploited at a level of culture somewhere below the depths of degradation.' In his heart of hearts, he knew that television, with its convenience and relative cheapness, must take over as the mass medium.

He tried to bring the two media together in 1948 by applying to the British Postmaster-General for a licence to operate a closed-circuit television system in Granada's cinemas. His plan was to record top-line plays at the end of their runs and then show them in the cinemas in parts of the country where the audiences would not have had the chance to see the live performances. His application was rejected, not surprisingly in view of the possible complications that it might have caused in the context of the wider plans that were taking shape.

The Early Years
of Television

From the start, the birth of commercial or independent television in Britain was intensely political, as was to be expected, for everyone in a position of power and influence, from politicians to the press, was secretly fearful that it could control people's minds and in the process woo them away from other 'responsible' media such as newspapers. This assumption has underlain official attitudes to television until very recently, when the technical ability to proliferate channels has both dissipated the fear and – like print after the invention of the Gutenberg press – solved the problem of control for governments by rendering them virtually helpless to stem the flow.

Initially, Sidney Bernstein professed himself to be against commercial television – just as he had at first been against talking films. He had seen in the United States how it could be trivialised, and proposed instead a kind of nonprofit mirror image of the BBC to provide an alternative competing service. He declared, 'The right of access to the domestic sound and television receivers of millions of people carries with it such great propaganda power that it cannot be entrusted to any person or bodies other than a public corporation.' But, just in case things worked out differently, he assembled a talented team of individuals capable of formulating a franchise-winning case. If the future of television was going to be commercial, he was determined that Granada would be part of it. As he wrote to the Labour politician, Herbert Morrison, 'I still think the country would be better off without it. However, if there is to be commercial television in this country, we think we should be in.'

In 1949 the Labour government set up an inquiry into television under Lord Beveridge, the founder of the welfare state. Predictably, his committee came down firmly in favour of the BBC continuing its state financed (and therefore ultimately state-controlled) monopoly. The only dissenting note on the committee came from Selwyn Lloyd, the future Conservative Chancellor of the Exchequer, who recommended what eventually happened – that commercial and public-service broadcasting should run side by side.

By the time Beveridge reported in January 1951 the Labour government's massive 1945 landslide majority had been slashed to just six seats. It published a White Paper broadly agreeing with Beveridge, but then lost that autumn's general election to the Conservatives, who themselves were returned with a slender majority of sixteen seats. That might see them through a full term, but it meant that any controversial legislation might be overturned by an incoming Labour administration. Indeed, Labour declared that if the Conservatives broke the BBC's monopoly, they would restore it if and when they returned to power. So there was considerable pressure to push the necessary legislation through as quickly as possible.

Meanwhile, television was becoming more and more popular as the country flocked to buy sets. Instead of the 20,000 solely in the London area who owned a TV in 1939, millions round the country were tuned in by the mid-1950s. The 1953 coronation of

Queen Elizabeth II sent set sales soaring, and surveys that year showed that the public would like more choice. So the Queen's Speech at the opening of Parliament that November promised legislation to establish independent television and, because of the Labour threat to repeal, an Act was rushed through the following summer.

The Independent Television Authority was set up under the chairmanship of Sir Kenneth Clark, father of the Conservative minister and diarist Alan Clark. Sir Kenneth had been Bernstein's old boss at the wartime Ministry of Information, and in August an advertisement was published in the newspapers inviting applications for franchises. Granada applied in September and was told in October that it had won the Monday–Friday franchise for the north of England, embracing Yorkshire as well as Lancashire, for no less than fourteen years. Only once more, while the franchise system operated, were the successful companies to be given such a lengthy tenure. That was from 1967 to 1981, and only then because of unpredictable extensions due to yet another Royal Commission and more legislation.

Despite the size of the prize, the application system was incredibly casual compared with the complex machinations demanded by later legislation. Until it could find premises of its own, the ITA was squatting in the then Arts Council offices in London's St James's Square. Sidney and Cecil Bernstein and two of their executives went along on 14 October and were questioned for an hour about the sort of programmes they intended to broadcast, and their financial backing. A week later they were told they had been successful, although they did not discover until later that someone in the government had tried to get Bernstein disqualified on the untrue grounds that he had once belonged to the Communist Party. The slur had arisen during the war, possibly because he had been a lifelong Labour voter and the prewar Film Society had attracted a fair crop of anti-Establishment figures. Sir Kenneth Clark threatened to resign if Granada was denied an ITV franchise, which would have exposed the nonsense, so the opposition backed off.

As it was, although this had nothing to do with the Bernstein witch hunt, Granada did not get all it asked for. The group was given the whole northern region, Yorkshire as well as Lancashire, but for only five days a week instead of the seven Bernstein had wanted. The weekend slot was initially awarded to a consortium of the Kemsley Press and Maurice Winnick Group, but this collapsed in June 1955, just three months before transmission was due to begin. The vacant franchise was picked up by ABC Television.

The government wanted transmission to begin within a year, calculating that there would be a public outcry if Labour was returned to power and tried to close it down after it had started operating. In fact, the Conservatives went back to the polls in May 1955, four months before the new service was due to begin, and won with a comfortable majority of sixty seats. Opposition to commercial television faded away, but the government could not have known that in 1954.

Bernstein had had no previous serious contact with the north, and once Granada was installed he was quite happy to let it be known that it was an unsentimental decision to apply for that region's franchise. He later told the Manchester Publicity Association,

> People have asked me why I applied for the northern region. I have answered that London is full of misplaced persons. The North is a close-knit, indigenous, industrial society, a homogenous, cultured group with a record for music, theatre, literature and newspapers not found elsewhere. These reasons are true. But I am now going to tell you how I really came to the decision. It was brought about by two maps: a population map of Great Britain and a rainfall map. Any sensible person, after studying these two maps for a few minutes, would realise that if commercial TV is going to be a success anyhere in the world, it would be in the industrial North of Engand.

While this is a shrewd explanation, and one that has gone

down in legend, Bernstein may have also calculated that there might be more competition for the prestige-laden London franchises and he could make a bigger splash in one of the more prosperous regions.

Granada Television was very much run in the early years by Sidney Bernstein and his brother Cecil, their production and technical expert Victor Peers, and Joe Warton in charge of accounts. Cecil attended the crucial network committee of the ITV companies, which decided which of the TV programmes produced by each region would be broadcast nationally for a fee that would make a huge difference to the economics of programme-making. Cecil and Sidney's background in music hall gave Granada a vital edge at these intensely political horse-trading sessions, at which they were often opposed by the pugnacious Lew Grade of Associated Television or ATV, the Midlands midweek and London weekend company.

But behind this top team was a talented group of individuals who responded to Sidney's rebellious spirit. Sir Denis Forman, co-founder and former chairman of Granada Television, said, 'It had a special quality that is not replicable today. What made it special was Sidney's selection of people, who together sparked an approach to television and an ethos that was particularly Granada. He had to like them.' Leslie Woodhead, who worked at Granada for twenty-eight years until 1989, said, 'The great joy of working there was a sense of shared purpose. It was never spelt out or laid down, but all of us knew why we were there and what we were doing – making good television for the widest possible audience without compromising standards.'

The Bernstein brothers toured Manchester and Liverpool in the urgent search for a headquarters site before finally settling on a collection of huts, workshops and cottages owned by the Manchester Ship Canal company in Quay Street, overlooking the canal. Manchester Corporation had made a bid for it as the home of an intended exhibition hall, but Sidney outbid them.

Year One, a 1958 Granada publication, said that Granada TV consisted of little more than a general idea of what the new television service should seek to attain. There were no tools with which to carry out this idea, no studio, no electronic equipment, not a single camera; no directors, electricians, cameramen, sound and vision mixers, typists or designers. The craftsmen, technologists, administrative and creative workers who were to create Granada Television were working at other jobs in Manchester, Toronto, London, Liverpool and New York, many of them unaware that their future lay in television. Just a year after the contract was signed, the first Granada transmission went on the air from the most modern television centre in Europe – a building which in eight months had risen on a waste plot of land in Quay Street, Manchester, the first building expressly designed for television.

There was then a delay because of the necessity of building separate transmitters to cover Lancashire and Yorkshire. The original idea had been for Granada to share the BBC's transmitter at Holme Moss, which transmitted coast to coast. But that turned out to be technically impossible, and the ITA's engineers insisted against Granada's opposition that it would take eighteen months to build another one as powerful. So they went for two, the first of which would cover Lancashire and be ready by early 1956. The Yorkshire one would take a further six months. Again the threat of a Labour election victory was the deciding factor. Sidney Bernstein was furious. On 17 March 1955, he wrote to Sir Robert Fraser, the ITA's director-general:

> Instead of starting commercial television with audience potential of twelve millions, we are now being asked to go into business with a potential of six millions. We cannot escape the impression that we are being asked to pay a very high price indeed to hasten the inauguration of the ITA service elsewhere. We have always reiterated our belief that starting commercial television in one region is extremely hazardous, and flouts the obvious foundation of good

programming. … The economic base of all our planning
has been continuously chipped away.

The episode did not endear Bernstein to the establishment,
and that, combined with his dislike of stuffed-shirt pomp, led him
to boycott the ceremony that opened ITV on Thursday, 22
September 1955, at London's Guildhall. When it finally came to
Granada's turn to open its own service the following year, he said as
much to Sir Robert. Instead, he fell back on the formula he had
used for opening new cinemas: a parade of those involved in starting the station.

So, at 7.30 p.m. on 3 May 1956, Victor Peers sat at a desk,
looked into the camera and said, 'From the north, this is Granada on
Channel 9. A year ago Granada was a blueprint, a promise. Tonight
the north has a new television service created by the devotion and
hard work of thousands of northerners and friends from all over the
world.'

After the parade of contributors, from Sir Kenneth Clark to
Jack Caine, the builders' foreman, the Liverpool comedian Arthur
Askey sang songs and the Lancashire-born singer Gracie Fields sent
a recorded message from Texas. There was a boxing match from
Liverpool, the first of a series called *Blue Murder*, a news bulletin
and a generous tribute to the BBC. And, just as Sidney Bernstein
had a tendency to upset the authorities, Granada's advertisers would
have been less than enthused by the message he had the station
broadcast at the end of that first night's transmission. It said, 'You can
use Granada advertisements as a trustworthy guide to wise spending. Wise spending eventually saves money. So, before we shop, let us
say to ourselves, "Is it essential?"' Bernstein himself spent the
evening alone, watching the proceedings on television.

Sidney's political and wartime background was to have a critical influence on the flavour of Granada Television, making it
much more like a campaigning newspaper than the other early
Independent Television franchises were and, indeed, than the

Television Act strictly allowed. But time and time again Bernstein was able to expose the absurdities of that Act's demand for balance and impartiality, a demand that was a blatant attempt to make commercial television as much as possible like the former BBC public-service monopoly, with its ponderous Reithian sense of self-importance. Sir Denis Forman recalled, 'We had rows with authority over everything. The Poulson affair, defence, security – I was often hauled up in Whitehall and given dire warnings by ministers and civil servants. We were regarded as a bit of a danger. That's quite gone – you can be much franker and more open today.'

In the early years of both BBC and ITV the most impressive programmes were those featuring live outside broadcasts, showing news events as they happened. Bernstein quickly realised that this was also an effective way of establishing Granada's regional credentials, and he made the most of it by having a fleet of Outside Broadcast (OB) vans driving around the area in distinctive light-blue livery. They also had that vital stroke of early luck. On the Saturday after the station opened one of the region's football teams, Manchester City, won the FA Cup at Wembley. It was not until the following year that the final would be shown live for the first time – another local team, Manchester United, played in that game and the 1958 final – but meanwhile Granada had the coup of live coverage of City's triumphant return to Manchester with the Cup.

Compared with the sophisticated equipment in modern television studios, Granada's early facilities were crude. Sir Denis Forman described the working conditions in those days:

> A general service producer ... might have four to six shows in the five working days, and all of them made on electronic cameras either in the studios or on OBs, for in those days the film camera was still regarded as an engine of the devil ... The day would often begin with a breakfast visit to the canteen to see the OB crew off, followed by a morning of script discussions and tumbles through in the studio. As each show neared its run-through the producer would spend more time in the box until actually during transmission, or in the rare event of taping, he

would be present throughout, standing behind the director, silent, concerned and supernumerary. It's hard to find much resemblance between today's shot-by-shot progress through the studio and the multiple camera live transmissions of 1959. First of all the camera itself, the old Mark III, built to withstand shell-fire … had a turret lens with a count of three seconds between one shot and the next should a lens change be required. Each camera had to be in position before its shot and if one camera went down, the flurry of rescheduling the remaining two or three would test the mettle of the PA and director. Everyone believed in those days – wrongly – in the magic of the uplift of on-air transmission. It is true that the adrenalin coursed through the veins of both crew and actors, but this did not always deliver a better performance. What it did ensure was a sense of climax and an enormous sense of release once the programme was over. If there had been no lens changes in shot, no booms in shot, no fluffs by actors and no over or underrun, then the show was generally regarded to be an unqualified success. A play was made or marred in the dry-rehearsal room and the only question that remained was how much of the performance the actors could keep and reproduce under the cameras on the night.

Nevertheless, the first few years were difficult financially. While the initial ITV levy was set at a level Granada and its rivals could only dream of before the open competition of the 1990 Broadcasting Act – 10p per head of population covered per year – advertising revenue was much lower than expected and Granada found itself losing money at the rate of £1 million a year, a far more serious amount in those days than it would be today. Sidney Bernstein tried to drum up business, openly asking local companies such as Beecham, Lever Brothers, Leyland Paint and Colgate to support Granada on a sale-or-return basis. If their advertisements did not reach a guaranteed minimum audience, Granada would pay rebates.

But it was not enough. Bernstein had to find a way of cutting the cost base. He therefore reached a deal with Associated-Rediffusion, the London midweek station, whereby AR would receive 85–90 per cent of Granada's net advertising revenue over the next four years in return for paying the total costs of all Granada-made programmes that AR broadcast. In fact, Granada's ad revenue reached viable levels much sooner than that, but it gave Bernstein a huge incentive to produce programmes that AR would want to run. That also gave Granada the 'window on London' that he wanted, which stood the company in good stead for winning future franchise applications. This arrangement was kept secret for many years after it came to an end, as it showed how close Granada came to going bust.

This was the schedule for Wednesday, 14 May 1958 – not beginning, note, until 4.30 in the afternoon: breakfast and daytime television were still many years away.

Amser Te, Welsh magazine programme
Junior Criss Cross Quiz with Jeremy Hawke
Adventures of Kit Carson, Western adventure
6.00 News
Melody Ranch, Western music programme
We Want An Answer, a Granada programme where youngsters
    interviewed experts about topical issues
The New Adventures of Charlie Chan, a US series about a Chinese
    detective
Boyd QC, courtroom drama with Michael Denison
Spot The Tune, musical quiz with Alfred Marks and Marion Ryan
Play of the Week, made by different companies, this week by
    Granada: *All My Sons* by Arthur Miller with Albert Dekker,
    Megs Jenkins, Betta St John and Patrick McGoohan
The Carrol Levis Discoveries, a talent show
Sports Outlook with Gerry Loftus
10.45 News
Palais Party from Hammersmith Palais in London, with Lou
    Preager and his orchestra

Major or popular programmes were networked, but there was scope for local initiative and the franchise terms, as well as insisting on a balanced output, also insisted on the schedules having a strong regional flavour. That was potentially expensive for the smaller ITV companies, so to save money they would affiliate to one of the bigger ones, and make all booking arrangements through that parent. All the parents made their programmes available to the smaller companies for the single fee paid each parent. The parents then shared the proceeds.

In 1960 the government set up another committee under the glassmaker Sir Harry Pilkington to look into the television industry, and to recommend what changes if any should be made to the franchise system the next time round. Granada told Pilkington that the big three companies had agreed to contribute live network programmes in proportion to their population coverage: weekdays, Granada two-fifths, Associated-Rediffusion two-fifths, ATV one-fifth. The general programming schedule was settled jointly, but each company had sovereign rights over its own programmes and could transmit them without vetting by the others.

As the typical night's schedule above shows, Granada transmitted a wide mixture of programmes, mostly light entertainment of one sort or another. However, it was its current-affairs coverage that attracted the most attention. This suited the buccaneering approach of Bernstein and his talented team of journalists, but it was also good business. Current affairs programmes are cheaper to make than drama or variety shows.

February 1958 was an early milestone in documentaries. Granada's local coverage of the Rochdale by-election that month led to the extensive national and regional coverage of the 1959 general election, when Granada covered all 229 candidates in northern England. The ITA's 1958 annual report said Rochdale was 'the first occasion in the whole history of broadcasting in Britain on which the issues of an election were expounded to audiences other than in party political broadcasts'. In one programme candidates discussed issues among themselves, in another they were interviewed by three journalists, and in a third Granada's *Under Fire* had two prominent people in the London studio interrogated by a Manchester studio audience. This was also the first campaign to be reported in ITN bulletins, which had previously ignored them in the belief that it would be breaking the law to do otherwise.

The early driving force behind Granada's current-affairs work was Tim Hewat, an Australian-born former *Daily Express* journalist. Sir Jeremy Isaacs, the first chairman of Channel Four, said, 'I learned more from him than from anyone else I've worked with in television. He taught me that it is primarily a mass-audience medium and that one must be understood. He wanted TV programmes to say something.' Hewat produced a regular half-hour midweek news documentary, *Searchlight*, which soon won a reputation for confronting social issues such as homosexuality, venereal disease and the contraceptive pill.

Searchlight ended in 1960 and was succeeded in 1962 by *World In Action*, more lavish and wider-ranging, with a format that lives on today in vigorous health. While other documentary programmes used anchormen, *World In Action* was narrated offscreen and there were no interviewers. Statements were made straight to camera without questions. Norman Swallow said in his book, *Factual Television*, 'It suggested, sometimes openly, sometimes obliquely, what the viewer should think about the subject under review. It did not leave him to make up his own mind. It made it up for him.'

Bernard Sendall, in his *History of Independent Television in Britain*, added, 'Neither in *Searchlight* nor in its more famous successor did Hewat make any bones about the fact he was editorialising. He did not try to suppress evidence which disagreed with his own conclusions, provided the latter emerged with unmistakable clarity.'

Popular and effective though this approach was – indeed, possibly *because* of its very popularity and effectiveness – it was bound to lead to a clash with the powers that be in London on the ground that it was breaching the ITV companies' obligation to be impartial. The Rochdale by-election, active and comprehensive coverage of the 1959 general election, and the incursions of *World In Action*, led Granada into several brushes with the ITA. Sidney Bernstein tried a touch of wide-eyed innocence when he told Sir Robert Fraser, ITA's director-general, 'But all we want to do, Bob, is what the newspapers do.' Granada basically got away with it and continued to do so. The requirements for balance and impartiality in the next Television Act were considerably toned down.

In 1962 all three main party conferences and the Trades Union Congress annual conference were held in Granada's territory. Granada televised them all live and at great length, showing that there was public demand for such treatment of political events, and paving the way for the eventual televising of Parliament. The following year, everyone else was understandably keen to get in on the act, but Granada still stole the show. On 10 October at the Conservative Party conference in Blackpool, the word went round the media that there would be an announcement at the end of the day's debates. No one had a clue about how important the announcement would be, and at 5 p.m. the other ITV stations duly switched over, on schedule, to *Junior Criss Cross Quiz*. Granada stayed with the Conservative conference, and televised live the scoop of Lord Home announcing the resignation of Harold Macmillan as Prime Minister.

Perhaps Granada felt it had a point to prove. When it was published in 1962 the Pilkington Report turned out to be at best patronising towards the ITV companies, and at worst hostile. As the *Daily Mail* TV critic, the late Peter Black, says in *Mirror in the Corner* (Hutchinson, 1972), 'The Pilkington Report thought that reform could be achieved by creating a service that was supported by advertising but not dependent on popular appeal. It is an attractive notion to those who dislike advertising and popular appeal.' ITV's critics felt they could take the gloves off because the companies were by this time in generally good financial health. They had been allowed to cut corners in the early days because several, including

Granada, had privately warned they faced financial collapse. So they were allowed to get away with cheap quiz and audience-participation shows as well as plenty of US-made crime and Western series.

Worse than that, however, Pilkington thought that ITV had failed to appreciate how far television could influence moral values and had therefore lapsed into too much low-grade and violent material. Range, variety and quality were too limited, and Pilkington thought minority-interest programmes were shown at 'unsuitable' times — a point of concern in the era before video recorders. To remedy these defects, Pilkington wanted far more power in the hands of the ITA, by making it the advertising salesman and the programme scheduler. Programme companies would merely sell programmes to the ITA and make what profit they could that way. Any extra profits would go to the Exchequer. It would be almost like the BBC, with advertising. The nannying theme of Pilkington would seem laughable in today's multichannel environment. But in 1962 it had to be taken deadly seriously, because another franchise round was coming up and any ITV company that was not seen to be giving the Report's findings at least serious consideration would be in danger of being dropped.

By the time of the next official report on British television, fifteen years later, the chattering classes had begun to embrace ITV. At fashionable dinner parties in Hampstead or Belgravia it was now acceptable to admit to watching, and even enjoying, ITV programmes. The ITA had been replaced as the ruling body by the Independent Broadcasting Authority, covering the many new commercial radio stations that were springing up round the country, and people realised that commercial broadcasters could be as good as, and at times better than, the BBC.

Sir Denis Forman, then chairman of Granada Television, was sufficiently relaxed about the competition in September 1976 to write,

The BBC ... is strong in Public Service Comedy, some of it very broad and very good, Public Service Olympics and sport in general, and with shows such as It's A (Public Service) Knockout and the like. Contrariwise ITV, once so clearly the People's Television, has the edge perhaps in popular history as treated in the excellent *The World At War*, and in contemplating our economy-ridden society in programmes like *Weekend World*, *The State of the Nation* and *Decision*. The admirable influence of the IBA has pushed ITV towards gravitas; reaction to the early years of ITV has pushed the BBC towards the box office ... But then, as we have discovered over the past 21 years, to provide good television for all of the people all of the time is not an easy thing.

By the 1970s Britain had become a much more turbulent place. Governments, Labour and Conservative, were constantly challenged by powerful trade unions and a more liberal attitude to the media. The innocent permissiveness of the 1960s had turned into a more violent mood in which all icons and taboos were liable to be kicked over. Broadcasters, much more than the press, felt that they could not be left behind in the race to shock, whether with swearing, nudity or just saying what had previously been unsayable. That in turn produced a backlash from a large minority concerned about the effect of all this on children.

But unemployment, a falling pound and raging inflation all gave rise to public anger and put Whitehall and Westminster on the back foot. The Northern Ireland conflict, which had broken surface once more in 1969, was by the 1970s filling TV screens with dramatic images of violence and destruction which it would have been ludicrous to ignore. Granada took full advantage of this atmosphere to produce some of its most controversial programmes, particularly in the *World In Action* series, helped by the move to colour television.

Significantly, when the government decided that it had to summon another report on broadcasting, it chose as chairman the ex-military intelligence officer turned liberal academic, Noel

Annan. He was almost bound to produce a more sympathetic doc-ument than Pilkington had, and so it proved. But the authors were still unable to keep a distinctly patronising tone out of their collec-tive voice. 'Commercial television has the defects of its merits,' the report declared in 1977. It continued,

> Its routine productions are on a lower level than those of the BBC, even in comedy, light entertainment and sport, the popular areas in which it might be expected to excel. But ... ITV has come a long way since the Pilkington Committee reported. They have made a real attempt to widen the subject matter of their programmes, particularly in current affairs and documen-taries, and the best of their programmes are as good as any made by the BBC ... What ITV needs to do is to give greater depth and subtlety to their popular series.

By this time Granada, having survived twenty-one years and had its franchise renewed twice, had become established as the *enfant terrible* of the ITV companies. There was little argument that it could and did produce some of the best of ITV's output. But the mere mention of Sidney Bernstein's name in the corridors of the IBA was enough to produce a shake of the head, eyes raised to heav-en and a wry, resigned smile. Sidney and his colleagues in Manchester were justifiably proud of their achievements, but they made little attempt to hide their arrogance towards the IBA or anyone else who dared to criticise them, let alone try to restrain them.

In its 1980 franchise application Granada said,

> Granada Television has conducted its affairs with a high degree of autonomy. Programmes were always a first charge on profits. The Group did not lay down criteria or targets: Television was asked to make its own budgets and forecasts and report them to the Group. The Group board as such has never imposed cash limits or other similar restrictions on the Television board, nor has it ever inhibited programme expenditure or programme policy. In the early days, however, Sidney and Cecil Bernstein and Joseph Wharton were directors both of Television and Group and there

was therefore a measure of common identity between the two boards.

In other words, Sidney, Cecil and Wharton had the power to give the TV business as much money as it needed. That was the historical background that laid the foundations for the clash between David Plowright and Gerry Robinson. By the time Robinson became group chief executive in 1991, the Television operation was just one among a portfolio of subsidiaries, and had to justify itself financially in just the same terms as TV Rentals, computer maintenance or motorway catering – all businesses that had been set up or bought to reinvest the vast profits that Television had generated.

Granada Group short to medium term review by G J Robinson

I have now completed an outline review of the main elements in Granada Group PLC and have had a chance to meet most of the senior management teams. In addition, we have carried out a first round of monthly detailed operational reviews on the performance of period 1 for each of the main divisions.

It is worth perhaps clarifying that I see my own initial task as one of settling the Group down to concentrating on running the main businesses that we now have (there are still a number of small potential disposals) in a much tighter and more profit/cost conscious way. This will inevitably involve a rather more hands-on approach than has been the case in the past which may, at least initially, lead to some discomfort in some areas.

The make up of the Group is as follows:

UK TV Rental (including Granada Business Communications)
Granada Television
Leisure including Motorways
                 Bowling

Nightclubs
Theme Parks
Travel
Other (Lakewoods, USA Bingo, Interactive
Video)
Computer Services
International (including Kapy)
Head Office

I outline below what I see as the key elements for each of these constituent parts of the Group.

UK TV Rental

I believe that we have an excellent business here which is capable of giving strong profits and cash flows long into the future. It is certainly true that it is likely, in the long run, to be in slow decline as prices for new televisions, video recorders and satellite installations fall in real terms and as their reliability improves. This makes the purchase option an easier one for the customer. Our management task, therefore, falls into four distinct parts:

Keep the decline in installation as low as possible and/or halt/reverse it should the opportunity present itself
Improve the pricing for greater margin at the same time as we reduce the capital spend
Gain an increasing share of the retail market, but only where it is clearly profitable to do so
Reduce costs vigorously

The profit history of the business (excluding GBC) has been as shown on the following page:

This a trend that, although a creditable performance, particularly against our major competitors, were it to continue in real terms would unacceptably reduce the value of the business over the

£m	1988/89	1989/90	%	1990/91	%	Budget 1991/92	%
Gross Income	316	329	+4	341	+4	356	+4
Depreciation	(74)	(65)	–12	(70)	+8	(75)	+7
Costs	(151)	(190)	+26	(197)	+4	(207)	+5
PBIT★	91	74	–19	74	Nil	74	Nil

★ Profit Before Interest and Tax

next ten years. I have agreed with the divisional management that we should seek, through a combination of intelligent price increases and vigorous cost-cutting, to reverse the trend. For example, an effective 2.5% price increase, combined with a 5% cost reduction, would move the 1991/2 PBIT to £99m compared to the £74m budgeted. These are not huge shifts and although undoubtedly painful are well within the boundaries of sensible targeting. This exercise is now being studied and plans for its execution should be available to be put into effect early in the new year. I do not anticipate that we will achieve the full £99m in the financial year for timing reasons, but we should take a worthwhile step along the way.

Strategically I believe that we should continue to buy small 'add-on' rental businesses as the opportunities present themselves, we should fully integrate the business rental side into the mainstream business and we should consider moving the non-TV/Video maintenance operation into the Computer Services division. I believe that the decision not to go into white goods rental is the right one. There is clearly considerable scope for profit growth in the next two to three years as we take the opportunity to reduce operating costs and to price upwards in a steady and intelligently controlled way. There may also be longer-term opportunities to rationalise the shop network, but this needs careful handling.

Granada Television

The recent award of the franchise at what is clearly an excellent price is a wonderful starting point for the future of this business. All other things being equal, we should manage to hold on to the franchise for the next twenty years. The TV operation as it now stands is made up of three separate, albeit inter-relating parts:

Broadcasting
Production & Distribution
The Studios Tour (and the Victoria & Albert Hotel)

Following the franchise debacle, there is little doubt, perhaps sadly, that the old, more comfortable, era of ever increasing advertising revenues, of selling at fixed prices to the network, of sharing often rapidly increasing network costs and of having a virtual monopoly in which to operate is over. The high prices paid for their franchises by a number of operators, together with the emergence of new operators, particularly Carlton in London, will change the face and pace of the industry. Increasingly too, the appearance of satellite in more and more homes will begin to eat into the monopoly advertising position. Tightly controlled budgets, particularly on the production side, with an increase in the use of independent producers for new material, will be the order of the day. Granada Television has a proud history of being a quality player as a producer/broadcaster, and its reputation and standing were undoubtedly key factors in winning its franchise on such favourable terms. Ironically, in the new scenario, that tradition may make it more difficult to adapt to the new commercial reality.

The profit history is shown in the table overleaf:

Here again is a downward trend that cannot be allowed to continue. There is little doubt that pressure on advertising income will continue as long as the recession does, and it is too early to know what kind of programme pricing structure will emerge among the franchise holders. Together with the rest of the industry,

£m	Actual 1988/89	Actual 1989/90	%	Actual 1990/91	%	Budget 1991/92	%
Total Income	252	250	–1	254	+2	257	+1
Granada Costs	(115)	(110)	–4	(120)	+9	(121)	+1
Industry/ Network Costs	(89)	(91)	+2	(102)	+12	(106)	+4
Profit Before Levy	47	49	+4	32	–35	30	–6
Levy	(16)	(17)		(12)		(14)★★	
PBIT★	31	32		20		16	

★ Profit Before Interest and Tax
★★ Excludes recent levy change.

we increased our programme expenditure in the run-up to the new franchise awards. We should, of course, adhere to any agreements with the ITC, but it is clear that we need now to tackle our own cost base firmly, and to contribute where we can to achieving an overall cost reduction in the network schedule costs. As examples, a 20% cost reduction in our own costs and a standstill on industry costs would produce a profit before levy of £54m in 91/92, a 10% own-cost reduction and similar standstill in industry costs would produce £43m. I believe that our cost base is high and that something of the order of a 20% real reduction is achievable, given the will to do so. As might be anticipated, there are conflicting views on this. The debate has begun – but clearly, we must get past that stage quickly if we are to make a worthwhile impact on this year's numbers.

Strategically I believe we have a powerful profit and cash producer in this division, and that that is not at all inconsistent with our wish to be the highest-quality operator in the network. If we are able to produce good returns from the business, we will be in a strong position in the medium term to acquire other operators, particularly locally, where combining them will give opportunities for cost rationalisation – a process that will almost certainly go on with or without us. We have a huge site in Manchester that, on balance, is something of a liability because it is far in excess of our needs and is expensive to operate. With the present state of the property market and our own shortage of funds it would be foolish to try to solve that problem now, but it is probable that over the coming years a new, much smaller facility would make sense. In the meantime we have developed a mini-theme park (Studios Tour) on the site and we are in the process of building a hotel (The Victoria & Albert). So far, despite a better-then-expected volume of visitors, the theme park loses money after interest and I am personally doubtful about the commercial viability of the hotel.

Our short-term aim should be to try to make a sensible return on our investment in the Studio Tour before we commit ourselves to further developments, and to review thoroughly our options on the hotel.

Leisure

We have a number of separate businesses of various sizes in this division. The key one is our motorway services operation, albeit that in some ways it is in fact two separate businesses, motorway service areas 'proper' and trunk road sites. It is no surprise that the motorway operations are relatively successful but the trunk road sites show very poor returns. The motorway operation is a sound business and, if average returns can be improved, it has good potential for steady long-term profits. The future of the trunk road sites and associated hotels is doubtful.

The profit history is shown in the table overleaf:

The picture here is of steadily increasing investment against static profits, again a picture that can not be allowed to continue. We have recently recruited Charles Allen, previously MD of Compass

£m	1989/90	1990/91	Budget 1991/2
Income	218	240	256
Cost of Sales	(181)	(200)	(213)
Gross Profit	37	40	43
Costs	(21)	(23)	(26)
PBIT	16	17	17
Interest	(5)	(9)	(8)
PBT	11	8	9
Average Capital Employed	155	164	182
Return on Capital Employed	10.3%	10.4%	9.3%
ROCE on Original Cost	15.5%	15.2%	13.1%

Catering, to head up the Leisure division and his first task will be to conduct a thorough review of the motorway operation with a view to significant margin improvement. Again, as an example some quite small improvements in market (+0.25% forecourt, +2.5% catering, +2% shops and +5% lodges) together with modest overhead reduction, will produce a PBIT of £23.1m, a PBT of £14.9m and a return on average capital employed of 12.7% which, although still unacceptable, would be beginning to look respectable.

Strategically we need to enchance greatly the returns we make from this business (20%+) before we commit further serious investment to it. We will probably need to spend a little more capital on bringing some of the existing locations up to scratch. We need to look at our options on the hotel front, although it is probable that we will seek to dispose of them in due course.

In Ten Pin Bowling, we are the largest operator in the UK with twenty-one sites up and running and a further three under construction. We currently have capital of £40m invested and this is expected to rise to £42.5m by the end of financial year 1992. Although there are obviously some grave doubts about the cyclical nature (faddiness?) of this business against the substantial investment in it, I honestly don't believe that we have seriously made the most of it. I am deeply unimpressed by the senior management here, and as an example of that we had recently eight sites without a general manager – a sorry state of affairs. I believe that we need to make some management changes and generally sharpen up our act before we give any further serious thought to our strategic options.

The picture in Nightclubs looks similar. We have ten clubs and five feeder bars with an overall capital investment of £15m. We are currently without a general manager for the operation and, in a business that needs controlling tightly, that is an unhappy situation. The strategy here too must be to run what we have well and consistently before we even begin to decide what our longer-term plans might be.

As at the end of last year we had some £43m invested in Theme Parks that yielded a 1.4% return on our investment, despite some enthusiastic work on improving attendances. There seems little doubt that our purchases in this area were a mistake and, although we may have to run them for some time to improve their selling profile, we should almost certainly seek to extricate ourselves from this area as soon as it is practicable.

In Travel, following earlier disposals, we are left with a collection of three businesses, Air Travel Group (ATG) that organises air travel holidays mainly to Italy, Budget Travel which operates holidays from Ireland, and Discovery Cruises. With the exception of Budget, which looks like a sound little business, the others produce small losses or minimum profits, huge accounting and administrative headaches and high ongoing risks. We should get out of the lot at the earliest sensible opportunity.

Computer services

Although this has been nothing short of a disaster for the Group, it is a delight to see the extent of the turnaround under John Curran's management. John's style is direct and, in a remarkably short time, he has imposed order on a business that was falling apart. It looks as though we have achieved a worthwhile profit in period 1 and John and his team are confident that that should continue for the rest of the year. That being so, we can take a breathing space to examine the longer-term outlook for the business. The key to that will be our ability to reduce the high level of non-renewal on maintenance contracts and to maintain/improve both the level and the quality of new gains. Alongside that issue is the one of establishing a 'permanently employed' management team for the longer term. Within the division, GIS, the in-house programming and processing service, needs to be examined as to its suitability to meet our longer-term needs.

1. International

There are four businesses that rightly belong in this 'division':

Business	Market	Capital Employed
US Hospitals ⎫	Short-term rental of	30
Canadian Hospitals ⎬	TVs to hospital patients	6
Telerent (Germany)	TV/Video rental to homes	19
Kapy (Spain)	Electrical goods retail	1 2
		£67m

All of these businesses are for sale in either the short or medium term. The two North American businesses are currently 'off the market' and John Curran and John O'Brien (to whom they currently report) have been asked to liaise on the short-term plans for them. I expect to have a clearer view by the end of the calendar year. Telerent in Germany is effectively to be run down and then the 'rump' is to be sold off. I have yet to decide whether it should report to John Curran, Tom Cole, or another after John O'Brien's departure in April 1992. The sale of Kapy is currently being negotiated, sadly with only one potential purchaser. The price looks dismal, as indeed does the prospect of continuing to run it. If necessary it will report to Charles Allen until we dispose of it.

Head Office

We are well on the way towards completing a major cost reduction programme for the head office. The revised ongoing annual central costs are now £5m compared to £6.5m originally, a reduction of 23%. The longer-term role of head office is to provide only those central services that are unavoidable and to manage the operating companies entirely through the directly reporting divisional managers. That being so, we will be seeking every opportunity to reduce costs further in the future.

Summary

It is of course early days, but I believe that the way forward in most areas is clear. With all the risks that it entails, I believe that our aim or target in profit terms for 1991/2 should be as shown in the table overleaf:

£m PBIT*	Latest Budget	Internal Annualised Target	Sensible Guess
UK Rental	82	99	90
Television	25**	46	30**
Leisure	25	32	29
Computer Services	9	9	9
International	1	1	1
Head Office – net	(10)	(9)	(5)
Pensions Credit	13	13	13
	145	195	167
Interest	(40)	(35)	(36)
	105	160	131

* Profit Before Interest and Tax
** includes a £6m reduction in Levy already achieved

We will certainly give it a good try.

Finally, on cash flow we were looking at a budgeted outflow of £105m. This has already been forecast to reduce to an £81m outflow and I hope that we can reduce that to below £50m. We will begin an exercise shortly to examine what options we have on this front.

G.J. Robinson
29.11.91

APPENDIX IV

Sources

Anonymous, *Creeslough-Dunfanaghy Guide Book*, Doe Historical Committee, 1988

Forte, C., *The Autobiography of Charles Forte*, Pan Books, 1987

Forman, D., *Persona Granada*, Andre Deutsh, 1997

Horsman, M., *Sky High*, Orion Business, 1997

Moorhead, C., *Sidney Bernstein, a Biography*, Macmillan, 1983

Potter, J., *Independent Television in Britain, Volume III & IV*, Macmillan, 1990

Sendall, B., *Independent Television in Britain, Volume I & II*, Macmillan, 1990

Snoddy, R., *Greenfinger*, Faber & Faber, 1996

Index